MINNESOTA BIRDS
Where, When, and How Many

Spruce Grouse. (Painting by W. J. Breckenridge.)

MINNESOTA BIRDS

Where, When, and How Many

JANET C. GREEN

and

ROBERT B. JANSSEN

Published by
the University of Minnesota Press, Minneapolis,
for the
James Ford Bell Museum of Natural History

Library of Congress Catalog Card Number 74-16980

ISBN 0-8166-0738-9

To MINNESOTA

for her prairies,
boreal forests,
deciduous woodlands,
and marshes;
her variety of birds;
and her human resources.
May they coexist in
ecological harmony.

Foreword

Ornithology has thrived on the contributions of amateur birders. Interest usually starts with local bird identification and often progresses to a preoccupation with rare birds and life lists. But pursuit of rarities produces diminishing returns as one's list grows. Some amateur birders find new satisfaction in serious study of nesting birds; examples are Margaret M. Nice's study of the Song Sparrow, Harold F. Mayfield's work on the Kirtland's Warbler, and Lawrence H. Walkinshaw's research on the Sandhill Crane. Other amateurs turn to detailed documentation of migration, distribution, and abundance. Janet C. Green and Robert B. Janssen have done so in this volume, the first statewide report on the Minnesota avifauna since publication of *The Birds of Minnesota* by Thomas S. Roberts in 1932.

State lists of birds become obsolete in surprisingly few years through the efficient efforts of armies of skilled birders. In the forty-two years since Roberts's book, birders have discovered additional species visiting the state and have improved our knowledge of the habits and movements of the regularly occurring birds. This book presents this new information on the birds of Minnesota. It is particularly appropriate that the authors are amateur ornithologists, since they are reporting largely on the work of amateur birders.

Jan Green lives in Duluth, Minnesota. Few birds visiting the North Shore escape her scrutiny. She braves the mosquitoes and deerflies of the northwoods in pursuit of breeding warblers. She is a fearless critic of sloppy sight records, perhaps not an endearing trait but an indispensable one in compiling accurate species accounts based largely on sight records. Her honesty and diligence are apparent throughout the book.

Bob Janssen, who lives in Minnetonka, Minnesota, is also a fanatic birder, ranging over the state wherever "good birds" show up. He has been at the focus of Minnesota field ornithology for over fourteen years as editor of *The Loon*, the journal published by the Minnesota Ornithologists' Union.

Together, Green and Janssen have produced a fresh view of Minnesota birds, entirely new in its wealth of detail on distribution and migration, estimates of abundance, and use of distribution maps. It is a book of high scientific standards, intended not to be read from cover to cover but to serve as an essential reference on Minnesota birds until the accomplishment of its

vii

purpose — the stimulation of field study of Minnesota birds — in time results in its own obsolescence.

Harrison B. Tordoff

James Ford Bell Museum of Natural History
University of Minnesota
September 1974

Preface

Minnesota is fortunate in that it was the subject of one of the early classic monographs on birdlife, Thomas Sadler Roberts's *The Birds of Minnesota*. In the decades since the appearance of Roberts's two-volume work in 1932 new field data have been published regularly in *The Loon* (first published in 1929 as *The Flicker*), the quarterly journal of the Minnesota Ornithologists' Union. Nevertheless, Roberts's monumental work has long been out of print, and so much additional information has accumulated that a new compilation of Minnesota bird records is needed. This book is an attempt to present these records in a form that can be used by both amateur and professional ornithologists.

The information collected herein tells the reader what species have been reported in Minnesota, in what parts of the state they are found, in what seasons they are present, and how abundant they are. Since it is intended that this book will be used in conjunction with standard field guides, no information on identification or habits is included. The discussion in the species accounts is usually divided into three sections: (1) migration, including distribution, abundance, and dates; (2) summer season, including breeding range and nesting records; and (3) winter season, including distribution and abundance. In a few species accounts the discussion format has been modified somewhat to accommodate additional information.

The 374 species that comprise the Minnesota list are divided into six status categories based on frequency of occurrence: regular (292 species), casual (23 species), accidental (44 species), hypothetical (12 species), extirpated (2 species), and extinct (1 species). Definitions of the status categories are given later in this section. The cutoff points for the records vary with the status: the information about species that are regular in occurrence applies to data collected through the end of 1970 with the addition of a few significant later observations; the information about species that are casual or accidental in occurrence applies to data (including unpublished information) collected through the end of 1973.

We stress that this compilation is just a step toward a detailed understanding of Minnesota's avifauna. In spite of the long history of bird study in the state, there is much to be learned about breeding ranges, migration timing and pathways, and relative abundance of all species. As we wrote the species accounts and prepared the range maps, we found many areas for which information is unavailable or incomplete. We hope that the gaps in knowledge revealed by this publication will inspire other students to make new field studies or to publish already accumulated data.

The Minnesota Ornithologists' Union, an organization of bird clubs and individuals devoted to the understanding, enjoyment, and protection of birdlife in the state, encourages the contribution of data and articles on Minnesota birds for publication in *The Loon* (permanent address: Minnesota Ornithologists' Union, Bell Museum of Natural History, University of Minnesota, Minneapolis, Minnesota 55455). The journal features a Seasonal Report (a summary of recent observations contributed by about a hundred birders) and articles about individual species and birdlife in different parts of the state.

The migration information presented here is largely from the Seasonal Report files of the Minnesota Ornithologists' Union. It should be remembered, however, that Minnesota is a large and ecologically varied state, and the migration patterns of its birdlife are very imperfectly known; as a result, the migration information given in this book cannot be regarded as definitive. Much remains to be learned about the timing of migration and about the peak periods that occur in the various regions of the state. For many species the end of spring migration and the beginning of fall migration are poorly known, and the assessment of differences in the preferred migration pathways within the state must await the availability of additional data. We know that some species (for instance, many shorebirds) migrate primarily through the prairie and that some northern passerines may also have preferred routes, but more information is needed from areas in the western two-thirds of the state, away from the human population centers, to confirm this.

Birding is an avocation that has many dimensions, from occasional backyard observation to species listing on a continental scale, but the thrill of discovery is common to all participants. Years ago, in the days of less rapid and convenient travel, the avid bird student collected eggs and bird skins; the same student today may be a full-time continental lister, striving for that magic number of six hundred — to become one of the elite few who have identified that many species in North America. For people who cannot travel as extensively as continental listing requires, local bird study can be just as exciting. When a local birder recognizes the possible significance of his discoveries and the importance of sharing them through publication, it becomes as great a challenge to him to find a new breeding locality for Sprague's Pipit on the Minnesota prairie as it might be to add the six hundredth species to the list of birds he has observed in his lifetime. The techniques of detailed bird study, especially the study of nesting birds, are rewarding in themselves, yet they are mastered by very few.

As the amateur ornithologist contends with the typical hazards of insects, heat, and brush to explore local habitats and acquires a detailed knowledge of natural history, he may find himself transformed into a modern-day pioneer. He learns that one does not have to go to a remote wilderness to find solitude — it is available in many marshes, fields, and woodlands throughout the state. Listening to the dawn bird-chorus in a forest in June or flushing broods of water birds by canoe in a marsh in July, he discovers the richness of nature that is available to those who seek it out.

We want to emphasize the contribution that amateur ornithologists, which we are, can make to general scientific knowledge. For instance, professional ornithologists need adequate information on bird distribution and abundance for their detailed studies of taxonomy, behavior, evolution, and ecology. These factors are not static; for example, birds expand or contract their ranges in response to changing climatic conditions. The environment is also being altered continually as a result of man's activities, and the ability of different species to adapt to the new conditions can best be documented by local field investigations. Avifaunal changes in an environment stressed by human activity (for example, the decline of species that are affected by the widespread use of persistent pesticides) also provide clues to the general health and stability of that environment and constitute an ecological early warning system. Finally, many breeding species reach the limit of their continental range in Minnesota, and data on their habitat preferences in the state are of great value in ecological and behavioral studies. In all of these areas amateur ornithologists can play a significant role by contributing the records of their field observations to the existing body of information.

Roberts's *The Birds of Minnesota* contained the first comprehensive documentation of the avifaunal history of Minnesota along with a thorough review of ornithology in the state up to that point. His personal records and the specimens he had collected since 1874 became the nucleus of the early collections in the University of Minnesota Museum of Natural History (now the Bell Museum of Natural History) after his appointment as director in 1915, and these materials were subsequently included in his book. Roberts was rigorously selective in choosing additional material for the book, relying to some extent upon the specimens and the notes of other early explorers and collectors and using many observations from bird students and Museum staff members who were active in field research throughout the state in the 1920s and the 1930s. The second edition of the book, published in 1936, included in an appendix a number of significant new records.

Although Roberts's work unquestionably laid the foundation for subsequent ornithological studies of Minnesota's avifauna, we must bear in mind that the data on breeding distribution available to him were limited, particularly for part of the prairie and for the northern coniferous forests. Subsequent fieldwork from these areas has either failed to confirm some of Roberts's assumptions or has uncovered new information, and the resulting data are discussed in the species accounts in this book. A few very unusual records used in *The Birds of Minnesota* have not been included here because substantiation of the records (the details of the reports or the specimens) could not be found in the files and the collections of the Bell Museum of Natural History.

Another important source of data is *The Loon*. This journal makes available the field data of the active observers in the state, but the coverage over the decades has not been uniform. In the late 1930s there was a peak of activity in ornithological investigation, and many useful records were obtained. The next two decades also produced some important information, but detailed field activity was spotty. In the early 1960s the record keeping by the Minnesota Ornithologists' Union became more thorough, and a detailed Seasonal Report column was begun in *The Loon* when Janssen became editor of the publication. Although the final form of this column has varied somewhat, reflecting the preferences of the numerous assistant editors who have volunteered to work on it, the records themselves have been maintained in a permanent file on special report forms that have been provided to the journal's contributors since 1965. Nesting data are kept on individual cards filed by species. The documentation for all records of species on the casual, accidental, and hypothetical lists is available in a separate file. The Bell Museum of Natural History and the Biology Department of the University of Minnesota at Duluth have been very helpful by allowing their facilities to be used for the storage of the files. Although the system for soliciting and filing data from contributors has added a great deal to our knowledge of Minnesota birdlife, there are still many areas of the state that have not been adequately covered.

Other journals that have furnished significant records of Minnesota birds are *The Auk*, *The Wilson Bulletin*, and *Audubon Field Notes* (now *American Birds*). Records published in these journals are cited in the species accounts. Finally, several books and pamphlets devoted to some aspect of birdlife in Minnesota have been published since *The Birds of Minnesota*, and these are listed in the bibliography.

The previously unpublished records included in this volume are principally those of the authors — Green's records, mostly from the northeastern region, for the period 1961–1972, and Janssen's records, from throughout the state but with a base in the Twin Cities area, for the period 1947–1972. Two other field ornithologists made their notebooks available for use in this book: P. B. Hofslund (records from Duluth and the adjacent areas, 1950–1964) and Nestor M. Hiemenz (records from the St. Cloud area, 1931–1968). In addition, we examined field notebooks donated to the University of Minnesota by E. D. Swedenborg (migration records from Hennepin County, 1921–1961) and by Mrs. C. E. Peterson (banding records from Madison, Lac qui Parle County, 1927–1960). The Migratory Bird Populations Station of the United States Fish and Wildlife Service provided a complete summary of all the Breeding Bird Survey routes covered in Minnesota between 1967 and 1972. The species files and the specimen collections of the Bell Museum of Natural History of the University of Minnesota were also examined; most of the material therein was published in *The Birds of Minnesota* or in *The Flicker*, but a few unpublished records were obtained.

In order to utilize most efficiently the existing knowledge of breeding bird distribution in Minnesota and to plan new field activities, the amateur ornithologist needs to know what parts of the state have been the subject of detailed summer field investigations. The information for several areas is available only in field notes and in the Seasonal Report columns in *The Loon*; other published reports on specific areas are listed in the bibliography. The major areas that have been surveyed since 1940 are listed below with the observers' names in parentheses:

> Winona County (Voelker)
> Fillmore County (Warner)
> Rice County (Rustad)
> Twin Cities area (many observers)
> Cedar Creek area, Anoka County (Breckenridge, Mitchell)
> Stearns and Sherburne counties (Hiemenz)
> Stevens County (Grant)
> Mahnomen and Norman counties (Kellehur)
> Itasca State Park, Clearwater County (Hickey, Lewis)
> Wadena County (Oehlenschlager)
> Crow Wing and Aitkin counties (Blanich, Savaloja)
> Duluth area (Carr, Green, Hofslund, Lakela)
> Gooseberry State Park, Lake County (Hofslund)
> Superior National Forest, St. Louis, Lake, and Cook
> counties (Beer, Cottrille, Green)

The responsibility for compiling information for the species accounts in the various families was divided as shown in the following lists:

Green		Janssen	
Cathartidae	Tyrannidae	Gaviidae	Cinclidae
Accipitridae	Corvidae	Podicipedidae	Troglodytidae
Pandionidae	Paridae	Pelecanidae	Icteridae (half)
Falconidae	Sittidae	Phalacrocoracidae	Thraupidae
Stercorariidae	Certhiidae	Ardeidae	Fringillidae
Laridae	Mimidae	Threskiornithidae	
Alcidae	Turdidae	Anatidae	
Columbidae	Sylviidae	Tetraonidae	
Cuculidae	Motacillidae	Phasianidae	
Tytonidae	Bombycillidae	Meleagrididae	
Strigidae	Laniidae	Rallidae	
Caprimulgidae	Sturnidae	Charadriidae	
Apodidae	Vireonidae	Scolopacidae	
Trochilidae	Parulidae	Phalaropodidae	
Alcedinidae	Ploceidae	Alaudidae	
Picidae	Icteridae (half)	Hirundinidae	

The final draft of the text and the appendixes was written by Green. The photographs were collected by Janssen. The manuscript as a whole was read critically by Harrison B. Tordoff, Dwain W. Warner, and John C. Green; their valuable comments are gratefully acknowledged.

We hope that this book will be informative and useful, and in particular we hope that it will serve to stimulate further fieldwork on the birdlife of Minnesota.

J. C. G.

R. B. J.

Contents

List of Maps

MINNESOTA BIRDS
Where, When, and How Many

Notes on Nomenclature, Terminology, and Maps

In condensing the information on Minnesota's avifauna into a format that would provide concise, easily accessible answers to questions of where, when, and how many for each species, we have aimed at consistency in the use of adjectives, in nomenclature, in the establishment of categories of information, and in the sequence in which the information is presented in the discussion of each species. The following comments on nomenclature, terminology, and maps will help the reader to interpret accurately the information in the species accounts.

Nomenclature. The nomenclature and taxonomic sequence in this book follow those of the fifth edition of the *Check-List of North American Birds* (published in 1957 by the American Ornithologists' Union) and the Thirty-second Supplement to the *Check-List* (April, 1973; *Auk* 90:411–419). The revised common names adopted by the American Ornithologists' Union in the Thirty-second Supplement are used in the headings of the species accounts and elsewhere in the text, but the earlier forms of the names are given in parentheses in the headings of the accounts.

Minnesota status. The following definitions are used in assigning each species to a particular status:

1. Regular: Occurs somewhere in the state every year (292 species)
2. Casual: Not known to occur every year but expected to occur at intervals of a few years; nine or more acceptable records for each species (23 species)
3. Accidental: Not expected to occur again or expected to occur again only very infrequently; eight or fewer acceptable records for each species (44 species)
4. Hypothetical: Probably has occurred in the state at least once but no substantiation in the form of a specimen or an identifiable photograph is available, or substantiation consists of three or fewer acceptable observations by a single observer, or substantiation consists of only one observation by fewer than three individuals (12 species)
5. Extirpated: Has not occurred in the state since 1900 but is extant elsewhere (2 species)
6. Extinct: No longer occurs anywhere in the world (1 species)

We seek to categorize species by their occurrence at present, as indicated by recent photographic records and observations, rather than by their occurrence at some point in the past, as confirmed by museum specimens. The collection of specimens for scientific purposes in Minnesota virtually stopped in the 1930s, except for a few special studies, and the occurrence of many species since then has been documented exclusively by photographic records. We have accepted observations if they have been accompanied by a written report including a detailed description of the bird and the circumstances of the observation. The substantiating details of almost all of the observations in the book have been published in *The Loon*, and appropriate source references are given in the species accounts. Not all published records have been judged acceptable. Some observations from before 1960 (when *The Loon* first began to solicit detailed reports of sightings) have been used if the competence of the observer is known and if the species is not easily confused with another. In the listing of species by category in Appendix I, the species name is followed by an asterisk (*) if the only proof is an identifiable photograph (either published or in the species files of the Minnesota Ornithologists' Union) or by a dagger (†) if there is no photograph or specimen on file.

Migration. The migration period for each species is discussed in the accounts. For summer residents and transient birds, the spring migration period is given first; for winter visitants, the fall migration period is given first. Since migration varies with the weather, normal and peak migration periods are described in terms of three ten-day segments for each month (for instance, early April, mid-April, and late April). The selection of the extreme dates from the material available was made according to our judgment of how representative they are. Usually three dates are given to define the extreme ranges of the normal migration; if two dates appear, it means that there were multiple arrivals on one date. Those dates that are regarded as extraordinary are set in italic type. Extreme dates that are hyphenated refer to successive observations of the same bird. Since Minnesota extends for some four hundred miles from Iowa to Canada, its latitudinal range affects the timing of migration, especially early in the spring and late in the fall. In recognition of this, dates are given for the northern and southern halves of the state. As shown on map I, the state is further divided into nine regions (using county lines as boundaries) that are relatively homogeneous seasonally and vegetatively. By referring to these regions we can discuss in greater detail the geographical variations in migration and range for each species.

Abundance. The following abundance terms (adapted from Wood, 1967) are used in discussing migration:

1. Abundant: Daily counts of as many as 50 birds; season counts of 250 or more birds
2. Common: Daily counts of 6 to 50 birds; season counts of as many as 250 birds by an active observer
3. Uncommon: Daily counts of 1 to 5 birds; season counts of 5 to 25 birds by an active observer

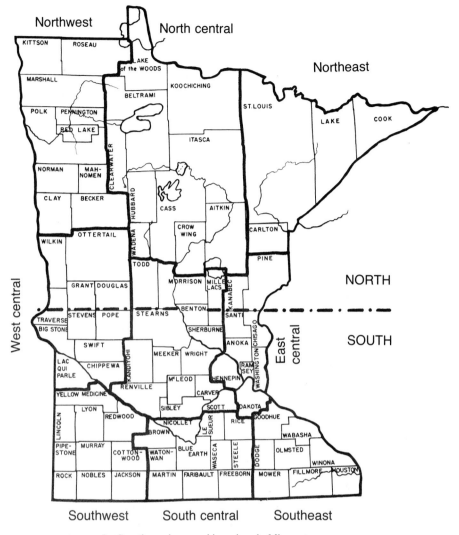

Northwest

North central

Northeast

KITTSON ROSEAU

LAKE of the WOODS

MARSHALL

KOOCHICHING

BELTRAMI

POLK PENNINGTON

ST.LOUIS

RED LAKE

LAKE COOK

ITASCA

NORMAN MAH-NOMEN

CLEARWATER

CLAY BECKER

HUBBARD

CASS AITKIN

CROW WING

CARLTON

OTTERTAIL

WILKIN

WADENA

PINE

TODD

West central

GRANT DOUGLAS

MORRISON MILLE LACS

KANABEC

NORTH

TRAVERSE BIG STONE

STEVENS POPE

STEARNS

BENTON

SANTI

SHERBURNE

SOUTH

SWIFT

ANOKA

CHISAGO

East central

LAC QUI PARLE

CHIPPEWA

KANDIYOHI

MEEKER WRIGHT

RAM SEY

WASHINGTON

HENNEPIN

McLEOD

RENVILLE

YELLOW MEDICINE

CARVER

LYON

REDWOOD

SIBLEY

SCOTT DAKOTA

LINCOLN

NICOLLET

LE SUEUR

RICE GOODHUE

BROWN

WABASHA

PIPE-STONE

MURRAY

COTTON-WOOD

WATON-WAN

BLUE EARTH

WASECA

STEELE

DODGE

OLMSTED

WINONA

ROCK NOBLES JACKSON MARTIN FARIBAULT FREEBORN MOWER FILLMORE HOUSTON

Southwest   South central   Southeast

I. Counties and geographic regions in Minnesota.

4. Rare: Season counts of no more than 5 birds by an active observer

5. Casual: Up to 3 birds seen in a decade by an active observer

6. Accidental: Up to 3 birds seen in a lifetime by an active observer

Obviously these terms are not absolute and are used only as general guides. The number of birds an observer sees depends a good deal on the amount of effort he expends, the degree of skill he possesses, and the kind of habitat he covers. For our purposes, an active observer is one who is afield for an average of one or more hours virtually every day.

Summer populations. Species present during the summer are classified as *residents* if they nest in the state and as *visitants* if they do not. Species that do not nest in the state every year are termed *casual summer residents*. The abundance of birds during the nesting season is determined by the amount of their preferred habitat that is available and the location of it. Since abundance can vary considerably over relatively short distances, no absolute abundance figures are included on the range maps or in the text. The only available data on the absolute abundance of species during the nesting season is from the Breeding Bird Survey conducted by volunteers for the Migratory Bird Populations Station of the United States Bureau of Sport Fisheries and Wildlife in Laurel, Maryland. Although information about many routes has become available since 1967 when the Minnesota surveys began, the coverage of the state is still incomplete. When more data from the surveys have accumulated, it will be possible to describe summer bird populations with greater precision.

Winter populations. Species that occur in the winter, either regularly or casually, are termed *winter visitants* if there are no data to prove that they breed locally. This term is also used for several species (for example, the Great Horned Owl and the American Robin) for which banding records or migration paths indicate that all or part of the winter population differs from the breeding population. If it is not known whether the winter population is different from the summer population, the phrase *regular in winter* is used. Species that are sedentary — that is, species in which most of the population remains in one area for the whole year — are classified as *permanent residents*. The terms used to describe the distribution and the abundance of each species in the winter are the same as those used for the migration seasons.

Seasonal occurrence. Almost all of the 292 species on the regular list occur in more than one season. Summer residents and winter visitants are also usually migrants because some of their movements in the state take place in fall and spring. Nevertheless, it is useful to divide the regular species by seasonal occurrence, assigning each species to the season when it is in the state for the longest period or when it is the most plentiful. Appendix III lists the regular species by seasonal occurrence as primarily *permanent residents*, *summer residents*, *migrants*, or *winter visitants*. Each species is assigned to only one category with emphasis on the status of the species as a breeding bird. A species is classified as a summer resident if it has a significant breeding range in Minnesota, even though most of the birds seen in the state might be migrants; this applies especially to many northern warblers. If a species has a very small breeding range (e.g., the Lesser Scaup), or only a few nesting sites (e.g., the White Pelican and the Sandhill Crane), or a very sparse breeding population (e.g., the Merlin and the Brown Creeper) in Minnesota but has a large migrant population, it is classified as a migrant. Similarly, certain species that are classified as winter visitants also have a very small breeding population; in such cases the assignment is determined by the season in which the largest numbers of birds are seen.

Maps of breeding ranges. Range maps are included in this book for almost all species which have a continental range boundary that cuts across the state. The ranges of about twenty-five other species that have very restricted breeding ranges within the state are not mapped, but they are described in the text. The boundaries on the range maps are generalized and do not contain fine details of locations, primarily because there is not sufficient information on which to base more precise delineations. (One of our purposes in presenting the maps is to stimulate fieldwork that will provide more data which can be used to correct any inaccuracies in the maps.) Those localities that represent the extreme ranges of various species are given in the text. The range maps utilize data on observations during the months of June and July only (in order to avoid the possibility that nesting birds might be confused with migrants), but they include nesting data from any month.

On the range maps nesting data (published or on file) are indicated by a symbol in the outline of each county for which such information is available. The larger counties (for example, Beltrami, Cass, St. Louis, and Lake counties) are divided into segments that approximate the size of the other counties, and more than one symbol may be used in each segment; otherwise, only one symbol is used for each county. The maps which have large areas without any nesting symbols indicate how little is known about many summer residents. Nesting data are particularly important because vagrant birds occurring far outside the regular breeding range of the species may remain unmated all summer. The range maps for ducks and geese were taken from *Waterfowl in Minnesota* (Moyle, 1964a), which was compiled from records of the Minnesota Department of Natural Resources (Division of Game and Fish), a source that offered more complete information than that available in the files of the Minnesota Ornithologists' Union. On these maps no nesting symbols are included within the primary range (the shaded area).

The map symbols and the corresponding definitions are adapted from *British Trust for Ornithology News* (Ornithological Atlas Supplement, 1971):

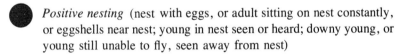

Positive nesting (nest with eggs, or adult sitting on nest constantly, or eggshells near nest; young in nest seen or heard; downy young, or young still unable to fly, seen away from nest)

Inferred nesting (nest-building or excavation of nest-hole in progress; adults seen in distraction display or feigning injury; used nest found; recently fledged young seen; adult seen carrying fecal sac; adult seen carrying food for young; adult seen entering or leaving nest site in circumstances indicating occupied nest)

Two additional symbols are used to show changes in the breeding range:

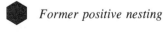

Former positive nesting

Former inferred nesting

The reference dates for former nesting records are given in parentheses in the captions of the maps.

Geography and Ecology
of Minnesota's Birdlife

An understanding of the geography of Minnesota enables the birder to relate the distribution of breeding birds and migration patterns to vegetation communities and landforms. For this reason we include in this section information on the landscape regions, the vegetation, and the diversity of the avifauna within the various geographic areas of the state.

Landscape regions. Most of the physiographic features of Minnesota are the result of glaciation during the Pleistocene epoch (about one million to ten thousand years ago), especially during the most recent series of advances of the Wisconsin glaciers (forty thousand to ten thousand years ago). For instance, the thousands of lakes for which Minnesota is famous are the result of erosion or deposition by glaciers and their meltwaters.

The landscape regions of Minnesota, formulated by Borchert and Yaeger in 1968, are presented in map II, which provides an overview of the physical geography of the state. The erosional activity of the ice sheets created only one major landscape region, the ICE SCOURED REGION along the Canadian border where the glaciers eroded the soil and some of the bedrock itself as they passed over the surface, leaving a country of many bare ledges and lake basins. Much of the rest of the state is blanketed by deposits of glacial origin. Large areas are covered by moraines consisting of unconsolidated material that was carried by the glaciers and deposited when the ice stagnated or melted. Borchert and Yaeger group the moraines into four landscape regions — the PINE MORAINE, the PARK REGION, the BIG WOODS MORAINE, and the WET PRAIRIE — all characterized by low, rolling hills with many lakes scattered among them. The Anoka SAND PLAIN and the WADENA DRUMLIN FIELD are other landscape features produced by glacial deposition.

As the glaciers melted, they released enormous amounts of water. In some instances the glacial meltwaters collected to form large lakes in which the accumulation of sediments over long periods of time eventually created flat beds. Two modern areas of very flat terrain — the BIG BOG and the RED RIVER VALLEY LAKE PLAIN (bounded on the east by ancient beach ridges as indicated in map II) — are the result of sediments deposited on the bottom of Glacial Lake Agassiz.

8

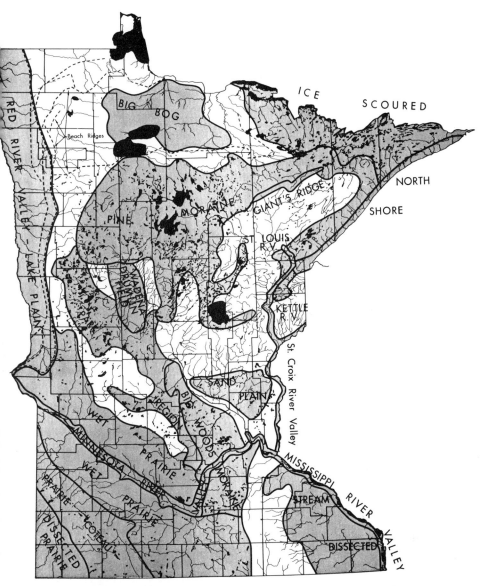

II. Landscape regions in Minnesota. (Prepared by Donald P. Yaeger and John R. Borchert; first published in *Minnesota Resource Potentials in State Outdoor Recreation*, Project 80 Staff Report No. 1, Minnesota Department of Natural Resources and Minnesota State Planning Agency, St. Paul, Minnesota, 1971.)

The largest of the glacial lakes were Glacial Lake Agassiz in the northwestern part of the state and Glacial Lake Duluth in the northeastern part. When the lakes filled to the brim, the meltwaters found outlets to the south, forming large rivers that eroded down through the glacial deposits into the bedrock beneath. Glacial River Warren, which carved out the modern Minnesota River valley, was the outlet for Glacial Lake Agassiz. In its course it eroded down into the Precambrian granites and gneisses (3.3 to 1.6 billion years old) that today are readily visible on the valley floor because the modern Minnesota River is much smaller than its torrential predecessor. Glacial Lake Duluth spilled over into what became the Kettle and St. Croix river valleys, exposing sedimentary rocks — sandstones and dolomites — of late Precambrian and early Paleozoic age (1 billion to 500 million years old). These swollen rivers ultimately drained into the Mississippi River as their descendants do today (Sims and Morey, 1972).

Preglacial erosion into the underlying bedrock also produced the topographic relief of the highlands along the North Shore of Lake Superior, the GIANT'S RIDGE in the Mesabi Range, the PRAIRIE COTEAU in the southwestern part of the state, and the STREAM DISSECTED REGION (or "driftless area") in the southeast (map II). The STREAM DISSECTED REGION and the DISSECTED PRAIRIE in the southwestern corner of the state were not covered by the Wisconsin glaciers, although these areas had been glaciated earlier in the Pleistocene. In the STREAM DISSECTED REGION, a country of steep valleys, bluffs, and flat uplands, almost all of the previous glacial drift deposits were removed by stream erosion, but drift material is still abundant in the DISSECTED PRAIRIE.

Vegetation. The various types of vegetation native to Minnesota developed in response to three elements in the environment: the topography of the land, including slope and drainage; the composition of the soils formed on the glacial deposits and the bedrock; and the climate, especially the amount of rainfall annually. Three of the main ecological units, or biomes, that make up the world's vegetation — the boreal forest, the deciduous forest, and the grassland — meet in Minnesota. Separating these biomes are two transitional areas, or ecotones, which cover large areas of the state. The ecotone between the grassland and the deciduous forest is represented on map III by the OAK AND OAK SAVANNA of the southeastern part of the state grading into the ASPEN PARKLAND of the northwestern corner. The complex ecotone between the boreal forest and the deciduous forest covers the northeastern and north central regions of the state with a complex mosaic of vegetation that intermingles with the boreal forest. This ecotone is described and mapped in different ways by various ecologists, and we find it useful to describe it as the white pine–northern hardwoods forest type. On map III the white pine–northern hardwoods forest type is represented by the PINE and MAPLE-BASSWOOD communities east of the Mississippi River, the boreal forest biome is represented by the SPRUCE-FIR community, and the deciduous forest biome is represented by the MAPLE-BASSWOOD forests west of the Mississippi River in the PARK REGION, the BIG WOODS MORAINE, and the STREAM DISSECTED REGION.

The presettlement vegetation types have been much changed by human activity since the beginning of intensive settlement in the middle of the nineteenth century. The coniferous forests (including the white pine–northern hardwoods and boreal forest types) have been the least modified, although

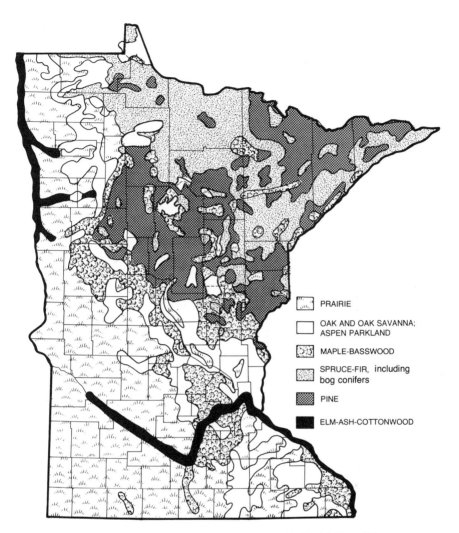

PRAIRIE

OAK AND OAK SAVANNA;
ASPEN PARKLAND

MAPLE-BASSWOOD

SPRUCE-FIR, including
bog conifers

PINE

ELM-ASH-COTTONWOOD

III. Presettlement vegetation types in Minnesota. (Adapted by Patricia Burwell from an unpublished map drawn by F. J. Marschner in 1930 for the United States Department of Agriculture, Washington, D.C.)

virgin forests survive only in Itasca State Park, in the Boundary Waters Canoe Area, and in many smaller remnant stands scattered throughout the area. Lumbering and (to a lesser extent) land clearing for agriculture are the two human activities that have resulted in the greatest modification of the forests. Both activities are frequently followed by severe fires that have an important influence on the nature of the present forest communities. Fire was always a factor in the virgin forest, and many species (pine, birch, and poplar) are especially well adapted to the forest environment produced by natural fires (Heinselman, 1973). Severe and repeated fires (such as those for clearing land), however, at times resulted in the complete destruction of the seed source of the conifers (and sometimes in the destruction of the soil itself) and produced the scrub forests of aspen, birch, and brush found in many areas. The white birch–aspen community, an early successional stage of the boreal forest, occupies disturbed sites formed by fire or land clearing. Eventually the white birch–aspen vegetation type is replaced by the white spruce–balsam fir type. This is now happening in many northern regions as the stands produced by fires early in this century mature. In areas of the coniferous forest where land cleared for farming was found to be unproductive, extensive cultivation has now been abandoned and the land is slowly returning to forest. The planting of commercially valuable species of conifers (especially red pine, jack pine, and white spruce) is rapidly accelerating reforestation in some places.

The communities in the coniferous forest that have changed least in the last one hundred years are the upland hardwoods and the swamp conifers. The former occupy well-drained ridges and hills and consist principally of sugar maple, basswood, and yellow birch. The two main areas of this type are the North Shore highlands and a belt trending westward from Duluth to Leech Lake, where the yellow birch drops out of the community (Flaccus and Ohmann, 1964). Other stands of northern hardwoods are found north and south of this belt (map III). Large white pines were among the original components of the northern hardwood stands, but they were subsequently removed through selective logging and they have not regenerated. Black spruce and tamarack are found in peat bogs scattered throughout the area, and black ash and white cedar occur in swamp forests where the soil is not acidic. The largest bogs have formed on the flat lake beds of Glacial Lake Agassiz (the BIG BOG area on map II), Glacial Lake Upham (central St. Louis County), and Glacial Lake Aitkin (northern Aitkin County). These peatlands consist of fen (grass-sedge), muskeg (thickets of leatherleaf, Labrador tea, and other ericaceous shrubs on sphagnum moss), and bog forest (tamarack–black spruce) and give a pronounced boreal aspect to much of northern Minnesota.

In contrast to the common assumption that the northern virgin forest consisted predominantly of old-growth stands of white pine and red pine, the communities of upland hardwoods and swamp conifers just described were well established in presettlement times. Before the advent of selective logging the stands of pine were indeed a more prominent part of the forest than they are now, but the other forest communities covered large areas as they do today.

The deciduous forests, including the OAK AND OAK SAVANNA and the MAPLE-BASSWOOD vegetation types on map III, have been permanently altered by land clearing for farming and urbanization, and only occasional remnant stands remain, particularly in the southern half of the state. In Minnesota the deciduous forest richest in species is found in the STREAM DISSECTED REGION of the southeast, where the deciduous forest intermingles with other forest communities in the Mississippi Valley. Rosendahl (1955) divides the southern forest areas into three types: bottomland forest, wooded slopes, and upland forest. He describes them as follows: "On the bottomlands of the Mississippi . . . the chief trees are cottonwoods and several species of willow. On slightly higher land the American elm and soft maple are abundant along with such trees as hackberry, green and black ash, box elder, river birch, and occasionally Kentucky coffee tree and swamp white oak. . . . The forest of the north- and northeast-facing slopes of the high bluffs is composed mainly of red oak, sugar maple, basswood, butternut, large-toothed aspen, pignut hickory, black cherry, and, less frequently, of white birch and black oak. Toward the base of the bluffs and ravines black walnut is common. Scattered groves of white pine occur throughout the region, usually well up the slopes or at the crest of the bluffs. . . . The upland forest is composed mainly of oak, in which Hill's oak, white oak, and bur oak predominate, with red oak, shellbark, and pignut hickory and black cherry occupying a secondary position. In abandoned fields and openings trembling aspen is fairly common." These forests are now best represented in the State Memorial Hardwood Forest of Wabasha, Winona, and Houston counties.

The thick deciduous forest of the BIG WOODS MORAINE from Stearns to Rice counties in the central part of the state was formed on rich calcareous soils and was composed mostly of sugar maple, basswood, white elm, red elm, and red oak (Rosendahl, 1955). This is fertile country and most of the land has been cleared for farming or has been urbanized. One of the best remnant stands is Nerstrand Woods in Rice County.

The combination of oak forest and oak savanna that once bordered the Big Woods on the less fertile soils to the northwest and the northeast has been entirely replaced by oak forest in areas where farming is not extensive. The oak savanna, a region of oak trees and oak groves on the prairie, needed fire for its perpetuation. In former times when fires on the prairie were less controlled by man than at present, the young oak trees were destroyed by the fires, although the older trees with their thick bark were able to survive. This created a more open vegetational community than that characteristic of the oak forest. To the east of the Big Woods, Rosendahl continues, the "dominant trees are oaks — bur oak on the more calcareous soils, white oak in great abundance on the heavier acid soils, and Hill's oak on the sandier areas. In some of these [soils] the trees reach good size, but often, over considerable areas, they are small and scarcely more than large shrubs. . . . In this area of open woods and groves conifers are rare but somewhat more common than in the region of the Big Woods. Red cedar and, less frequently, juniper and yew occur around lakes and on the bluffs of the Mississippi and St. Croix rivers. White pine is fairly common along the St. Croix and occurs in a few situations along the bluffs of the Mississippi. Tamarack bogs are frequent and may be regarded as local islands of the northeastern forest surrounded by the more southern general vegetation."

Of the three biomes that occur in Minnesota, the grassland biome has been the most disturbed and has been destroyed almost completely by farming. The prairie is an area of very fertile soils, and except for some small patches of virgin prairie preserved in parks, cemeteries, waterfowl areas, and holdings of The Nature Conservancy it is under intense cultivation. Some rocky areas that are too rough to plow, principally in the PRAIRIE COTEAU and on the beach ridges of Glacial Lake Agassiz, remain as pasture, but the rest is cropland. According to Smith (1966), the Minnesota grassland was originally part of the tall-grass prairie, "a narrow belt running north and south next to the deciduous forests. In fact, it was well developed within a region that could support forests. Oak-hickory forests did extend into the grassland along streams and rivers, on well-drained soils, sandy areas, and hills. Prairie fires often set by Indians in the fall stimulated a vigorous growth of grass and eliminated the encroaching forest. . . . Big bluestem was the dominant grass of moist soils and occupied the valleys of rivers and streams and the lower slopes of the hills. The foliage stood two to three feet tall and the flower stalks three to twelve feet, so high that cattle were hidden in the grass. . . . Associated with bluestem were a number of forbs, goldenrods, compass plants, snakeroot, and bedstraw. . . . Drier uplands in the tall-grass country were dominated by the bunch-forming needlegrass, side-oats grama, and prairie dropseed. Like the lowland, the drier prairie contained many species other than grass. . . . The suggestion has been made that perhaps the xeric prairie might be more appropriately called 'daisyland.' "

Ecology and breeding avifauna. Because of the great diversity of vegetation in Minnesota, an impressive variety of birds breed in the state. Of the 292 species that occur in the state regularly, 220 species nest in the state every year, and 8 species nest in the state occasionally; in addition, 5 species on the casual list nest in the state occasionally. Paradoxically, in spite of the complex vegetational pattern, almost half of the regular breeding species occur either throughout the state or over most of its geographical area (Appendix II). This is because the habitat requirements of these species are widely available; most of the species occupy aerial or aquatic niches, successional stages within the forest (for example, thickets or deciduous communities of any type), or grasslands (native prairie, hayfields, or pastures within the forested areas). As the notations on the lists in Appendix II indicate, a number of species that are thought to breed generally throughout Minnesota (that is, species that do not have a range boundary within the state) become very scarce or do not occur at all in the northeastern boreal forest and the southwestern prairie. The following species that occupy specialized or successional habitats are found only in the southern half of the state:

Great Egret	Dickcissel (usually)·
King Rail	Henslow's Sparrow
Common Gallinule	Field Sparrow

The grassland habitats that occur throughout the state harbor particularly distinctive species of birds. These species do not all occur together, however, because they have different requirements for such things as the extent of bare ground, the amount of litter, the degree of wetness, and the height and density of grasses:

Upland Sandpiper	Dickcissel
Horned Lark	Savannah Sparrow
Bobolink	Grasshopper Sparrow
Eastern Meadowlark	Henslow's Sparrow
Western Meadowlark	Vesper Sparrow

Other grassland species are found on the native upland prairie of the northwestern region:

Marbled Godwit	Baird's Sparrow
Sprague's Pipit	Chestnut-collared Longspur

The aquatic environments in the state vary from wooded swamps to large, open lakes and seasonally flooded meadows, and the ranges of many species overlap in them. A typical aquatic environment is the shallow marsh with vegetation composed principally of cattails, bulrushes, grasses, and sedges. The following species are usually found in cattail marshes in south and central Minnesota:

Least Bittern	Common Gallinule (south)
Redhead	American Coot
Canvasback (now rare;	Black Tern
adjacent to open water)	Long-billed Marsh Wren
Ruddy Duck	Yellow-headed Blackbird
King Rail (south)	Red-winged Blackbird
Virginia Rail	

Another aquatic community — characterized by sedges, grasses, and rushes — is the northern sedge meadow found in the north and central parts of the state. The avifauna of the northern sedge meadow includes several distinctive species:

Sora	Le Conte's Sparrow
Yellow Rail	Sharp-tailed Sparrow (northwest)
Short-billed Marsh Wren	

Almost all species that have a range boundary within Minnesota have a preference for one of the three major biomes or the associated ecotones that meet within the state. It is useful to assign these species to one of three ecological categories based on the location of their primary breeding ranges in the northern coniferous forest, the southeastern deciduous forest, or the prairie (Appendix II). It must be stressed that this division is not absolute, and a number of species (especially those typical of the deciduous forest) have ranges that cover more than one biome. Only those species in the southeast and the river bottomlands are particularly distinctive. As the qualifiers on the ecological distribution list in Appendix II show, the ranges of these species are less stable than the ranges of species in the other two areas. In none of the three areas do the ranges of the listed species overlap one another completely.

1. *Northern coniferous forest.* The list of species that breed primarily in this area is long because the area is large and contains a complex pattern of vegetation. The area includes the northeastern and north central regions, but not all of the species on the list occur throughout these regions. Several species are so rare that they cannot be found regularly every summer; those designated (? casual) have not yet been found breeding in Minnesota. Although early ornithological investigations were scanty, several historical changes in the avifauna are evident. For instance, the range of the Common Raven was sharply reduced as a result of lumbering operations early in the century, but since the mid-1950s the range and the abundance of the species have increased again. Many northern passerines (Winter Wren, Hermit Thrush, Golden-crowned Kinglet, Black-throated Green Warbler, Blackburnian Warbler) that used to occur regularly south of Mille Lacs Lake no longer are found there. The gradual elimination of natural pine in the forests and the widespread clearing of woods for farms and suburbs may have been factors in the disappearance of these northern passerines from the southern part of the state.

In general, the number of northern forest species is greatest in northern St. Louis, Koochiching, Lake, and Cook counties. Within the northern coniferous forest regions the species most characteristic of the boreal forest are usually found in the muskeg–black spruce bogs formed on the peatlands of former glacial lakes of various sizes. These species include:

Spruce Grouse	Nashville Warbler
Yellow-bellied Flycatcher	Cape May Warbler
Gray Jay	Yellow-rumped Warbler
Boreal Chickadee	Bay-breasted Warbler
Hermit Thrush	Palm Warbler
Golden-crowned Kinglet	Connecticut Warbler
Ruby-crowned Kinglet	Dark-eyed Junco
Solitary Vireo	Lincoln's Sparrow
Tennessee Warbler	

Many other species that are more typical of the deciduous forest occur throughout the coniferous forest regions, and in areas where two or more forest communities intermingle the avifauna may be correspondingly diverse. For example, during a survey of breeding birds in the Superior National Forest (Sawbill Landing) a Whip-poor-will and an Olive-sided Flycatcher were heard together at one stop and a Brown Thrasher and a Connecticut Warbler were heard at another stop.

2. Southeastern deciduous forest. The species listed for this area are generally restricted to the bottomland forests and the remnant deciduous woods and their brushy openings in the southeastern quarter of the state. Many other species (not listed) occur here as well as in wooded areas elsewhere in the state. The ranges of most species typical of the southeastern deciduous forest have undergone some change since the settlement of the state. Currently the Red-shouldered Hawk, the Red-bellied Woodpecker, and the Cardinal are rapidly expanding their ranges into the northern and western regions of the state, a trend that began early in this century. The Mockingbird is also extending its range in the state, but it is still rare and local in occurrence; it nests more often in the central and northern regions (to Cook County) than in the southern regions of the state. The Bewick's Wren, the Carolina Wren, and the Yellow-breasted Chat were numerous at one time, but at present they are only casual in occurrence in the southeastern deciduous forest. Roberts believed that the Blue-gray Gnatcatcher, the Bell's Vireo, the Blue-winged Warbler, and the Cerulean Warbler had expanded their ranges into southeastern Minnesota within the historical period. These species currently occupy about the same territory that they did in the 1930s, and they may have been overlooked before then. The population of the Tufted Titmouse is particularly variable from year to year. Wintering groups occasionally occur as far north as Duluth, but in other years few wintering birds are present in the center of their range along the lower Mississippi River valley. The Bobwhite, which was once stocked in the state by the Minnesota Department of Conservation as a game bird, is rare now, and its numbers seem to be restricted by the severity of the winters. The Yellow-crowned Night Heron and the Acadian Flycatcher have been recorded as breeding species only during the past twenty-five years. The populations of both species are small and local, occurring primarily in Houston County.

3. Prairie. The avifauna in this area can be divided into aquatic species that occupy prairie marshes and lakes and grassland species of the native prairie. The wetlands of the prairie have been much reduced by draining for agricultural purposes, especially south of the Minnesota River and in the Red River Valley. Most of the prairie pothole country that remains is in the west central part of the state from Kandiyohi to Mahnomen counties, where the state and federal governments own many acres of wetlands. Although the destruction of habitat as a result of draining continues, grebes, ducks, phalaropes, gulls, and terns still occupy these areas. The Willet and the American Avocet may always have been rare and local in occurrence there. The Trumpeter Swan and the Whooping Crane once nested on wetlands of the Minnesota prairie, but these species were extirpated during the nineteenth century. The White Pelican also was more widespread than it is now; currently it is known to breed in only three localities. The Short-eared Owl of the prairie marshes and meadows has suffered a decline since the early 1960s with the expansion of intensive agriculture. It is possible that the Burrowing Owl, which was found locally in fairly large numbers as recently as the early 1960s, no longer nests in the state. Two grassland species, the Long-billed Curlew and the McCown's Longspur, were extirpated as breeding species before the turn of the century. Other species have retreated to the northwestern region as the grasslands farther south have been put under the plow; these species include the Upland Sandpiper, the Marbled Godwit, the Sprague's Pipit, the Baird's Sparrow, and the Chestnut-collared Longspur. As the world's need for food increases, the demand for agricultural land on the fertile Minnesota prairie will also increase. Although little native habitat for birds now remains there, even that small fraction is likely to be threatened in the future.

The variety of landscape regions in Minnesota and the resulting ecological diversity combine to make the state an area of special interest to birders throughout the United States. Amateur and professional ornithologists come to Minnesota to seek out species such as the Common Loon in quiet wilderness habitats, the Greater Prairie Chicken, the Marbled Godwit, and the Yellow Rail in the prairie marshes and grasslands, and the Connecticut Warbler in the boreal forest. These and other representative species and the typical ecological settings they occupy are illustrated in the following section of photographs.

Common Loon on nest, Hubbard County. (Photo by Paul W. Harrison.)

Greater Prairie Chicken, Wilkin County. (Photo by Lloyd Paynter.)

Marbled Godwit, Wilkin County. (Photo by Lloyd Paynter.)

Yellow Rail; adult male, photographed in captivity. (Photo by Scott Stalheim.)

Glaucous Gull and Herring Gulls, Lake County. (Photo by Janet C. Green.)

Franklin's Gulls, Marshall County. (Photo by Lloyd Paynter.)

Great Gray Owl, St. Louis County. (Photo by Janet C. Green.)

Gray Jay, Lake County. (Photo by Craig R. Borck.)

Connecticut Warbler at nest, Lake County. (Photo by Betty Darling Cottrille.)

Mourning Warbler at nest, Lake County. (Photo by Betty Darling Cottrille.)

Evening Grosbeak, St. Louis County. (Photo by Marj Carr.)

Le Conte's Sparrow, St. Louis County. (Photo by Marj Carr.)

Typical spruce bog habitat, Lake County. (Photo by Betty Darling Cottrille.)

Boreal watercourse habitat, Jasper Creek, Lake County. (Photo by Betty Darling Cottrille.)

Northern forest mosaic, Teal Lake, Cook County. (Photo by John C. Green.)

Northern deciduous forest habitat, Cook County. (Photo by Marj Carr.)

Northern coniferous forest habitat, Misquah Lake and Misquah Hill, Cook County. (Photo by John C. Green.)

Typical grassland habitat, Pope County. (Photo by John C. Green.)

Marsh habitat of Yellow Rail, Mahnomen County. (Photo by Scott Stalheim.)

Heron rookery island, Lake Johanna, Pope County. (Photo by Bruce A. Hitman.)

Family GAVIIDAE: Loons

COMMON LOON *Gavia immer*

1. Common Loon (1930)

Minnesota status. Regular. Migrant and summer resident.
Migration. Common spring and fall migrant in the eastern and central regions; uncommon in the western regions. Concentrations of several hundred to a thousand birds have been noted, especially on Mille Lacs Lake in the fall. *Spring migration period:* Late March through late May with the bulk of the migration from mid-April through early May. Earliest dates: SOUTH, March *12*, 25, 26; NORTH, March *28*, *30*, April 4, 5, 7. *Fall migration period:* Late August through early December with a peak in mid-October. Latest dates: NORTH, December 1, 3, *22*; SOUTH, December 6, 8, 9, *26*.
Summer. Resident throughout most of the state except the southern regions and the Red River Valley (see map 1); most numerous in the north central and northeastern regions. Formerly (in about 1900) the species nested as far south as the Iowa border. Nonbreeding birds have been reported recently in the southern regions; many nonbreeding pairs summer on Lake Superior.

ARCTIC LOON *Gavia arctica*

Minnesota status. Accidental. One spring record and six fall records.
Records. Six fall observations from Lake Superior in St. Louis County: September 10, 1973, bird in winter plumage (*Loon* 46:39); September 16–20, 1973, bird in winter plumage (*Loon* 46:58); September 17–24, 1972, bird in breeding plumage (*Loon* 44:116–117); October 3–4, 1973, bird in breeding plumage; October 22–23, 1973, bird in winter plumage; November 22, 1969, bird in winter plumage (*Loon* 43:19). The spring record was the sighting of an adult bird near Duluth on May 3, 1973 (*Loon* 45:61–62).

RED-THROATED LOON *Gavia stellata*

Minnesota status. Regular. Migrant; accidental in summer and winter.
Migration. Uncommon spring migrant and rare fall migrant throughout the eastern part of the state (east of the Mississippi River); casual or absent elsewhere. *Spring migration period:* Late April through mid-June with a peak from late May through early June on Lake Superior. Earliest dates: SOUTH, April 17, 22, 28; NORTH, April 30, May 1, 6. Latest dates: SOUTH, May 20 (only date); NORTH, June 15, 17, *22*. *Fall migration period:* Mid-September through late November. Earliest dates: NORTH, September 16, 19,

26; SOUTH, October 30 (only date). Latest dates: NORTH, November 7, 23 (only dates); SOUTH, November 17, 26 (only dates).

Summer. Two midsummer observations, both from Lake Superior: July 8, 1945, Duluth; July 3, 1952, Cook County.

Winter. Three records: January 1, 1954, Duluth; February 22, 1942, one bird in spring plumage, St. Cloud; March 9, 1952, two birds, Lake Superior, St. Louis County.

Family PODICIPEDIDAE: Grebes

RED-NECKED GREBE *Podiceps grisegena*

Minnesota status. Regular. Migrant and summer resident; accidental in winter.

Migration. In the spring common throughout the state, becoming abundant on Lake Superior at Duluth at the migration peak. In the fall uncommon throughout the state. *Spring migration period:* Early April through late May with a peak in late April. Earliest dates: SOUTH, April 5, 7, 8; NORTH, April 5, 8, 14. *Fall migration period:* Late August through early December; no peaks or concentrations noted. Latest dates: NORTH, November 11, 23, December 6, 27; SOUTH, December 1, 8, 13.

Summer. Resident primarily in the northwestern, central, and east central regions; occurs sparingly in other parts of the state (see map 2). There are breeding records from as far east as Lake Vermilion, St. Louis County, and as far south as Swan Lake, Nicollet County; Albert Lea, Freeborn County; and Heron Lake, Jackson County.

2. Red-necked Grebe (1930)

Winter. The winter records are all of single birds on Lake Superior: January 1, 1954, Duluth; January 4 and February 15, 1964, Two Harbors; January 6, 1963, Knife River; February 19, 1962, Duluth.

HORNED GREBE *Podiceps auritus*

Minnesota status. Regular. Migrant and summer resident; casual in winter on Lake Superior.

Migration. Common spring and fall migrant throughout the state. Peak concentrations of one thousand to five thousand birds occur at Duluth at the time of the smelt run in late April. *Spring migration period:* Late March through early June with a peak in late April. Earliest dates: SOUTH, March 19, 25, 30; NORTH, April 3, 5, 9. Latest dates (beyond breeding areas): SOUTH, May 14, 16, 24; NORTH, June 2, 6, 9. *Fall migration period:* Mid-August through mid-December with the bulk of the migration from early October through mid-November. Earliest dates: None can be given because of postbreeding wanderers. Latest dates: NORTH (with the exception of Lake Superior), November 14, 17, 19; SOUTH, December 4, 6, 8.

Summer. Resident in the northwestern region with breeding reported from Kittson, Roseau, Marshall, and Mahnomen counties. Formerly more widespread with nesting documented for Jackson County (1885, 1900), McLeod County (1926), and Kandiyohi County (1944). There are a number of recent summer observations from the central and northeastern regions, but these probably represent postbreeding dispersal or nonbreeding birds.

Winter. Casual visitant on Lake Superior with four observations in the second half of December, three in January, and two in February; all observations were of one or two birds.

EARED GREBE *Podiceps nigricollis*

Minnesota status. Regular. Migrant and summer resident.
Migration. In the spring uncommon in the western regions; rare in the central, east central, and south central regions; casual elsewhere. In the fall rare in the western regions; casual to accidental elsewhere. *Spring migration period:* Mid-April through late May with a peak probably in early May. Earliest dates: SOUTH, March *30*, April 12, 13, 16; NORTH, April 11, 19, 22. *Fall migration period:* The bulk of the population probably leaves the nesting areas in September or early October; very little information is available. Latest dates: NORTH, November *29* (only date); SOUTH, October 2, 11, 14, November *7*.
Summer. Resident primarily in the western regions and through the central part of the state as far east as Swan Lake, Nicollet County (see map 3). In the last twenty-five years nesting for this colonial bird has been reported only from Alberta, Stevens County; Swan Lake, Nicollet County; and Agassiz National Wildlife Refuge, Marshall County.

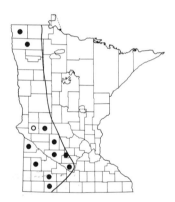

3. Eared Grebe

WESTERN GREBE *Aechmophorus occidentalis*

Minnesota status. Regular. Migrant and summer resident.
Migration. Common spring and fall migrant in the western regions; locally abundant, especially in the fall. Casual elsewhere, except for breeding locations in the central regions, in both seasons. *Spring migration period:* Mid-April through early June with a peak in early May. Earliest dates: SOUTH, April 15, 16; NORTH, April 29 (only date). Latest dates (beyond breeding areas): June 2, 6, *19*. *Fall migration period:* Probably from sometime in September through

mid-November. Latest dates: NORTH, no data; SOUTH, November 11, 15, 17.

Summer. Resident primarily in the western regions and eastward through the central region to Swan Lake, Nicollet County (see map 4). In the last ten years breeding has been reported from Lake Traverse, Traverse County; Frog Lake, Stevens County; Sundberg Lake, Kandiyohi County; Agassiz National Wildlife Refuge, Marshall County; and Swan Lake, Nicollet County (*Flicker* 33:93–94). Large numbers (100 to 150 birds) have been seen at the last two locations, and the population in the state seems to be increasing.

PIED-BILLED GREBE *Podilymbus podiceps*

Minnesota status. Regular. Migrant and summer resident; casual in winter.

Migration. Common spring and fall migrant throughout the state; least numerous in the northeastern region in the fall. *Spring migration period:* Mid-March through mid-May with a peak in mid-April. Earliest dates: SOUTH, March 8, 13, 14; NORTH, March *16*, 22, 25, 27. *Fall migration period:* Late August through mid-December with a peak in mid-October. Latest dates: NORTH, November 29, December 4, *26*; SOUTH, December 12, 19, 20.

Summer. Resident throughout the state but very scarce in Cook, Lake, and northern St. Louis counties because of the lack of suitable habitat.

Winter. There are eight records of birds attempting to overwinter in the southeastern region and in adjacent Dakota and Hennepin counties. Three of these birds are known to have survived until mid- or late February.

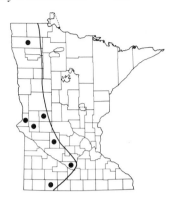

4. Western Grebe

Family PELECANIDAE: Pelicans

WHITE PELICAN *Pelecanus erythrorhynchos*

Minnesota status. Regular. Migrant, summer resident, and summer visitant.

Migration. Common migrant in the west central, southwestern, and south central regions and in the adjacent counties in the central region; locally abundant (with concentrations of as many as five thousand birds) in the southwestern region, especially in the fall; rare in the north central and northeastern regions; usually uncommon elsewhere in the state. *Spring migration period:* Early April through late May with a peak in the third week of April. Earliest dates: SOUTH, March 20, April 2, 4, 5; NORTH, April 15, 21, 24. *Fall migration period:* Possibly August through early November with a peak in the second half of September.

Latest dates: NORTH, November 5, 8, 12; SOUTH, November 1, 3, 10, December *1*.

Summer. The species currently breeds on Marsh Lake, Lac qui Parle County (1943, 1968–1972), and Heron Lake, Jackson County (1972). Roberts (1932) stated that it was formerly a fairly common summer resident throughout Minnesota, although he listed breeding data only from Grant County (1878) and Sandy Lake, Aitkin County (1904), and mentioned possible former nestings on Leech Lake, Lake Shetek, and Heron Lake. The species is now a common summer visitant near the headwaters of the Minnesota River (Traverse, Big Stone, and Lac qui Parle counties), near Heron Lake (Jackson and Nobles counties), and at Agassiz National Wildlife Refuge (Marshall County); it is occasionally seen farther east (Aitkin, St. Louis, Crow Wing, Freeborn, Rice, Nicollet, and Houston counties).

Family PHALACROCORACIDAE: Cormorants

DOUBLE-CRESTED CORMORANT
Phalacrocorax auritus

Minnesota status. Regular. Migrant and summer resident.
Migration. Common spring and fall migrant throughout most of the state; uncommon in the spring and rare in the fall in the northeastern region. Until the early 1950s the species was abundant, and flocks of one thousand to five thousand birds were observed; peak flock size now is usually two hundred to five hundred birds. *Spring migration period:* Late March through early June with a peak in the second half of April. Earliest dates: SOUTH, March *15*, *19*, 28, 30, April 1; NORTH, April 11, 14, 16. *Fall migration period:* Mid-September through early December with a peak in the third week of October; almost all birds leave by early November (formerly a few birds stayed longer). Latest dates: NORTH, October 21, 29 (only dates), November *29*; SOUTH, currently November 6, 7, 8, *17* (formerly December 3, 4, 5, *11*, *17*).

Summer. Resident with active colonies in Marshall, Pope, and Lac qui Parle counties. The species has bred in all regions of the state but only sparingly in the north central region (Lake of the Woods, Rice Lake National Wildlife Refuge) and in the northeastern region (Kawishiwi Lake). Nonbreeding birds (or birds from undiscovered colonies) may be seen in any part of the state in summer. Recent observations are mostly from the vicinity of the active colonies mentioned above and near the large lakes in the west central region.

Family ARDEIDAE: Herons and Bitterns

GREAT BLUE HERON *Ardea herodias*

Minnesota status. Regular. Migrant and summer resident; casual in winter.

Migration. Common spring and fall migrant throughout the state; least numerous in the heavily wooded areas. *Spring migration period:* Mid-March through mid-May with a peak in early April. Earliest dates: SOUTH, March 12, 14; NORTH, March 25, 27, April 1, 2, 3. *Fall migration period:* Late July through mid-December with the bulk of the migration in August and early September. Latest dates: NORTH, October 31, November 5, 8, *18*, December *1*; SOUTH, none can be given because of late-lingering birds, most of which leave by late November.

Summer. Resident throughout the state. The colonies are small and scarce in the northwestern region, and none are known in the southwestern region. The number of breeding birds contained in a colony varies considerably. The largest colonies (more than two hundred nests) occur in the southeastern, east central, central, and south central regions.

Winter. Stragglers remain in the southeastern part of the state (from the Twin Cities southward) through mid-January. There are only two February records: February 13, 1965, Winona County; February 13, 1967, Cotton, St. Louis County.

GREEN HERON *Butorides virescens*

Minnesota status. Regular. Migrant and summer resident.

Migration. Common migrant in the southeastern, east central, and central regions; uncommon in the south central, southwestern, and west central regions; rare to casual in the northern regions. *Spring migration period:* Mid-April through late May with a peak in the first week of May. Earliest dates: SOUTH, April 6, 10, 12; NORTH, April 27, 30, May 5. *Fall migration period:* Probably from sometime in August through late October; birds leave breeding areas gradually (no concentrations noted). Latest dates: NORTH, September 1 (only date); SOUTH, October 26, 27, 30, November 9.

Summer. Resident primarily in the southern half of the state with breeding confirmed as far north as Pine County (1919) and Crosby, Crow Wing County (1969). Since 1960 quite a number of observations (but no nesting data) have been reported from farther north (see map 5). There are also single observations from Lake of the Woods, Lake of the Woods County (1939); Agassiz National Wildlife Refuge, Marshall County (1966); and Trout Lake, St. Louis County (1969).

5. Green Heron

LITTLE BLUE HERON *Florida caerulea*

Minnesota status. Casual. Spring migrant, summer visitant, and resident.

Records. Seven of the records are from the spring migration (April 18 to May 21, with a peak between May 8 and May 10) and occur south of a line between Lac qui Parle and Goodhue counties. One bird was seen in Hennepin County on June 5, 1973 (*Loon* 45:62–63). The only northern record is from the vicinity of Virginia, St. Louis County, May 27–29, 1972 (*Loon* 44:123). Five late summer records: August 17, 1956, Wabasha County; August 5 and August 13 (two adults), 1972, and August 25, 1973, near Ashby, Grant County; and August 11, 1973, Pope County. During the summers of 1971 and 1972 this species established itself as a breeding species at the heronry at Lake Johanna, Pope County; in 1971 one pair fledged two young (*Loon* 44:36–43), and in 1972 eight nests produced thirty-one young (*Loon* 44:107). The birds remained at this colony until September 9, 1972. During 1973 eight young were produced from three nests at the Lake Johanna colony (*Loon* 46:17). Nesting was suspected at Pelican Lake, Grant County, during 1972 (*Loon* 45:21–22). A late bird was seen at Weaver, Wabasha County, on October 3, 1973.

CATTLE EGRET *Bubulcus ibis*

Minnesota status. Regular. Migrant and summer resident.

Migration. Very rare spring migrant in the southern half of the state and in the adjacent counties northward in the west central region; accidental in the northern half of the state. In the fall casual (near breeding areas) to accidental. *Spring migration period:* Mid-April through late May with a peak in mid-May. Earliest dates: April 15, 17, 20. Latest dates (beyond breeding areas): May 26, 27, 30. *Fall migration period:* Birds leave breeding colonies in the second half of August; postbreeding congregations remain throughout September. Latest dates: September 29, October 1, 10, 27.

Summer. The first report of this species in Minnesota was on June 29, 1959, near Glenwood, Pope County (*Flicker* 31:103–104). Subsequent reports during the 1960s were from the spring migration and were scattered around the southern half of the state; this species was considered casual in Minnesota at that time. In 1970 the number of reports sharply increased, and breeding was suspected in Pope and Grant counties. Nesting was confirmed in 1971 at the heronry at Lake Johanna, Pope County (*Loon* 44:36–43), and in 1972 at the heronry at Pelican Lake, Grant County (*Loon* 44:107). Birds again nested at the Pelican Lake colony during 1973 (*Loon* 45:100). There have been several

spring reports and one summer report from near the Mississippi River in Houston County, possibly indicating that an
undiscovered colony exists in that area.

GREAT EGRET (Common Egret)
Casmerodius albus

Minnesota status. Regular. Migrant and summer resident.
Migration. Common spring and fall migrant in the southern part of the state (south of a line between Grant and
Anoka counties); locally abundant in the fall. In the north
the species is casual in the spring and accidental in the fall;
there are no records from northeast of a line between
Roseau and southern St. Louis counties. *Spring migration
period:* Late March through late May with a peak in mid-
May. Earliest dates: SOUTH, March 24, 29, 31; NORTH,
April 2, 10, 11, 12. *Fall migration period:* Late July
through late October with concentrations in August and the
first week of September. Latest dates: NORTH, September
17, 29, October 5; SOUTH, October 22, 25, 26, November
1, 5.

6. Great Egret

Summer. Resident in the southern half of the state and in
the adjacent counties in the west central region (see map 6).
This species was casual in Minnesota until the 1930s;
breeding was first recorded in Martin County (1938) and
Winona County (1939). The largest colonies (from fifty to a
hundred nests) have been found in Washington, Dakota,
Houston, LeSueur, Pope, and Grant counties. Since there
are recent summer records for Otter Tail, Clearwater, and
Marshall counties, it would appear that the species is extending its range northwestward.

SNOWY EGRET *Egretta thula*

Minnesota status. Casual. Migrant and summer visitant.
Records. Two records in the 1950s (Faribault County and
Traverse County); four records in the 1960s (Nicollet
County, Hennepin County, and Marshall County [two
records]); four records in the early 1970s (Lyon County
[two records], Ramsey County, and Pope County). Over
half of these are summer records, including two reports
from Agassiz National Wildlife Refuge in Marshall County
and several observations in 1971 of at least one adult (possibly nesting) at the Lake Johanna heronry in Pope County
(*Loon* 44:36–43). Earliest dates: April 30, May 10, 14.
Latest dates: August 14, 28, September 1.

LOUISIANA HERON *Hydranassa tricolor*

Minnesota status. Accidental. One spring record and one
summer record.

Records. Both observations are of single birds from Marshall County: May 10–24, 1963, Agassiz National Wildlife Refuge (*Loon* 36:106); June 12, 1971, Thief Lake (*Loon* 43:93).

BLACK-CROWNED NIGHT HERON
Nycticorax nycticorax

Minnesota status. Regular. Migrant and summer resident; casual in winter.

Migration. Common spring and fall migrant in the southern half of the state and in the west central and northwestern regions. Abundance increases from rare to casual in the parts of the range that extend to the north and east. *Spring migration period:* Late March through mid-May with a peak in late April. Earliest dates: SOUTH, March 25, 28, 30; NORTH, April 12, 14, 29. *Fall migration period:* Early September through late November; no peak period noted. Latest dates: NORTH, November 5, 17 (only dates); SOUTH, November 23, 26, 28.

Summer. Resident primarily in the southern half of the state (see map 7). Apparently the species does not breed in the southeastern tip of the state, although one nest was found near Winona in 1939. The only known nesting colony north of Grant County is one that was first discovered in 1963 at Agassiz National Wildlife Refuge, but there are summer observations from Clearwater and Pine counties.

Winter. In December and January stragglers have been seen very occasionally in the Twin Cities area and in Rice and McLeod counties. Most reports consist of single observations from one locality, but one bird was present at Black Dog Lake, Dakota County, from December 6, 1970, to January 23, 1971. The only February report is of a single bird in St. Paul on February 7, 1942.

YELLOW-CROWNED NIGHT HERON
Nyctanassa violacea

Minnesota status. Regular. Migrant; summer resident in Houston and Dakota counties.

Migration. Uncommon spring migrant from the Twin Cities southward and eastward; rare elsewhere in the southern half of the state; accidental in the north. The species is very seldom seen in the fall. *Spring migration period:* Early April through early June with a peak during the first half of May. Earliest dates: April 7, 9, 15. Latest date (beyond breeding areas): June 6. *Fall migration period:* Probably from sometime in July through late September; most birds leave the nesting areas by mid-August. Latest dates: September 16, 17, 18, *27, 28*.

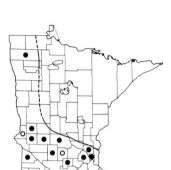

7. Black-crowned Night Heron

Summer. Resident in Houston and Dakota counties. The first observations and the first breeding record for the state were reported in the summer of 1955 near LaCrescent, Houston County (*Flicker* 27:171–172); this small colony (two to five nests) has remained regularly active since then. In addition, single nests have been found near Reno, Houston County (1960), and near South St. Paul, Dakota County (1964). Summer observations of fully fledged immatures have been made in Jackson and Redwood counties, and an adult was regularly seen at the Lake Johanna heronry, Pope County, in the summer of 1972. Other summer records of single adult birds: St. Croix State Park, Pine County, June 6, 1964; Anoka County, June 15, 1971; in rice beds near Aitkin, Aitkin County, in early July, 1972.

LEAST BITTERN *Ixobrychus exilis*

Minnesota status. Regular. Migrant and summer resident.
Migration. Uncommon spring and fall migrant in the southern half of the state; rare in the west central and southwestern regions. Rare migrant in the northern half of the state; absent in the northeastern region, north of Duluth, and in adjacent Itasca and Koochiching counties. *Spring migration period:* Early May through early June with a peak in late May. Earliest dates: SOUTH, May 1, 5, 10; NORTH, May 18 (only date). *Fall migration period:* Mid-September through early October; no peak period noted. Latest dates: NORTH, September 16 (only date); SOUTH, October 1, 5, 12, November 5, December 23 (injured bird).
Summer. Resident throughout most of the state; not known in the northeastern region, north of Duluth, or in adjacent Koochiching and Itasca counties (see map 8). The only records east and north of Mille Lacs County are recent observations in Duluth (1973) and in Aitkin County (1971).

8. Least Bittern

AMERICAN BITTERN *Botaurus lentiginosus*

Minnesota status. Regular. Migrant and summer resident.
Migration. Common spring and fall migrant throughout most of the state; uncommon in the northeastern region. Recently this species has become less numerous in many parts of its range. *Spring migration period:* Late March through late May with a peak in early May. Earliest dates: SOUTH, March 23, 25, 26; NORTH, April 7, 12, 15. *Fall migration period:* Early September through early November; no peak period noted. Latest dates: NORTH, October 21, 26, 29, November 5; SOUTH, November 4, 6, 11, 25, December 20.
Summer. Resident throughout the state; most numerous in the central regions.

Family THRESKIORNITHIDAE: Ibises

GLOSSY IBIS *Plegadis falcinellus*

Minnesota status. Hypothetical.

Records. One observation of an adult bird that was identified as belonging to this species was reported at Heron Lake, Jackson County, on June 16, 1939 (*Wilson Bulletin* 51:183). All other observations are discussed in the account for the White-faced Ibis.

WHITE-FACED IBIS *Plegadis chihi*

Minnesota status. Casual. Migrant and summer visitant. In the nineteenth century a summer resident in Jackson County.

Records. The first recent record was one bird seen on October 6–7, 1956, near Weaver, Wabasha County. Other recent reports: one or two birds from two localities in 1962; two birds from one locality in 1965; two birds from one locality in 1967; one to three birds from four localities in 1971 (photographed on April 13 near Lake Ocheda, Nobles County); one bird from one locality in 1972. Six of the records are from the southwestern quarter of the state (Traverse, Lac qui Parle, Jackson, Nobles, and Watonwan counties). The other records are from Marshall, Ramsey, and Goodhue counties. Earliest dates (recent): April 13, 24, May 10. Latest dates (recent): September 25, October 7. There are three recent July and August records.

Former status. In the nineteenth century the species was known to breed at Heron Lake, Jackson County. A nest found in 1895 and an observation in 1910 were the most recent records from the area until those of the late 1950s and 1960s were reported.

Family ANATIDAE: Swans, Geese, and Ducks

WHISTLING SWAN *Olor columbianus*

Minnesota status. Regular. Migrant, casual summer visitant, and accidental winter visitant.

Migration. Common to abundant spring and fall migrant throughout the state. Concentrations of one thousand to five thousand birds may occur in the spring. Traditional spring stopping places include Mud Lake and Lake Traverse in Traverse County, Long Meadow Lake and Rice Lake in Hennepin County, Fisher Lake in Scott County, the Weaver marshes in Wabasha County, and the St. Louis River estuary at Duluth. In the fall flocks normally pass through the state quickly, and congregations do not usually appear except in the Weaver marshes where flocks linger into early winter. *Spring migration period:* Late March through late May with a peak in the second week of April. Earliest dates: SOUTH, March *10, 14, 15,* 19, 20, 21; NORTH, March *31,* April 4, 6, 7. Latest dates: SOUTH, May 16, 17, 18; NORTH, May 28, 29, June *17, 24, 28. Fall migration period:* Early October through late December with a peak in mid-November. Earliest dates: NORTH, September *22, 29,* October 2, 12, 19; SOUTH, October 7, 9, 13. Latest dates: NORTH, November 16, 24 (only dates), early January; SOUTH, December 21, 22, 25, *29.*

Summer. There are several records of birds lingering into June and July in the northern regions. Some of these birds are know to have been injured; in two instances in which one member of a pair was injured, the pairs remained and nested — in Mahnomen County (1932) and Otter Tail County (1956), respectively. Other locations include Agassiz National Wildlife Refuge (three records), Lake Superior (Duluth, Schroeder), and Britt and Virginia, St. Louis County.

Winter. In January and February single wintering birds have been reported from the Mississippi River (Sartell, Hastings, and Wabasha), Silver Lake at Rochester, Olmsted County, and Carver Park, Hennepin County. This species is occasionally confused with the free-flying Trumpeter Swans that have been introduced in the state.

TRUMPETER SWAN *Olor buccinator*

Minnesota status. Extirpated; migrant and summer resident in the nineteenth century. Recently introduced in Carver County.

Discussion. According to Roberts (1932), the species probably bred in many places throughout the prairie and the sparsely wooded parts of the state in the 1800s. No specimens are available from this era. Roberts listed nesting records for Nicollet County (1823); Pike Lake in central Minnesota, probably Hennepin County (1853); Heron Lake, Jackson County (1883); and Meeker County (1884 or 1885). A previously unpublished breeding record for northeastern Minnesota (possibly Aitkin County) in 1798 is mentioned in the *Wilson Bulletin* (76:331–332). Banko (1960) cited a field report of a pair of Trumpeter Swans that spent the summer of 1937 on a small marshy lake in Beltrami County. No details of identification were given in the original report, and the birds described in the report may have been Whistling Swans. All summer observations of swans should be very carefully checked for accuracy of identification. In 1969 and 1970 a captive flock of

Trumpeter Swans was introduced at the Carver Park Nature Center, Carver County, and several pairs nested in that area in 1971 and 1972. In 1972 the young left the refuge by early December; perhaps these birds will establish a migratory pattern into the state.

CANADA GOOSE *Branta canadensis*

Minnesota status. Regular. Migrant, summer resident, and winter visitant.

Migration. Common to abundant migrant throughout the state; especially numerous in the western regions. The traditional congregating areas for flocks of five thousand to twenty thousand birds include Lake Traverse and Mud Lake, Traverse County; Lac qui Parle Refuge, Lac qui Parle County; and Agassiz National Wildlife Refuge, Marshall County. *Spring migration period:* Late February through early May with the bulk of the migration from late March through early April. Earliest dates: None can be given because of wintering birds; early arrivals in the south are in late February, and those in the north are in mid-March. *Fall migration period:* Early September through early December with a peak in mid-October. Earliest dates: None can be given because of breeding birds; early arrivals in the north are usually in mid-September. Latest dates: None can be given because of stragglers and wintering birds.

Summer. The species formerly nested throughout Minnesota with the probable exception of the northeastern region; the last reliable breeding record was in 1929 (Roberts, 1932). In the 1940s and 1950s the United States Bureau of Sport Fisheries and Wildlife conducted a project for the restoration of breeding flocks (principally *B. c. maxima*), at Agassiz National Wildlife Refuge, Rice Lake National Wildlife Refuge, and Tamarac National Wildlife Refuge. More recently state and local agencies have introduced breeding flocks at a number of refuges, notably Lac qui Parle Refuge, Carlos Avery Game Refuge, and Carver Park Nature Reserve. Currently this goose is established as a breeding bird in all regions of the state except the northeastern region. Most nesting is on or near major wildlife refuges, although the species also breeds elsewhere.

Winter. Regular winter visitant wherever there is sufficient open water and food. Most numerous in the south, but flocks of fifty to five hundred birds have overwintered in Otter Tail and St. Louis counties. One of the principal winter locations since 1947 is Silver Lake (near Rochester in Olmsted County); the population there increased from about five thousand birds in the early 1960s to about fifteen thousand birds in the late 1960s. Lac qui Parle Refuge is also an important winter location for flocks of about two thousand birds.

BRANT *Branta bernicla*

Minnesota status. Accidental. Two fall records.

Records. One bird was shot near Pierce Lake, Martin County, on November 23, 1956 (*Flicker* 29:85; MMNH #12696). Another was seen and photographed in Rochester, Olmsted County, October 7–13, 1973; the bird remained in Rochester through October and November and was last seen on December 8, 1973 (*Loon* 46:33–34). In addition, a flock of about eighteen brant (species unknown) was seen at Buffalo Bay, Lake of the Woods, Lake of the Woods County, on November 2, 1963.

BLACK BRANT *Branta nigricans*

Minnesota status. Accidental. One spring record and one fall record.

Records. One bird was seen and photographed at Rice Lake National Wildlife Refuge, Aitkin County, May 17–31, 1966 (*Loon* 38:105), and one bird was seen at Agassiz National Wildlife Refuge, Marshall County, October 31, 1972 (*Loon* 45:24).

WHITE-FRONTED GOOSE *Anser albifrons*

Minnesota status. Regular. Migrant; accidental in winter.

Migration. Common spring migrant and uncommon fall migrant in the western regions. Rare to casual in the spring and accidental in the fall in the central and eastern regions. *Spring migration period:* Mid-March through mid-May with a peak in mid-April. Earliest dates: SOUTH, March *1*, 15, 16; NORTH, March *26*, April 10, 12, 18. Latest dates: SOUTH, May 11 (only date), *21*, *31*; NORTH, May 8, 11, *28*. *Fall migration period:* Late September through late November. Earliest dates: NORTH, September *9*, October 11 (only dates); SOUTH, September *27*, October 11 (only dates). Latest dates: NORTH, October 22 (only date); SOUTH, November 22, 26, December *7*.

Winter. At Silver Lake (Rochester, Olmsted County) a single bird wintered with the Canada Geese from December 2, 1968, to February 16, 1969; a single bird was also seen there in January, 1970, and in 1972.

SNOW GOOSE (Snow Goose; Blue Goose)
Chen caerulescens

Minnesota status. Regular. Migrant; casual summer and winter visitant.

Migration. Common spring and fall migrant throughout the state; abundant in the western regions. Concentrations of twenty-five thousand birds gather at Mud Lake and Lake Traverse, Traverse County, and flocks of five thousand to ten thousand birds occur at Lac qui Parle Refuge, Lac qui Parle County, and at Agassiz National Wildlife Refuge, Marshall County. *Spring migration period:* Mid-March through late May with the bulk of the migration from early April through early May. Earliest dates: SOUTH, March 10, 12, 15; NORTH, March *11*, 17, 18, 19. Latest dates: SOUTH, May 23, 28, 31, June *3*; NORTH, May 27, 29, June *1–13*. *Fall migration period:* Mid-September through early December with a peak in mid-October. Earliest dates: NORTH, Sept. *5*, *11*, 19, 22; SOUTH, July *28*, August *7*, *11*, September *7*, *8*, 17, 21. Latest dates: NORTH, November 12, 14, 19; SOUTH, November 27, December 1, 7, *16*.

Summer. Nonbreeding birds occasionally spend the summer months in Minnesota; single birds and pairs have been recorded in Lac qui Parle, Olmsted, and Aitkin counties, and a flock of eighteen birds stayed at Mud Lake, Traverse County, all summer in 1941. (Additional summer dates are listed under **Migration.**)

Winter. Occasionally individuals or small flocks (four to six birds) have wintered with other geese at Silver Lake (Rochester, Olmsted County). Single birds have also remained throughout the winter at Howard Lake, Wright County; Watab Lake, Stearns County; and Silver Lake (Virginia, St. Louis County).

Taxonomic note. The color phases of this species were formerly regarded as separate species: Snow Goose, *C. hyperborea*, and Blue Goose, *C. caerulescens*.

ROSS' GOOSE *Chen rossii*

Minnesota status. Accidental. Six fall and winter records.

Records. Half of the six records are reports of single birds seen in the wintering flock at Silver Lake (Rochester, Olmsted County): October 20, 1964, to January 8, 1965 (photographed; *Loon* 37:79); December 2, 1968, to March 1, 1969; December 20, 1969, to January 11, 1970. It is possible that the same individual was seen each year. Two of the other records are also of birds attempting to winter: November 18 to December 2, 1962, Jackson County (*Flicker* 35:94–95); December 5, 1965, to early January, 1966, Wright County (two birds; *Loon* 38:36–37). The last record is of a single bird seen on October 2, 1966, at Swan Lake, Nicollet County.

FULVOUS TREE DUCK *Dendrocygna bicolor*

Minnesota status. Accidental. One spring record and one fall record.

Records. Two birds were seen on May 24, 1929, near Arco, Lincoln County (*Wilson Bulletin* 42:58), and one bird was shot from a flock of eight birds (species undetermined) on Lake Onamia, Mille Lacs County, on October 20, 1950 (photograph of specimen; *Loon* 36:107).

MALLARD *Anas platyrhynchos*

Minnesota status. Regular. Migrant and summer resident; regular in winter.

Migration. Abundant spring and fall migrant throughout the state; most numerous in the western regions and least numerous in the northeastern region. Peak numbers (thirty thousand to sixty thousand birds) can be seen at Agassiz National Wildlife Refuge, Marshall County. *Spring migration period:* Early March through early May with a peak in early April. Earliest dates: None can be given because of wintering birds; early arrivals in the north occur in late March. *Fall migration period:* Early September through late November; peak numbers depend on weather conditions but normally occur in late October and early November. Latest dates: None can be given because of wintering birds.

Summer. Resident throughout the state; most numerous in the western regions. Second only to the Blue-winged Teal as a resident breeding duck.

Winter. Common to locally abundant in the southern half of the state. Usually uncommon or rare in the north but may be common where there is sufficient open water (usually near power plants).

BLACK DUCK *Anas rubripes*

Minnesota status. Regular. Migrant, summer resident, and winter visitant.

Migration. Common spring and fall migrant in the eastern and northern regions; uncommon to rare in the other regions. Peak numbers (one thousand to five thousand birds) can be seen at Rice Lake National Wildlife Refuge, Aitkin County, and Agassiz National Wildlife Refuge, Marshall County. During the fall hunting season this species makes up only 1 percent of the annual duck bag in Minnesota (Moyle, 1964a). *Spring migration period:* Late March through early May with a peak in mid-April. Earliest dates: None can be given because of wintering birds; early arrivals in the north occur in late March. *Fall migration period:* Early September through early December; peak numbers occur in October. Latest dates: None can be given because of wintering birds.

Summer. Resident primarily in the northeastern region and

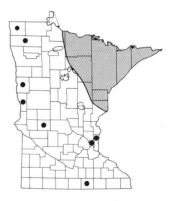

9. Black Duck (1930)

in Koochiching and Itasca counties. Breeds regularly, but sparsely, as far south as Ramsey and Washington counties; also has nested farther south and west (see map 9).

Winter. Uncommon to locally common winter visitant in the southeastern quarter of the state. In the northeastern region the species is rare but regular, occurring primarily at Virginia, St. Louis County, and Grand Marais, Cook County. The only other known wintering locality is in the vicinity of Fergus Falls, Otter Tail County.

GADWALL *Anas strepera*

Minnesota status. Regular. Migrant and summer resident; casual in winter.

Migration. Common spring and fall migrant throughout most of the state; rare in the northeastern and north central regions. Peak numbers (ten thousand to thirty thousand birds) can be seen at Agassiz National Wildlife Refuge, Marshall County, in the fall. *Spring migration period:* Mid-March through late May with peaks in mid-April (south) and mid-May (north). Earliest dates: SOUTH, March 7, 10, 12, 14; NORTH, March *29, 31,* April 8, 10, 11. *Fall migration period:* Early October through early December with a peak in mid-October. Latest dates: NORTH, November 8, 12, 14, December *18;* SOUTH, December 7, 8, 12, *17.*

Summer. Resident primarily in the western and southern prairie regions (see map 10). Most numerous at Agassiz National Wildlife Refuge, Marshall County, where the species sometimes outnumbers the Mallard. In the west central counties it makes up only 1 percent of the breeding duck population (Moyle, 1964a).

Winter. Stragglers are occasionally present from late December through early January from the Twin Cities area southeastward. The species has overwintered in Scott and Winona counties.

10. Gadwall

PINTAIL *Anas acuta*

Minnesota status. Regular. Migrant and summer resident; regular in winter.

Migration. Common spring and fall migrant throughout most of the state; uncommon in the spring and rare in the fall in the northeastern region. Most numerous in the western regions. Peak concentrations (five thousand to ten thousand birds) occur from Wabasha to Marshall counties. *Spring migration period:* Early March through mid-May with a peak in mid-April. Earliest dates: SOUTH, March 4, 6; NORTH, March 18, 25, 29. *Fall migration period:* Early September through early December; an early peak occurs in

late September and a late peak, depending on weather conditions, normally occurs in late October and early
November. Latest dates: NORTH, November 1, 4 (only
dates), 26; SOUTH, December 10, 11.
Summer. Resident primarily in the western and southern
prairie regions (see map 11). During annual breeding
ground surveys that were made around 1960 only 3 or 4
percent of the ducks noted were of this species (Moyle,
1964a).
Winter. Rare in late winter in the southeastern and south
central regions and in the Twin Cities area. There is one
record from an area farther north: February 12, 1969,
Grand Marais, Cook County.

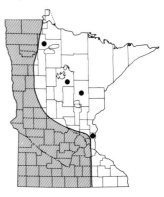

11. Pintail

GREEN-WINGED TEAL *Anas crecca*

Minnesota status. Regular. Migrant and summer resident;
casual in winter.
Migration. Common spring and fall migrant throughout
most of the state; uncommon in both seasons in the northeastern region. Peak numbers (ten thousand to fifteen
thousand birds) can be seen at Rice Lake National Wildlife
Refuge, Aitkin County, and Agassiz National Wildlife Refuge, Marshall County. Hunting bag checks in the 1950s
showed that the species was the fourth most abundant duck
taken, comprising 6 percent of the total bag (Moyle,
1964a). *Spring migration period:* Mid-March through late
May with a peak in early April. Earliest dates: SOUTH,
March 6, 9, 11, 13; NORTH, March 30, April 5, 8, 11. *Fall
migration period:* Late August through early December;
peak numbers occur in October. Latest dates: NORTH,
November 6, 10, 14; SOUTH, December 13, 15, 19, 26.
Summer. Resident throughout most of the state but very
scarce. The species is one of the rarest breeding ducks in the
state. Nesting evidence has been recorded in the following
counties: Marshall, Polk, Otter Tail, Stevens, Yellow
Medicine, Nobles, Wabasha, Rice, Hennepin, Washington, Mille Lacs, Aitkin, Crow Wing, and Itasca.
Winter. Overwintering birds are occasionally seen in the
southern half of the state with records from Hennepin,
Dakota, Winona, and Freeborn counties. There are two
records for the northern half of the state: December 31,
1950, Walker, Cass County; January 24, 1970, Virginia,
St. Louis County.

BLUE-WINGED TEAL *Anas discors*

Minnesota status. Regular. Migrant and summer resident;
accidental in winter.
Migration. Common to abundant spring and fall migrant

throughout the state. The species makes up at least 15 percent of the total fall hunting bag in Minnesota (Moyle, 1964a). *Spring migration period:* Late March through late May; peak numbers occur in April. Earliest dates: SOUTH, March *10*, *13*, *14*, 20, 23, 25; NORTH, April *6*, 12, 13, 14. *Fall migration period:* August through late November; peak numbers occur in September, and most birds leave by mid-October. Latest dates: NORTH, October 30, November 4, 7, *19*, *27*; SOUTH, November 27, 30, December 4, *28*, *29*.

Summer. Resident throughout the state. The species is the most abundant breeding duck in the state; during six annual breeding ground counts ending in 1963, an average of 49 percent of all breeding pairs were Blue-winged Teals. (Moyle, 1964a).

Winter. There are two records of uninjured birds that have wintered in the state: February 3, 1940, Hennepin County; 1941–1942, Morris, Stevens County (fifteen birds).

CINNAMON TEAL *Anas cyanoptera*

Minnesota status. Casual. Migrant.

Records. Twenty-four records (sixteen of them since 1960). Eighteen records are from the spring migration. Earliest dates: April 9, 12, 15. Latest dates: June 4, 8, 13. The few fall records range from August 27 to October 29. A few of the spring observations are of one or two pairs; the rest are of individual birds. There is one specimen for the state (MMNH #3711). Half of the records are for the western regions from Nobles County to Marshall County; most of the others cluster in the central and east central regions between Washington County and Meeker County and between Hennepin County and Sherburne County. The remaining records are from Nicollet County, Goodhue County, and St. Louis County (Duluth). The geographical patterns for the spring and fall observations are similar.

EUROPEAN WIGEON (European Widgeon) *Anas penelope*

Minnesota status. Casual. Spring migrant.

Records. Fourteen records (three since 1960). All the records are from the spring migration. Earliest dates: March 26, April 6, 17. Latest dates: June 4, 5, *15*. No specimen is available for the state, but there is one photograph on file (June 5, 1973, Big Sandy Lake, Aitkin County; L. Paynter). The observations are scattered throughout the state with the following counties represented: Kittson, Hennepin, Stearns, Marshall (twice), Goodhue (twice), St. Louis (Duluth), Aitkin (twice), Jackson, Benton, Houston, and Mille Lacs. Three of the observations are of two birds; the rest are of individuals.

AMERICAN WIGEON (American Widgeon)
Anas americana

Minnesota status. Regular. Migrant and summer resident; casual in winter.

Migration. Common spring and fall migrant throughout most of the state; uncommon in the fall in the northeast. Peak numbers (ten thousand to forty thousand birds) occur at the Weaver marshes, Wabasha County, and at Agassiz National Wildlife Refuge, Marshall County. The species normally makes up 2 percent of the fall hunting bag in Minnesota (Moyle, 1964a). *Spring migration period:* Mid-March through early June with a peak in mid- to late April. Earliest dates: SOUTH, March 10, 12; NORTH, March 29, 31, April 3. Latest dates: SOUTH, June 2, 3, 6; NORTH, none can be given because of breeding birds. *Fall migration period:* Late August through early December with a peak in late September and early October. Earliest dates: NORTH, none can be given because of breeding birds; SOUTH, August *18*, 24, 25. Latest dates: NORTH, October 29, 30, November 5, *25*, December *17*; SOUTH, December 8, 11, 12, *19*, *20*.

Summer. Resident primarily in the north central region and in the adjacent counties in the northwestern and northeastern regions; occasionally breeds outside this area (see map 12). The species is most numerous in Itasca and Beltrami counties.

Winter. Casual in late winter (January and February) from the Twin Cities area southeastward; not known elsewhere during this season.

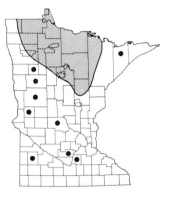

12. American Wigeon

NORTHERN SHOVELER (Shoveler)
Anas clypeata

Minnesota status. Regular. Migrant and summer resident; accidental in winter.

Migration. Common spring and fall migrant throughout most of the state; uncommon in the spring and rare in the fall in the north central and northeastern regions. Peak numbers at Agassiz National Wildlife Refuge, Marshall County, are in the range of one thousand to two thousand birds. *Spring migration period:* Mid-March through mid-May with a peak in mid-April. Earliest dates: SOUTH, March *3*, 14, 15, 16; NORTH, April 3, 8, 11. *Fall migration period:* Early September through early December with a peak in early October. Latest dates: NORTH, November 1, 5 (only dates), *24*; SOUTH, December 8, 10, 11.

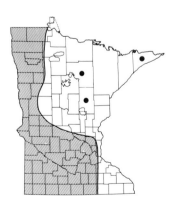

13. Northern Shoveler

Summer. Resident primarily in the prairie regions and in the southern part of the central and east central regions (see map 13). The breeding records outside this range represent only single occurrences: Devil Track Lake, Cook County (1922); White Oak Lake, Itasca County (1949); rice paddies at Aitkin, Aitkin County (1972).

Winter. Stragglers have been reported in late December and early January south and east of the Twin Cities area, but there are only two records of overwintering birds (in 1940–1941 and 1941–1942, in each case a single bird in Hennepin County).

WOOD DUCK *Aix sponsa*

Minnesota status. Regular. Migrant and summer resident; regular in winter.

Migration. Common spring and fall migrant in the deciduous woodlands of the state. Uncommon migrant on the prairie and in the northeastern region. Peak numbers (one thousand to fifteen hundred birds) can be seen at Rice Lake National Wildlife Refuge, Aitkin County, and at the Upper Mississippi National Wildlife Refuge. *Spring migration period:* Mid-March through late May with a peak in early May. Earliest dates: SOUTH, March *3*, 8, 10; NORTH, March *25*, April 4, 6, 8. *Fall migration period:* Late August through early December with the bulk of the migration in late September and early October. Latest dates: NORTH, October 15, 19, 28, November *28*, December *6*; SOUTH, December 7, 8, *25*, *27*.

Summer. Resident throughout the state wherever there is suitable wooded habitat along streams and lakes. Mostly absent from the Red River Valley and the southwestern region; scarce in the northeastern region. The species is the fourth most numerous nesting duck in the state (Moyle, 1964a).

Winter. Regular but rare as an overwintering species in the southeastern quarter of the state; it is not known whether the overwintering birds are local breeding residents. In the northern half of the state there are late winter records from Virginia, St. Louis County; Pine River, Cass County; and Fergus Falls, Otter Tail County.

REDHEAD *Aythya americana*

Minnesota status. Regular. Migrant and summer resident; accidental in winter.

Migration. Common spring and fall migrant throughout most of the state; rare in the fall in the northeastern region. Most numerous in the western prairie regions. During the

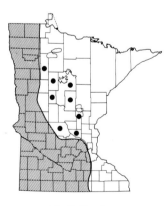

14. Redhead

last ten to fifteen years the species has been greatly reduced in numbers. Peak concentrations of about two thousand birds have been observed recently at Agassiz National Wildlife Refuge. The species comprises about 5 percent of the total waterfowl bag in Minnesota (Moyle, 1964a). *Spring migration period:* Early March through late May; peak numbers in mid-May. Earliest dates: SOUTH, March 4, 7; NORTH, April *3*, 11, 12. *Fall migration period:* Late September through early December with peak numbers in mid-October. Latest dates: NORTH, November 13, 20, 24; SOUTH, December 11, 12, 13, *23*.

Summer. Resident primarily in the prairie regions and in the central region as far east as the Twin Cities (see map 14). During a six-year period ending in 1963 the species made up about 6 percent of the breeding pairs recorded on the breeding ground transects in Minnesota (Moyle, 1964a).

Winter. There are three records of stragglers in early January (latest date: January 9) from Dakota, Stearns, and Ramsey counties.

RING-NECKED DUCK *Aythya collaris*

Minnesota status. Regular. Migrant and summer resident; casual in winter.

Migration. Common spring and fall migrant throughout the state; most numerous in the eastern and central regions, least numerous on the prairie. Concentrations of one thousand to five thousand birds occur on many lakes in the northern regions from western St. Louis County to eastern Marshall County. Normally the species is the eighth most important species in the hunting bag in Minnesota (Moyle, 1964a). *Spring migration period:* Mid-March through late May with a peak in mid-April. Earliest dates: SOUTH, March *4*, 8, 10, 11; NORTH, March *23*, 29, April 3. *Fall migration period:* Late September through early December with a peak in mid-October. Latest dates: NORTH, November 20, 24, December 3, *12*, *18*; SOUTH, December 9, 10, 11.

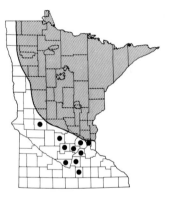

15. Ring-necked Duck

Summer. Resident primarily in the forested and forest-prairie transition areas of the state (see map 15). The species is the third most numerous nesting duck, ranking behind the Mallard and the Blue-winged Teal in abundance (Moyle, 1964a).

Winter. Stragglers are regularly observed in early winter (Late December through mid-January) from the Twin Cities area southward; there are also two records from Lake Superior. Overwintering birds have been reported only from

Black Dog Lake, Dakota County, and Virginia, St. Louis County.

CANVASBACK *Aythya valisineria*

Minnesota status. Regular. Migrant and summer resident; accidental in winter.

Migration. Common spring and fall migrant throughout most of the state; uncommon in the spring and rare in the fall in the northeastern region. Formerly the species was much more numerous in Minnesota. In the early 1950s peak concentrations were on the order of fifty thousand birds; at present peak flocks usually contain five hundred to one thousand birds. *Spring migration period:* Mid-March through late May with a peak in mid-April. Earliest dates: SOUTH, March 6, 7, 12, 13, 14; NORTH, April 5, 9, 10. *Fall migration period:* Late September through mid-December with a peak in mid-October. Latest dates: NORTH, November 12, 14 (only dates), 28, December 1; SOUTH, December 10, 11, 15, 23.

Summer. Resident primarily in the northwestern region, although the species does breed sparingly as far east as Hennepin County and as far south as Lyon County (see map 16).

Winter. Stragglers remain through early winter (late December and early January) in the southeastern quarter of the state. The only late winter records are for January 3 to January 23, 1971, French River, St. Louis County, and for January 13 to February 3, 1962, Black Dog Lake, Dakota County.

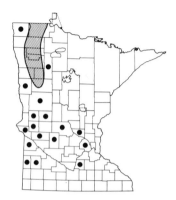

16. Canvasback

GREATER SCAUP *Aythya marila*

Minnesota status. Regular. Migrant.

Migration. Uncommon spring and fall migrant throughout most of the state; abundant in the spring and common in the fall in the northeastern region, especially at Duluth. *Spring migration period:* Late March through late May with the bulk of the migration in early April through early May. Earliest dates: SOUTH, March 19, 23, 25; NORTH, March 30, 31, April 2. Latest dates: SOUTH, May 6, 7, 10, 21, 23; NORTH, May 28, 29, June 1, 6, 8, 13. *Fall migration period:* Early October through early December with a peak in late October and early November. Earliest dates: NORTH, September 17, 20, October 8, 15, 18; SOUTH, September 26, October 8, 9, 10.

Winter. There are reports during the Christmas Count period, but no substantiating details are available for any of them; confusion of this species with the Lesser Scaup is likely.

LESSER SCAUP *Aythya affinis*

Minnesota status. Regular. Migrant, summer resident, and visitant; casual in winter.

Migration. Abundant spring and fall migrant throughout the state. Peak numbers are usually in the range of fifteen thousand to twenty-five thousand birds. Hunting bag checks for a ten-year period in the 1950s showed that this species constituted about 11 percent of the kill, ranking third behind the Mallard and the Blue-winged Teal (Moyle, 1964a). *Spring migration period:* Late February through mid-June with the bulk of the migration in April. Earliest dates: SOUTH, February *12*, *13*, *22*, *23*, 28, March 3; NORTH, March *19*, 27, 28, 30. *Fall migration period:* Mid-September through early December with the bulk of the migration from mid-October through mid-November. Latest dates: NORTH, November 28, 29, 30; SOUTH, December 18, 19, 23.

Summer. Resident in the northwestern region (see map 17). Scarce; the species is the rarest breeding duck in the state. Records from Kandiyohi County (1942), Meeker County (1903), and Otter Tail County (1893) represent single nesting occurrences. Nonbreeding birds are regularly present in June and July in the northern regions and also as far south as the Iowa border.

Winter. Stragglers linger regularly through December and into early January, especially in the eastern part of the state. Latest dates: Lake Superior, December 29, January 5, 6. Two February records for the northern half of the state: February 1, 1969, Virginia, St. Louis County; February 24, 1970, Cass County. February dates for the southern half of the state are given with the dates for the spring migration period.

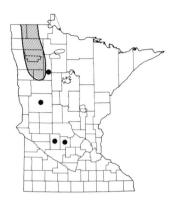

17. Lesser Scaup

COMMON GOLDENEYE *Bucephala clangula*

Minnesota status. Regular. Migrant, summer resident, and winter visitant.

Migration. Common spring and fall migrant in the eastern and central regions, becoming abundant at Duluth in the spring; uncommon in the western regions but common in the northwestern region. *Spring migration period:* Late February through late May with the bulk of the migration in late March and early April. Earliest dates: None can be given because of wintering birds. Latest dates: SOUTH, May 9, 16, 20; NORTH, none can be given because of breeding birds. *Fall migration period:* Early October through mid-December with the bulk of the migration in November and early December. Earliest dates: NORTH, none can be given

18. Common Goldeneye

because of breeding birds; SOUTH, October 9, 10, 12. Latest dates: None can be given because of wintering birds. **Summer.** Resident primarily in the northeastern and north central regions (see map 18); highest breeding densities occur in Itasca and Beltrami counties.
Winter. Common winter visitant along the Mississippi River and eastward where there is open water (for instance, on Lake Superior) as far north as Beltrami and Cook counties. Most numerous in the southeastern region.

BARROW'S GOLDENEYE *Bucephala islandica*

Minnesota status. Casual. Migrant and winter visitant.
Records. All records are based on sightings; there are no specimens or photographs for the state. Most of the records are from Lake Superior and the Mississippi River (Dakota, Ramsey, and Hennepin counties); one to three birds stayed in the latter area each winter from 1965 through early 1970 and again in the winter of 1972–1973. Other localities: Rainy River, Lake of the Woods County; Cass Lake; Otter Lake, Ramsey County; Chisholm, St. Louis County. Earliest dates: November *30*, December *13*, 27, 31. Latest dates: April 12, 13, *22*, 23, May *5–7*. The best published descriptions are found in *Flicker* 28:79; *Loon* 37:84–85; *Loon* 39:49, 103–104; and *Loon* 39:136–137.

BUFFLEHEAD *Bucephala albeola*

Minnesota status. Regular. Migrant; casual summer and regular winter visitant.
Migration. Common spring and fall migrant throughout the state; most numerous in the northern regions. Large flocks contain from twenty to sixty birds, and peak counts at Agassiz National Wildlife Refuge, Marshall County, range from five hundred to fifteen hundred birds. *Spring migration period:* Mid-March through late May with a peak in mid-April. Earliest dates: SOUTH, March *6*, 13, 20, 24; NORTH, March 12, 13, 16. Latest dates: SOUTH, May 16, 19, 24, *30*; NORTH, May 26, 27. *Fall migration period:* Early October through early December with the bulk of the migration from late October through mid-November. Earliest dates: NORTH, August *31*, September *2*, *17*, October 6, 9, 15; SOUTH, September *20*, 27, October 2, 3. Latest dates: NORTH, November 29, 30, December 3; SOUTH, December 8, 9, 12.
Summer. Casual visitant in the northern half of the state. Single stragglers have been seen in June and July in Cook, St. Louis, Clearwater, Mahnomen, Cass, Douglas, Marshall, and Kittson counties. On August 9, 1963, three birds were seen in Chisholm, St. Louis County. Not known to nest in the state.

Winter. Rare winter visitant on Lake Superior and in the southeastern part of the state from the Twin Cities area southeastward; unknown elsewhere. Most records are from early winter, but the species has overwintered in both areas.

OLDSQUAW *Clangula hyemalis*

Minnesota status. Regular. Migrant and winter visitant.
Migration. On Lake Superior a common migrant; rare elsewhere in the northern and central regions of the state; casual in the southern regions. *Fall migration period:* Late October through early December. Earliest dates: October *13*, 21, 25, 28. *Spring migration period:* March and April with stragglers present on Lake Superior throughout May and into early June. Latest dates: May 29, June 1, 2.
Winter. Common winter visitant on Lake Superior; unknown elsewhere. Most numerous in Cook County where normal flock size is thirty to one hundred birds. A peak count of over a thousand birds between Tofte and Grand Marais was made on February 12, 1961.

HARLEQUIN DUCK *Histrionicus histrionicus*

Minnesota status. Regular. Migrant and winter visitant.
Migration and winter. Very rare visitant on Lake Superior during these seasons; accidental elsewhere. Inland records: during migration in Cass County (Lake Winnibigoshish, Kabekena River); June 5–7, 1956, St. Louis River near Eveleth, St. Louis County (*Flicker* 32:35); winter of 1966–1967, subadult male, and winter of 1967–1968, adult male (same bird?), Silver Lake (Virginia), St. Louis County. On Lake Superior most records are of single birds, but groups of two or three have been seen a few times. Earliest dates: October 16, 20, November 3. Latest dates: April 10, 16, 18, May *1*, June *5–7*.

COMMON EIDER *Somateria mollissima*

Minnesota status. Accidental. Five fall records.
Records. The following specimens are in the Bell Museum of Natural History: MMNH #15812 and #15813, October 25, 1959, Warroad, Roseau County; MMNH #22157, shot from a flock of four birds, November 5, 1966, Lake Reno, Pope County; MMNH #16400, November 7, 1959, Squaw Lake, Itasca County. In addition, a single female was seen at very close range and identified as belonging to this species in Grand Marais, Cook County, on November 7, 1953 (*Flicker* 25:141–142). Another eider, either a female or an immature, was seen on January 16, 1966, at Two Harbors, Lake County, but weather conditions made exact identification impossible.

KING EIDER *Somateria spectabilis*

Minnesota status. Accidental. One spring record, two fall records, and one winter record.

Records. On May 9, 1971, two pairs were seen at Lower Red Lake, Beltrami County (*Loon* 43:90–91). A female or immature bird was seen on Mille Lacs Lake on October 16, 1973 (*Loon* 46:34). One bird was shot out of a flock of five or six birds on October 29, 1964, at Lost Lake, St. Louis County (*Loon* 36:136). The winter record is of a specimen (MMNH #18635) obtained at Knife River, Lake County, on January 13, 1963 (*Flicker* 35:70).

WHITE-WINGED SCOTER *Melanitta deglandi*

Minnesota status. Regular. Migrant; casual visitant in winter and summer.

Migration. Uncommon spring and fall migrant on Lake Superior and in the western regions of the state; rare migrant elsewhere. Peak flocks of thirty to fifty birds are seen on Lake Superior. *Spring migration period:* Early April through early June with a peak in mid-May. Earliest dates: SOUTH, March *21*, April 4, 8, 9; NORTH, April 11, 12, 13. Latest dates: SOUTH, April 23 (only date), May *22, 24*; NORTH, June 3, 6, 10, *17*. *Fall migration period:* Mid-October through early December with stragglers still present through early January. Earliest dates: NORTH, October 6, 10, 12; SOUTH, October 10, 11, 13. Latest dates: SOUTH, December 1, 4, 6, *15, 20*; NORTH, December 1, 3, 6.

Summer. Casual summer visitant in the northern regions. There are records of single birds and a small flock (once) from late June through late August in Lake, Cook, Cass, Clearwater, Marshall, Roseau, and Lake of the Woods counties.

Winter. Casual winter visitant on Lake Superior; accidental elsewhere. There are records, usually of one or two birds, for all the winter months on Lake Superior, although the species is most often seen during the first half of the winter. The only other record is from Grey Cloud Island, Ramsey County, where five birds were seen on January 16, 1943.

SURF SCOTER *Melanitta perspicillata*

Minnesota status. Regular. Migrant; accidental in winter.
Migration. Rare spring migrant on Lake Superior; accidental at Mille Lacs Lake. In the fall uncommon on Lake Superior and rare elsewhere. *Spring migration period:* Late April through early June with a peak in late May. Earliest dates: SOUTH, no data; NORTH, April *25*, May 6, 7, 11. Latest dates: SOUTH, no data; NORTH, May 31, June 1, 3.

Fall migration period: Late September through mid-November with a peak in mid- and late October. Earliest dates: NORTH, September *23*, October 1, 6, 8; SOUTH, October 1, 15, 31. Latest dates: NORTH, November 14 (twice), December *16*; SOUTH, November 4, 18, *28*–December *5*.
Winter. Two winter records: one bird seen January 18–19, 1964, at Two Harbors, Lake County; one bird (possibly injured) seen February 11, 1934, near St. Paul.

BLACK SCOTER (Common Scoter)
Melanitta nigra

Minnesota status. Regular. Migrant; accidental in winter.
Migration. Rare spring migrant on Lake Superior; accidental in Hennepin and Kandiyohi counties. In the fall uncommon on Lake Superior; rare elsewhere. *Spring migration period:* Late April through early June. Earliest dates: SOUTH, April 17, 30 (only dates); NORTH, April *5*, 28, 29 (only dates). Latest dates: SOUTH, no data; NORTH, May 23, 27, June 2, *8*, *14*. *Fall migration period:* Early October through late November. Earliest dates: NORTH, October 8, 10; SOUTH, November 6, 7 (only dates). Latest dates: SOUTH, November 14 (only date); NORTH, November 18, 22, 25.
Winter. Observation of one bird on January 1, 1972, at Grand Marais, Cook County.

RUDDY DUCK *Oxyura jamaicensis*

Minnesota status. Regular. Migrant and summer resident; accidental in winter.
Migration. Common spring and fall migrant throughout most of the state; rare in the north central and northeastern regions. Normal flock size is fifteen to thirty birds; peak concentrations of one thousand to fifteen hundred birds. *Spring migration period:* Mid-March through late May with a peak in mid- and late April. Earliest dates: SOUTH, February *26*, March 7, 10, 14, 17; NORTH, April 10, 11, 18. *Fall migration period:* Early September through mid-December with a peak in October. Latest dates: NORTH, November 20, 23, December 5; SOUTH, December 12, 14.
Summer. Resident primarily in the prairie regions and in the central region as far east as the Twin Cities (see map 19). In breeding ground transects conducted for six years around 1960, the species made up 2 percent of the breeding population (Moyle, 1964a).
Winter. In the southeastern quarter of the state stragglers are present in late December and early January. Latest dates: January 3, 4.

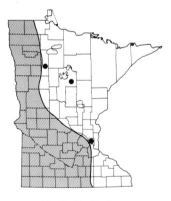

19. Ruddy Duck

HOODED MERGANSER *Lophodytes cucullatus*

Minnesota status. Regular. Migrant and summer resident; casual in winter.

Migration. Common spring and fall migrant throughout most of the state; uncommon in the western prairie regions. Normal flock size is fifteen to twenty birds; peak concentrations of one hundred to three hundred birds. *Spring migration period:* Mid-March through mid-May with a peak in mid-April. Earliest dates: SOUTH, March *4, 5*, 15, 16, 18; NORTH, March *11, 19*, 25, 27, 30. *Fall migration period:* Early September through mid-December with a peak in October. Latest dates: NORTH, November 13, 15, 20, *28*, December *1*; SOUTH, December 11, 17, 19.

Summer. Resident throughout the state; very scarce in the southwestern quarter (summer occurrences reported only from Jackson, Lyon, Lac qui Parle, and Stevens counties). No breeding evidence on record. Most numerous in the southeastern and north central regions.

Winter. Stragglers linger regularly into late December and early January, and a few remain throughout the winter in the southeastern quarter of the state. One other record: January 23 and February 13, 1972, Pine River, Crow Wing County.

COMMON MERGANSER *Mergus merganser*

Minnesota status. Regular. Migrant, summer resident, and winter visitant.

Migration. Common spring and fall migrant throughout the state; least numerous in the west. Peak flocks usually contain one hundred to two hundred birds, but late fall congregations along the lower Mississippi River may range from one thousand to four thousand birds. *Spring migration period:* Mid-February through mid-May with a peak in late March and early April. Earliest dates: SOUTH, none can be given because of wintering birds, but early arrivals usually occur during the first two weeks in March; NORTH, none can be given because of wintering birds, but early arrivals usually occur in late March. Latest dates: SOUTH, April 26,

20. Common Merganser

29, May 2; NORTH, none can be given because of breeding birds. *Fall migration period:* Mid-September (north) through mid-December with a peak in late November. Earliest dates: NORTH, none can be given because of breeding birds; SOUTH, November 8, 12, 19. Latest dates: None can be given because of wintering birds.

Summer. Resident in the north central and northeastern regions (see map 20). Roberts (1932) mentioned three nineteenth-century records for Fillmore, Jackson, and Hennepin counties, but there is no subsequent information to indicate that the species once nested, even sparingly, in the southern

and central regions as Roberts assumed. In view of recent summer observations in Clearwater and Otter Tail counties, however, breeding should be looked for in these counties.
Winter. Common winter visitant in the southeastern quarter of the state; most numerous along the Mississippi River below the Twin Cities. Uncommon winter visitant on Lake Superior; rare elsewhere in the northeastern quarter of the state. Casual in the western half of the state.

RED-BREASTED MERGANSER
Mergus serrator

Minnesota status. Regular. Migrant and summer resident; accidental in winter.
Migration. Common spring and fall migrant in the central and eastern regions, becoming abundant on Lake Superior in the spring. Uncommon migrant in the western regions. *Spring migration period:* Mid-March through late May; the bulk of the migration is from mid-April through early May. Earliest dates: SOUTH, March 13, 14, 15; NORTH, March 28, 31, April 4. Latest dates: SOUTH, May 14, 15, 16; NORTH, none can be given because of breeding birds. *Fall migration period:* Early September through mid-December; the bulk of the migration is from late October through early December. Earliest dates: NORTH, none can be given because of breeding birds; SOUTH, October 1, 9, 20. Latest dates: Stragglers remain through early January in both north and south.
Summer. Resident along the shore of Lake Superior in Cook, Lake, and St. Louis counties. Good breeding evidence is available for Mille Lacs Lake and for Big Sandy Lake, Aitkin County, but the species is very scarce there. Published nesting records exist for inland St. Louis County, Beltrami County, and Houston County, but the records include no details and confusion with females of other merganser species is possible.
Winter. Stragglers remain throughout December and early January in the Lake Superior area and in the southeastern quarter of the state. Because juvenile Common Mergansers are frequently mistaken for Red-breasted Mergansers, the latest dates are based on observations of males (all from Lake Superior): January 5, 9, 12, 27.

Family CATHARTIDAE:
American Vultures

TURKEY VULTURE *Cathartes aura*

Minnesota status. Regular. Migrant and summer resident; accidental in winter.

Migration. Uncommon spring and fall migrant throughout the state, becoming common at Duluth in the fall. *Spring migration period:* Mid-March through mid-May with the bulk of the migration in the last three weeks of April. Earliest dates: SOUTH, March 16, 17; NORTH, March *22*, April 1, 6, 7. *Fall migration period:* Late August through late October with the bulk of the migration from early September through early October. Latest dates: NORTH, October 18, 21, 26, November *6*; SOUTH, October 20, 28, 31, November *26*.

Summer. Resident throughout the forested part of the northern regions and along the St. Croix and lower Mississippi rivers. Formerly more widespread with nineteenth-century nesting records from Traverse, Jackson, Nicollet, and Hennepin counties. Most numerous now along the lower Mississippi River (Goodhue to Houston counties), in the north central region, and along the border lakes in the northeastern region.

Winter. There are several late December and early January records for the lower Mississippi River. Latest date: January 5. In addition, there is a specimen (MMNH #8670) from Lyon County, December 27, 1937, and a record (J. C. Hvoslef) for February 23 and February 28, 1884, in Fillmore County.

Family ACCIPITRIDAE:
Hawks, Eagles, and Harriers

SWALLOW-TAILED KITE *Elanoïdes forficatus*

Minnesota status. Accidental. Summer resident in the nineteenth century. Since the 1920s, one summer record and one spring record.

Records. One bird found dead in Washington County, April 29, 1966 (MMNH #23152; *Loon* 39:67); another bird shot by a farmer near Spring Valley, Fillmore County, about August 18, 1949 (MMNH #9555; *Flicker* 21:71–72).

Former status. In the nineteenth century the species was found breeding in the deciduous forest belt from the Twin Cities area at least as far north as Itasca State Park, Clearwater County. There are several nesting records from Becker and Hennepin counties. Around the turn of the century the species decreased rapidly in numbers and was last reported during the breeding season in about 1907. There are only a few additional reports: Cass County, September 14, 1914; Hennepin County, March 20, 1916; Sherburne County, May 18, 1921; McLeod County, July 29, 1923.

MISSISSIPPI KITE *Ictinia misisippiensis*

Minnesota status. Hypothetical.

Records. Observation of one bird near Arco, Lincoln County, August 31, 1973 (*Loon* 45:131).

GOSHAWK *Accipiter gentilis*

Minnesota status. Regular. Migrant, summer resident, and winter visitant.

Migration. Rare spring and fall migrant throughout most of the state; usually uncommon on the hawk flyway at Duluth in the fall but may be common to abundant there in invasion years. At Duluth peak fall daily counts of two hundred to eight hundred birds in invasion years; peak spring daily counts of about fifty birds after an invasion. *Fall migration period:* Mid-September through early December (normal years) and late August through late December (invasion years) with a peak from mid-October through mid-November. Earliest dates: NORTH, none can be given because of breeding birds; SOUTH, September *1*, *16*, *21*, October 1, 8, 9. *Spring migration period:* Probably late February through early May with the bulk of the migration in March and early April. Latest dates: SOUTH, April 8, 12, 14, May *16*; NORTH, none can be given because of breeding birds.

Winter. Rare visitant throughout the state; least numerous on the prairie. In invasion years uncommon in the eastern half of the state. Recent invasion years: 1962–1963, 1963–1964, and 1972–1973 (the last invasion is the largest on record).

Summer. Resident in the forested part of the northern regions (see map 21). The species very rarely nests farther south. There is a nineteenth-century breeding record from Hennepin County, and breeding was suspected near Pine Center, Morrison County, in 1938.

21. Goshawk (1900)

SHARP-SHINNED HAWK *Accipiter striatus*

Minnesota status. Regular. Migrant and summer resident; regular in winter.

Migration. Usually an uncommon spring and fall migrant except on the hawk flyway at Duluth (abundant in both seasons) and along the shores of large lakes elsewhere in the state (common in the fall). Peak fall daily counts at Duluth range from one thousand to fifteen hundred birds. *Spring migration period:* Early March through late May with the bulk of the migration during April and the first week of May. Earliest dates: SOUTH, none can be given because of wintering birds; NORTH, March *18*, 28, 31, April 1. *Fall mi-*

gration period: Early August through late November with the bulk of the migration from early September through mid-October. Latest dates: NORTH, November 3, 4, 10, *26*, 28; SOUTH, none can be given because of wintering birds.

Summer. Resident throughout the state; no records since the 1930s from west of Fillmore, Rice, Stearns, Becker, and Roseau counties. One nesting record from Murray County in 1921. Most numerous in the north central, northeastern, central, and southeastern regions; generally scarce everywhere.

Winter. Uncommon in winter in the southeastern quarter of the state; rare to casual farther north and west. It is not known whether birds seen in winter are residents of the same area in summer.

COOPER'S HAWK *Accipiter cooperii*

Minnesota status. Regular. Migrant and summer resident; regular in winter.

Migration. Uncommon spring and fall migrant throughout the state. Since the hawk flyway at Duluth is north of the main breeding range, the species is normally uncommon there (common on peak fall days). It may also be common along the shores of some of the other large lakes in the fall. *Spring migration period:* Early March through mid-May with the bulk of the migration in April. Earliest dates: SOUTH, none can be given because of wintering birds; NORTH, March *17*, 23, 30, 31. *Fall migration period:* Mid-August through late November with the bulk of the migration from early September through early October. Latest dates: NORTH, October 22, 23, 25, November *8*; SOUTH, none can be given because of wintering birds.

Summer. Resident throughout the state; very scarce on the prairie in the west central, southwestern, and south central regions. Most numerous in the central, east central, and southeastern regions. More numerous than the Sharp-shinned Hawk everywhere except in the north central and northeastern regions.

Winter. Uncommon in winter in the southern half of the state; accidental in the northern half. It is not known whether the birds seen in winter are residents of the same area in summer.

RED-TAILED HAWK *Buteo jamaicensis*

Minnesota status. Regular. Migrant, summer resident, and winter visitant.

Migration. Common spring and fall migrant throughout the state, becoming abundant on peak days along the major rivers in the spring and along the shore of Lake Superior in the fall. At Duluth peak fall daily counts of five hundred to eight hundred birds. *Spring migration period:* Mid-February through early May with a peak in early April. Earliest dates: SOUTH, none can be given because of wintering birds; residents move back to their territories in February and early March; NORTH, March *11*, 18, 22, 24. *Fall migration period:* Early August through late December; the bulk of the migration is from mid-September through mid-November with a peak in October. Latest dates: None can be given because of wintering birds in the south and stragglers in the north in early winter.

Summer. Resident throughout the state. The species is the third most numerous breeding hawk (after the Marsh Hawk and the American Kestrel) in most areas except the heavily forested northern regions where the Broad-winged Hawk is more numerous.

Winter. Uncommon in winter in the southern half of the state; rare in early winter and casual in late winter in the northern half. Although there are no conclusive data to show whether wintering birds are local summer residents, the population changes in fall and spring indicate that many birds are visitants.

Taxonomic note. Three subspecies — Harlan's Hawk, *Buteo jamaicensis harlani*, once considered a full species; Western Red-tailed Hawk, *B. j. calurus*; and Krider's Hawk, *B. j. kriderii* — are migrants throughout the state. At Duluth in the fall the black phase of the Western Red-tailed Hawk is regular, the Krider's Hawk is casual, and the Harlan's Hawk is accidental. Nothing is known about their relative abundance elsewhere. The Eastern Red-tailed Hawk, *B. j. borealis*, is the breeding race in the state.

RED-SHOULDERED HAWK *Buteo lineatus*

Minnesota status. Regular. Migrant and summer resident; regular in winter.

Migration. Uncommon spring and fall migrant in the southeastern quarter of the state and in the adjacent areas to the west (Stearns County) and to the north (Mille Lacs and Crow Wing counties); rare (farther west) to casual (farther north) in the rest of the state. *Spring migration period:* Probably mid-February through early May; most first arrivals are in March. Earliest dates: SOUTH, none can be given because of wintering birds; NORTH, March *14*, 20, 27, 30. *Fall migration period:* Early September through early November with stragglers into December; most birds depart by late October. Latest dates: NORTH, October 3, 10, 13, November *6*; SOUTH, none can be given because of wintering birds.

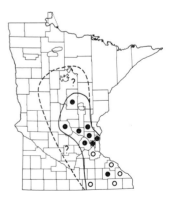

22. Red-shouldered Hawk

Summer. Resident primarily in the southeastern quarter of the state and in the adjacent counties to the northwest (see map 22). The species is known to breed as far north as Crow Wing County (Deerwood, Brainerd) and as far west as Stearns County (Grand Lake, St. Johns); summer occurrence has been reported as far north as Cass County (Leech Lake, Woman Lake) and Becker County (Tamarac National Wildlife Refuge) and as far south and west as Nicollet County (Swan Lake). Roberts believed that the species had increased in numbers and had expanded its range in Minnesota since the early 1930s (*Flicker* 16:31), although there were observations as far north as Cass County in 1902. The species has never been numerous and could have been missed in the ornithological reconnaissance early in this century.

Winter. Uncommon in winter in the southeastern part of the state as far north as Anoka and Chisago counties and as far west as Nicollet County. Whether some birds remain on their summer territory for all or part of the winter is not known, but a few observations (especially those from the Whitewater Wildlife Area) hint at this. It is evident that some birds leave the state, because the number of observations increases after the middle of February.

BROAD-WINGED HAWK *Buteo platypterus*

Minnesota status. Regular. Migrant and summer resident.
Migration. Common migrant throughout the state, becoming abundant in the fall on the hawk flyway at Duluth and elsewhere on rare occasions when birds are grounded by unfavorable weather during the migration peak. Peak fall daily counts at Duluth of twelve thousand to twenty-four thousand birds. *Spring migration period:* Late March through mid-May with a sharp peak in late April. Earliest dates: SOUTH, March *22*, *24*, *28*, *31*, April 5, 6, 11; NORTH, March *30*, April *2*, *3*, 6, 8, 11. *Fall migration period:* Mid-August through late October with a sharp peak in mid-September. Latest dates: NORTH, October 11, 12, *18*, *19*, *27*, *28*; SOUTH, October 21, 22, 23, *30*. Many extreme spring and fall dates have been discarded because the records are not sufficiently detailed to eliminate the possibility of confusion with the Red-shouldered Hawk.

Summer. Resident throughout the forested portions of the state. There are no summer records for the prairie in the west central, southwestern, and south central regions, and the species is scarce in the southeastern region. In the northern forested areas it is the most numerous breeding hawk.

SWAINSON'S HAWK *Buteo swainsoni*

Minnesota status. Regular. Migrant and summer resident.
Migration. Rare spring and fall migrant in the southern half

of the state south of the Minnesota River. Uncommon in the west central and northwestern regions along the Red River Valley. Casual elsewhere with records from Stearns, Pine, Lake of the Woods, and St. Louis counties. *Spring migration period:* April and May with the bulk of the migration from mid-April through mid-May. Earliest dates: SOUTH, April *2*, 9 (three years); NORTH, April 9 (only date). *Fall migration period:* Late August through early October. Latest dates: NORTH, September 30, October 4, 8; SOUTH, October 3, 5, 6.

Summer. Resident on the prairie but very scarce except in the eastern part of the range (see map 23). Almost all recent summer observations and the only modern breeding record are from Dakota, Goodhue, Olmsted, and Dodge counties. The species was formerly more numerous on the western prairie and scarce in the east (Roberts, 1932).

23. Swainson's Hawk

ROUGH-LEGGED HAWK *Buteo lagopus*

Minnesota status. Regular. Migrant and winter visitant; accidental in summer.

Migration. Common spring and fall migrant throughout the state, becoming occasionally abundant along the shore of Lake Superior in the fall. Peak fall daily counts at Duluth of two hundred birds. *Fall migration period:* Mid-September through early December with stragglers into late December; the bulk of the migration occurs from mid-October through mid-November. Earliest dates: NORTH, September *5*, 12, 13, 14; SOUTH, September *8*, *10*, 20, 23. *Spring migration period:* Probably from sometime in February through mid-May with the bulk of the migration from mid-March through late April. Latest dates: SOUTH, May 2, 5, *15*, *17*; NORTH, May 20, 23, 24, *30*.

Winter. Uncommon winter visitant in the southern half of the state; rare in the northern half. The species winters in open country or where there is an exceptionally good food supply (for instance, near the Duluth harbor).

Summer. Four records, all from the northern regions: June 2 and July 10, 1950, Duluth (*Flicker* 22:127); June 16, 1894, Lake Vermilion, St. Louis County (Roberts, 1932); June 28, 1967, Lude, Lake of the Woods County (P. E. Bremer); August 26, 1941, Waskish, Beltrami County (M. Brooks).

FERRUGINOUS HAWK *Buteo regalis*

Minnesota status. Regular. Migrant; accidental in summer.

Migration. Very rare spring and fall migrant west of the Mississippi River; accidental farther north and east. No reports for the years 1968 through 1970, but three reports during 1971 and 1972. *Spring migration period:* Probably mid-March through mid-May. Earliest dates: SOUTH, March *10*, 31, April 3, 8; NORTH, March 18, 24, April 7. Latest dates: SOUTH, May 6, 19 (only dates); NORTH, May 24, 29, 31. *Fall migration period:* Late September through early November. Earliest dates: NORTH, September 28 (only date); SOUTH, September 25 (only date). Latest dates: NORTH, October 21, 23 (only dates); SOUTH, October 24, 31, November 5.

Summer. Although no positive breeding evidence has been obtained, there are a number of single summer observations for the western counties: Lac qui Parle (1891), Kittson (1895, 1896), Roseau (1948), Mahnomen (1964), and Traverse (1966).

GOLDEN EAGLE *Aquila chrysaëtos*

Minnesota status. Regular. Migrant and winter visitant.
Migration. Uncommon fall migrant and rare spring migrant throughout the state. Most frequently seen at the various national wildlife refuges, at Duluth in the fall, and along the lower Mississippi River. *Fall migration period:* Mid-September through December with the bulk of the migration from mid-October through late November. Earliest dates: NORTH, September 13, 15, 16; SOUTH, October 12, 13, 14. *Spring migration period:* Probably from sometime in February through mid-April. Latest dates: SOUTH, April 12, 13, 18, *28*, *30*; NORTH, April 7, 14; May *4*, *5*.
Winter. Rare winter visitant throughout the state. Most frequently seen at the large wildlife refuges.

BALD EAGLE *Haliaeetus leucocephalus*

Minnesota status. Regular. Migrant, summer resident, and winter visitant.
Migration. Uncommon spring and fall migrant throughout the state. Most often seen along rivers, large lakes, and marshes where waterfowl congregate. Peak fall daily counts at the Duluth flyway of twenty to twenty-five birds in late November or early December. The largest concentrations in the state occur along the lower Mississippi River (below Hastings) with peak flocks of fifty to one hundred birds from late February through early April and from late November through late December. *Spring migration period:* Mid-February through late April with the bulk of the migration during March. Extreme dates: None can be given because of wintering birds throughout the state. *Fall migration period:* Late August through late December with the bulk of the migration from mid-September through early

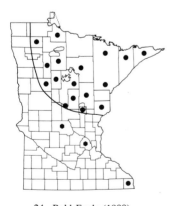

24. Bald Eagle (1900)

December. Extreme dates: None can be given because of wintering birds throughout the state.

Summer. Resident primarily in the northern regions of the state (see map 24). The area producing the most young is the Chippewa National Forest (*Loon* 41:84–87; 42:84–87). In presettlement times the species nested throughout the state; the early records include nesting data from Hennepin and Stearns counties and observations from the Des Moines River and the Red River Valley. In modern times the only known active nesting site in the southern half of the state is in the Upper Mississippi National Wildlife Refuge (Houston County, 1960s and 1970s). Immature birds are very rare summer visitants in the southern half of the state along large rivers and lakes.

Winter. Common winter visitant along the lower Mississippi River, rare or occasionally uncommon at wildlife refuges elsewhere. Most birds leave the northern regions in midwinter, but a few remain through the winter in areas where there is open water.

MARSH HAWK *Circus cyaneus*

Minnesota status. Regular. Migrant and summer resident; regular in winter.

Migration. Common spring and fall migrant throughout the state. Peak fall daily counts at the Duluth flyway of 100 to 150 birds. *Spring migration period:* Mid-February through mid-May with the bulk of the migration from late March through late April. Earliest dates: SOUTH, none can be given because of wintering birds; NORTH, March 5, 7, 8, 11, 12, 15. *Fall migration period:* Mid-August through late November with the bulk of the migration from early September through mid-October. Latest dates: NORTH, November 10, 12, 13, 21; SOUTH, none can be given because of wintering birds.

Summer. Resident, breeding throughout the state. One of the three most numerous nesting hawks (along with the Red-tailed Hawk and the American Kestrel); in heavily forested areas, where openings of marsh and meadow are rare, the Marsh Hawk is outnumbered by other species. There is recent evidence that in some areas the population has declined sharply, probably because the nesting habitat of the species has been destroyed.

Winter. Uncommon in winter in the southern half of the state; casual in the northern half (records from Polk, Clay, Aitkin, Wadena, and St. Louis counties). More often seen in December than in January and early February, although some birds remain throughout the season even in the northern regions. It is not known whether the birds seen in winter are breeding residents.

Family PANDIONIDAE: Ospreys

OSPREY *Pandion haliaetus*

Minnesota status. Regular. Migrant and summer resident.

Migration. Uncommon spring and fall migrant throughout the state. Peak fall daily counts at the Duluth flyway of twenty to twenty-five birds. *Spring migration period:* Early April through late May with a peak in late April and early May. Earliest dates: SOUTH, March *25*, *26*, April 1, 2, 3; NORTH, March *27*, April 11, 12. *Fall migration period:* Mid-August through early November with the bulk of the migration from early September through early October. Latest dates: NORTH, October 18, 22, November *6*; SOUTH, October 29, November 5, 10, *23*, *25*, *27*.

Summer. Resident in the north central and northeastern regions and in adjacent Becker, Mille Lacs, and Pine counties (see map 25). In presettlement times the species nested throughout the state (Roberts, 1932), but information gathered during the twentieth century indicates that the present range of the species is restricted to the area shown on the map. Single birds have been seen in the Upper Mississippi National Wildlife Refuge, but no nest sites are known.

25. Osprey

Family FALCONIDAE: Falcons

GYRFALCON *Falco rusticolus*

Minnesota status. Casual. Winter visitant.

Records. From early November through early March this falcon may be seen anywhere in the state. The records are concentrated near the population centers of Duluth and the Twin Cities, which probably reflects the distribution of observers more than the distribution of the species. Although two-thirds of the observations are from the northern half of the state, a few records have been reported as far south as the Iowa border. In recent years the species has been seen with some regularity along the shore of Lake Superior, especially in the Duluth-Superior harbor. There are five specimens in the Bell Museum of Natural History: MMNH #4080, #8676, #8677, #25727, #25728. Earliest dates: NORTH, September *16*, October *10*, November 3, 5; SOUTH, September *22*, November 5, 26. Latest dates: SOUTH, March 10, *26*; NORTH, March 3, 10, *31*.

PRAIRIE FALCON *Falco mexicanus*

Minnesota status. Accidental. Three summer records since the late 1930s. Regular fall migrant during the 1930s.

Records. Three recent summer observations: July 18,

1949, two birds seen at Mound Springs Recreation Area, Rock County (H. Gunderson and B. Hayward); August 15, 1959, near Waubun, Mahnomen County; August 15, 1959, near St. Hilaire, Pennington County (*Flicker* 31:135).

Former status. Before 1938 there were three periods when this species was recorded as a fall migrant on the prairie in the southwestern quarter of the state: 1890–1895, 1922–1926, and 1930–1937. In the last period the species was seen often enough to be considered regular. All but two of the earlier reports are from August 23 through December 27. The exceptions are spring migrants: March 26, 1935, Traverse County; April 7, 1933, Pipestone County (Roberts, 1936). There are six specimens in the Bell Museum of Natural History: MMNH #3484, #4081, #7707, #7884, #8244, and #8245.

PEREGRINE FALCON *Falco peregrinus*

Minnesota status. Regular. Migrant; accidental in winter. Regular summer resident until 1960.

Migration. Rare spring and fall migrant throughout the state. Highest fall daily counts (at Duluth) of ten birds in 1952 and fourteen birds in 1961. *Spring migration period:* Mid-March through late May with the bulk of the migration from late March through early May. Resident birds are the earliest to arrive. Earliest dates: SOUTH, March 11, 12, 14; NORTH, March 17, April 4 (complete clutch, North Shore). Latest date (beyond breeding areas): May 31. *Fall migration period:* Mid-August through late November with the bulk of the migration from mid-September through late October. Earliest dates (beyond breeding areas): August 11, 27. Latest dates: NORTH, October 26, November 3, *21*; SOUTH, November 19, 24, 26.

Summer. Formerly a resident along the bluffs of the Mississippi River south of Red Wing (nesting last reported in 1962), along the upper St. Croix River (nesting last reported in 1945), along the North Shore of Lake Superior (adults last observed near an eyrie in the summer of 1964), and in the Boundary Waters Canoe Area (nesting last reported in 1964). From 1965 through 1969 there were no summer reports, but in 1970 and in 1971 there were observations of a single bird in two localities in the Twin Cities area.

Winter. Secondhand reports from falconers and local residents indicate that some resident peregrines along the Mississippi River remain all winter. Only four confirmed winter observations: Hennepin County (December 13, 1941; January 10, 1959; January 28, 1968); Duluth (December 23, 1969).

26. Merlin

MERLIN (Pigeon Hawk) *Falco columbarius*

Minnesota status. Regular. Migrant and summer resident; casual in winter.

Migration. Rare spring and fall migrant throughout the state (including the prairie). In the 1950s peak fall daily counts at the Duluth flyway of fifteen to twenty-five birds, declining to only three to five birds in the 1960s. *Spring migration period:* Late March through mid-May with a peak during the last two weeks of April. Earliest dates: SOUTH, March *15*, 20, 22; NORTH, March *11*, 29, 31, April 6. Latest dates: SOUTH, May 3, 5, 16; NORTH, none can be given because of breeding birds. *Fall migration period:* Mid-August through early November with the bulk of the migration in September and early October. Earliest dates: NORTH, none can be given because of breeding birds; SOUTH, August 5 (only date). Latest dates: NORTH, October 17, 18, 30, November *26*; SOUTH, October 20, 24, November 3.

Summer. Resident in the northeastern and north central regions and adjacent counties in the northwestern region (see map 26). Very scarce throughout most of this area except along the Canadian border in Lake and Cook counties and also possibly in Kittson and Roseau counties.

Winter. Casual in winter with records from the following counties: Fillmore (December 6, 1969), Hennepin (December 26, 1931), Cook (December 28, 1952), St. Louis (December 28, 1963), Lake (January 3, 1970), and Stearns (February 5 and February 25, 1966, in different locations). Some of the extreme migration dates for the northern half of the state may represent wintering birds.

AMERICAN KESTREL (Sparrow Hawk) *Falco sparverius*

Minnesota status. Regular. Migrant and summer resident; regular in winter.

Migration. Common spring and fall migrant throughout the state; abundant along the shore of Lake Superior in the fall with peak daily counts of 150 to 250 birds. *Spring migration period:* Early March through mid-May with the bulk of the migration from late March through late April. Earliest dates: SOUTH, none can be given because of wintering birds; NORTH, March 12, 15, 16. *Fall migration period:* Early August through late October with the bulk of the migration from late August through late September. Latest dates: NORTH, October 21, 22, 27, November *22*, *23*; SOUTH, none can be given because of wintering birds.

Summer. Resident throughout the state. One of the most numerous breeding hawks (along with the Red-tailed Hawk and the Marsh Hawk), the American Kestrel is an open-country bird and is least numerous in the heavily wooded portions of the state, especially since increaesd fire protection has almost eliminated burned-over woodland.

Winter. Uncommon in winter in the southern half of the state, especially from Washington and Kandiyohi counties southward. Casual in the northern half of the state. Records (mostly from the early part of the winter) from Clay, Clearwater, Morrison, Pine, and southern St. Louis counties.

Family TETRAONIDAE: Grouse and Ptarmigan

SPRUCE GROUSE *Canachites canadensis*

Minnesota status. Regular. Permanent resident.

Distribution. Permanent resident in the northeastern and north central regions and in adjacent Roseau County (see map 27). In the nineteenth century the species was found as far south as Mille Lacs Lake and Wadena and Carlton counties (Roberts, 1932); it is now found primarily in counties adjacent to the Canadian border, although other populations were observed between 1960 and 1972 in northern Hubbard County. There are no recent published records from central or southern St. Louis County, despite an abundance of spruce bog habitat in these areas.

27. Spruce Grouse

RUFFED GROUSE *Bonasa umbellus*

Minnesota status. Regular. Permanent resident.

Distribution. Permanent resident throughout most of the forested portions of the state (see map 28; data from the Minnesota Department of Natural Resources). Along the western fringe of the range in the Twin Cities area the species has been extirpated by development; there have been no reports from Hennepin County in twenty-five years. The species is also scarce in the west central region. Its abundance varies with peaks occurring in ten-year cycles.

WILLOW PTARMIGAN *Lagopus lagopus*

Minnesota status. Accidental. Two spring records, and many records from the winter invasion of 1933–1934.

Records. The records for this species occurred in three winters, many years apart. One bird was collected on April 20, 1914, on Springsteel Island, Lake of the Woods County (MMNH #8479). During the winter of 1933–1934 an invasion occurred in Roseau, Lake of the Woods, and northern St. Louis counties; three specimens were collected (MMNH

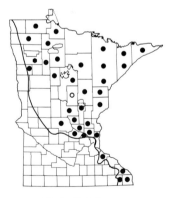

28. Ruffed Grouse

#8024, #8030, #8031), and over two hundred observations were reported between December 7 and April 25. The most recent observation, in 1964, was of two birds that came to a feeder at Graceton, Lake of the Woods County, between February 27 and March 12 (*Loon* 36:66).

GREATER PRAIRIE CHICKEN
Tympanuchus cupido

Minnesota status. Regular. Permanent resident; casual winter visitant.

Distribution. Resident primarily on the prairie in the northwestern region (see map 29). A small population in Wadena and adjacent Cass counties was still extant in 1973 (R. Oehlenschlager, personal communication). The general population, even on the main range, declined sharply in the 1960s, owing to the destruction of the preferred habitat of the species. During the same period an outlying population in Morrison County disappeared entirely (last seen in 1965; M. Partch, personal communication). The population decline is the continuation of a trend that was first noted in the 1930s. Roberts (1932) described the Prairie Chicken as breeding throughout the prairie and the open woodlands of the state and also in areas where the forest had been cleared in the northeast. Resident flocks were present in Fillmore and Mower counties until the late 1930s (*Wilson Bulletin* 51:242–43). Birds were last seen in the northeastern region (near Duluth) in 1952. In presettlement times this species did not occur in the state (see the discussion of the Sharp-tailed Grouse).

Migration. In fall and winter a few birds are seen in the west central and southwestern regions. They arrive in September (earliest dates: September 7, 8) and probably depart in February and March.

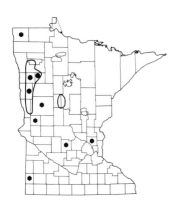

29. Greater Prairie Chicken (1930)

SHARP-TAILED GROUSE
Pedioecetes phasianellus

Minnesota status. Regular. Permanent resident.

Distribution. Permanent resident in the northern regions and in adjacent Pine County (see map 30; data from the Minnesota Department of Natural Resources). The population in the state was reduced to the lowest known level in the mid-1960s, but a slight increase in population has occurred since then. The species is most numerous in the northwestern part of the state in Roseau, Lake of the Woods, Beltrami, and Marshall counties. There is another population center in the area of Carlton County, Aitkin County, and west central St. Louis County (Floodwood to Zim). Casual in Cook County (possibly vagrants from the Thunder Bay population). The species was formerly more wide-spread, and a nest was found in Swift County as recently as 1942. In presettlement times this species was commonly termed "Prairie Chicken" (the species we now call by that name had not yet moved into the state). According to Roberts (1932), the Sharp-tailed Grouse lived on the prairies in the summer and retreated to the brushlands and open forests in the winter, and the early explorers and settlers found the species to be abundant everywhere. When the prairie was converted to grain fields, the Prairie Chicken moved in and the Sharp-tailed Grouse retreated to the north.

30. Sharp-tailed Grouse

Family PHASIANIDAE:
Quails and Pheasants

BOBWHITE *Colinus virginianus*

Minnesota status. Regular. Permanent resident.
Distribution. Resident primarily in the southeastern region, in adjacent counties in the south central region, and in Dakota County (see map 31). It is not known whether the birds observed recently farther west and north were wild birds, escapees from captive flocks, or stock released by game farms. The species is very scarce even in its primary range; formerly it was more numerous and widespread, although it was very rare or perhaps even absent in presettlement times. Introductions of the species were begun in the nineteenth century. The Division of Game and Fish of the Minnesota Department of Natural Resources stopped releasing these birds in 1952, and the hunting season has been closed since 1958. The peak period of abundance was in the 1920s, and the numbers have continued to decline since then (*Loon* 36:60–62). The species has been reported as far north as Pine, Morrison, Stearns, Pope, and Big Stone counties.

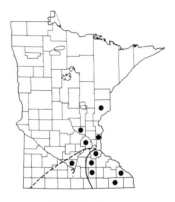

31. Bobwhite

RING-NECKED PHEASANT *Phasianus colchicus*

Minnesota status. Regular; introduced. Permanent resident.
Distribution. Permanent resident throughout much of the state; absent from most of the northeastern and north central regions and very scarce in the northern part of the northwestern region (see map 32). The best pheasant range occurs in the southern part of the central region and in the south central, southwestern, and west central regions, but "clean farming" practices in recent years have resulted in a reduction of the population. Most numerous in the Twin Cities suburban area where there is sufficient cover and artificial feeding by the local residents. This species was not

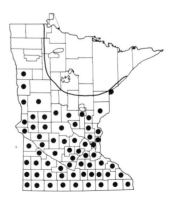

32. Ring-necked Pheasant

part of the native avifauna but was introduced into the state in 1905. Large-scale releases of birds were begun in 1915, and the first hunting season was opened in 1924; peak populations occurred in the early 1940s.

CHUKAR *Alectoris chukar*

Minnesota status. Regular; introduced. Permanent resident in Ely, St. Louis County.

Distribution. A remnant population of the large-scale releases that were made throughout the state in the 1930s and 1940s exists near the abandoned open-pit iron ore mines in Ely, St. Louis County. The population is small but has persisted because of suitable breeding habitat and artificial winter feeding by the town's residents. The last observation of a brood was in 1966, but the area is not regularly checked in summer. Winter flocks of six to ten birds have been observed recently. Introductions of this species were made in all but two of Minnesota's counties thirty-five years ago; although the birds established themselves for a short time in Stearns, Benton, Sherburne, Wright, Hennepin, Anoka, Chisago, Pine, Itasca, St. Louis, and Lake counties (*Flicker* 32:64), on the whole the introductions were not successful.

GRAY PARTRIDGE *Perdix perdix*

Minnesota status. Regular; introduced. Permanent resident.

Distribution. Permanent resident generally west of the Mississippi River (see map 33). Most numerous in the southwestern part of the central region and in the west central and southwestern regions; scarce north of Polk County, southeast of Olmsted County, and along the eastern margin of the central region. This species was not part of the native avifauna but entered Jackson and Nobles counties from Iowa (where it had been introduced) sometime after 1914. It also spread into the northwestern part of the state from North Dakota and Canada between 1926 and 1929. Birds were released by the Minnesota Department of Natural Resources in Martin County in 1926, in Hennepin County in 1927, and later in various other parts of southern and western Minnesota. The first hunting season was in 1939, and peak numbers were harvested in 1958.

33. Gray Partridge

Family MELEAGRIDIDAE: Turkeys

TURKEY *Meleagris gallopavo*

Minnesota status. Hypothetical.

Discussion. Roberts (1932) concluded that there was no

positive evidence that the species had ever existed in Minnesota. None of the explorers after 1800 made reference to this bird, and the few earlier accounts do not offer reliable data on location and species. Sporadic attempts have been made by the Minnesota Division of Game and Fish to introduce the species, most recently in the Whitewater Game Refuge in Winona and Wabasha counties. Releases there in 1936 and between 1955 and 1959 of game-farm birds were not successful. Stocking, using wild-trapped birds, was attempted again in 1964, 1965, and 1968, and the birds are still present and breeding in the refuge and the surrounding farmland. Various sportsmen's clubs have tried to stock the species elsewhere in the state (Clay, Becker, Sherburne, Otter Tail, Brown, Blue Earth, Rice, and Houston counties), and some of these projects appear to be successful.

Family GRUIDAE: Cranes

WHOOPING CRANE *Grus americana*

Minnesota status. Accidental. One fall record. Migrant and summer resident in the nineteenth century.

Records. The only verified modern sighting was of one bird on November 7, 1951, by the manager of the Rice Lake National Wildlife Refuge, Aitkin County. (*Loon* 40:21). There are a few newspaper accounts which indicate that the species may still pass over the western regions of the state in April and October.

Former status. In the nineteenth century this crane was a regular migrant and summer resident, breeding throughout the prairie; there are six specimens from the same era in the Bell Museum of Natural History. The most recent nest in the State was found in Grant County in 1876; the most recent regular sighting of birds was in Roseau County on April 23, 1917.

SANDHILL CRANE *Grus canadensis*

Minnesota status. Regular. Migrant and summer resident.

Migration. Common spring and fall migrant in the northwestern region and in adjacent Wilkin County; rare elsewhere. Peak fall concentrations of one thousand to five thousand birds. Congregating points: Roseau River Wildlife Area, Roseau County; near Borup, Norman County; and near Rothsay, Wilkin County. *Spring migration period:* Late March through early May with a peak in early and mid-April. Earliest dates: SOUTH, March 22, 23; NORTH, none can be given because of breeding birds. *Fall migration period:* Early September through mid-November with a peak in October. Earliest dates: NORTH, none can be given because of breeding birds; SOUTH, September 26 (only date). Latest dates: NORTH, November 11, 14, 15; SOUTH, October 31, November 8, 9, *20*.

Summer. Resident primarily in the northwestern region and in a few localities in the central part of the state. Recent summer observations in Kittson and Marshall counties and breeding evidence from Roseau County (1954, 1966) and northern Clearwater County (1972). Recent summer observations also in Mille Lacs and Sherburne counties and breeding evidence from Aitkin County (near McGregor, 1972), Morrison County (near Buckman, 1968, 1969), and Pine County (near Beroun, 1950). There are probably undiscovered breeding sites in both the northwestern and central areas. At Carlos Avery Wildlife Area, Anoka County, a wild female successfully bred with a captive male in 1964 and 1965. The species was formerly more abundant and widespread, nesting in swamps and muskeg throughout most of the state. Roberts (1932) lists breeding records from Jackson County (Loon Lake, 1883) and Pennington County (Goose Lake, 1920s).

Winter. At Carlos Avery Wildlife Area the female mentioned above spent the winter of 1968–1969 with the flightless male.

Family RALLIDAE: Rails, Gallinules, and Coots

KING RAIL *Rallus elegans*

Minnesota status. Regular. Migrant and summer resident.

Migration. Rare during the migration seasons in the southern half of the state; most birds encountered are on breeding territories. Accidental in the northern half of the state; one spring record (Agassiz National Wildlife Refuge, Marshall County, May 25, 1968) and one fall record (near Hackensack, Cass County, August 5, 1936). *Spring migration period:* Probably mid-April through mid-May. Earliest dates: April 10, 11 (only dates). *Fall migration period:* Probably August and September. Latest dates: September 11, 16, 23, October *1*, *21*.

Summer. Resident in the southern half of the state (see map 34); probably most numerous in the southern regions. Little is known about actual breeding densities or about the apparent variations from year to year in the number of birds present in the state.

34. King Rail

VIRGINIA RAIL *Rallus limicola*

Minnesota status. Regular. Migrant and summer resident; accidental in winter.

Migration. Uncommon spring and fall migrant throughout most of the state; rare in the north central and northeastern regions. *Spring migration period:* Mid-April through late May with a peak in late April and early May. Earliest dates: SOUTH, April 15, 16, 18; NORTH, April *15*, May 2, 4. *Fall migration period:* gradual exodus from nesting areas probably in August and September. Latest dates: NORTH, September 6, 15 (only dates), October *16*; SOUTH, October 12, 25, 30, November *6*, *11*, *13*.

Summer. Resident throughout most of the state. The species breeds at Duluth and Virginia, St. Louis County, but not farther northeast in Lake and Cook counties. Generally scarce in the northern counties of the north central region.

Winter. Three records: Hennepin County (December 30, 1960; January 10 to February 7, 1959); Winona County (January 8, 1972).

SORA *Porzana carolina*

Minnesota status. Regular. Migrant and summer resident; accidental in winter.

Migration. Common during the spring and uncommon during the fall throughout most of state except in heavily wooded portions of the northeastern region where there is little suitable habitat. *Spring migration period:* Mid-April through late May with a peak in early May. Earliest dates: SOUTH, April *1*, *4*, 12, 13; NORTH, April *20*, 27, 30, May 3. *Fall migration period:* Mid-August through mid-October with no noticeable peak. Latest dates: NORTH, October 10, 15; SOUTH, October 24, 25, November *21*, December *7*, *12*.

Summer. Resident throughout the state; scarce in the heavily wooded and rocky lake country along the Canadian border in the eastern part of the state.

Winter. One record of a wintering bird: November 30, 1893, to January 24, 1894, at Lanesboro, Fillmore County.

YELLOW RAIL *Coturnicops noveboracensis*

Minnesota status. Regular. Migrant and summer resident.

Migration. Rare migrant throughout the state. Little is known of the migratory habits of the species, but there are records of its presence in all regions. *Spring migration period:* Probably late April through late May. Earliest dates: SOUTH, April 26, May 3 (only dates); NORTH, April 26 (only date). *Fall migration period:* Probably late August through early October. Latest dates: NORTH, October 2, 3 (only dates), *16*; SOUTH, September 21, 24, 26, October *26*.

Summer. It is not possible to map the breeding distribution of this rail because of the paucity of records. There are nesting records from four locations: Murray County (Lake Wilson, 1917); Sherburne County (near St. Cloud, 1952); Becker and Mahnomen counties (county line road near Waubun, 1962, 1964); Aitkin County (near McGregor, 1973). In addition, there are summer records from Kittson, Marshall, Clearwater, Traverse, and Crow Wing counties. The species is most numerous in the northwestern and north central regions.

BLACK RAIL *Laterallus jamaicensis*

Minnesota status. Accidental. Four spring records and two fall records.

Records. All the records for this elusive species are observations, but those listed below are sufficiently detailed to be considered reliable. Four spring observations: May 1, 1951, Fox Lake, Rice County (D. W. Warner shot one bird, but the specimen could not be found; a single feather was recovered which compared favorably with existing specimens); May 12, 1962, Long Meadow Slough, Hennepin County (W. E. Parrish; details on file, MMNH); May 12, 1971, Frontenac, Goodhue County (*Loon* 43:58); May 25, 1934, Little Rock Lake, Benton County (*Loon* 37:52). A research study for a University of Minnesota Master's thesis on rails in the marshes of northern Ramsey County listed this species as a migrant (*Flicker* 26:4), but no details are given. Two fall records: August 14, 1968, Martin Lake, Anoka County (*Loon* 40:101); October 1, 1972, Girard Lake, Hennepin County (*Loon* 44:121). All the records are clustered in the central and east central parts of the state.

PURPLE GALLINULE *Porphyrula martinica*

Minnesota status. Accidental. Two fall records and one summer record.

Records. Two specimens, both adult birds that were found dead: June 11 or June 12, 1967, Sheldon Township, Houston County (MMNH #23021); November 11, 1963, near Toivola, St. Louis County (MMNH #19754). In addition, one immature bird was seen and photographed on September 5, 1970, at Oak Leaf Lake near St. Peter, Nicollet County (*Loon* 42:119; photographs on file).

COMMON GALLINULE *Gallinula chloropus*

Minnesota status. Regular. Migrant and summer resident; accidental in winter.

Migration. Uncommon spring and fall migrant in the southern half of the state; casual in the western regions (Becker, Mahnomen, and Marshall counties), and accidental elsewhere in the northern half of the state (Duluth).

Spring migration period: Late April through late May with a peak in early May. Earliest dates: SOUTH, April 2, 21, 24; NORTH, April 21, May 7, 10. *Fall migration period:* Probably from sometime in August through mid-October. Latest dates: NORTH, no data; SOUTH, October 9, 12, 13, 25. **Summer.** Resident primarily in the southern half of the state (see map 35). Along the western margin of the state nesting has been reported as far north as Parker's Prairie, Otter Tail County (1903); May and August records from Becker, Mahnomen, and Marshall counties suggest that the species may breed farther north. A single bird was seen at the Mud-Goose Wildlife Area, Cass County, on July 11, 1966 (*Loon* 38:109).

Winter. One record: one bird captured in Minneapolis on January 23, 1915.

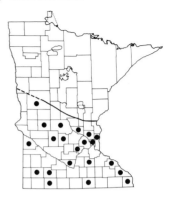

35. Common Gallinule

AMERICAN COOT *Fulica americana*

Minnesota status. Regular. Migrant and summer resident; regular in winter.

Migration. Abundant spring and fall migrant throughout most of the state; usually uncommon in the spring and common in the fall near Duluth and less numerous farther northeastward. *Spring migration period:* Mid-March through late May with the bulk of the migration from early April through early May. Earliest dates: SOUTH, March 11, 15, 16; NORTH, April 7, 9. *Fall migration period:* Mid-September through early December with a peak in mid- and late October. Latest dates: NORTH, November 19, 20, 26; SOUTH, December 11, 13, 18.

Summer. Resident throughout the state; scarce in the northeastern region (one breeding record from Palo, St. Louis County) and in the adjacent counties in the north central region. The main breeding range is west of the Mississippi River in the northern and central regions and west of Dodge County in the southern regions.

Winter. In the southeastern quarter of the state stragglers are regularly present in December and early January, and a few birds overwinter. For the northern half of the state there is one record of nine birds at Fergus Falls, Otter Tail County, during the winter of 1971–1972.

Family CHARADRIIDAE:
Plovers and Turnstones

SEMIPALMATED PLOVER
Charadrius semipalmatus

Minnesota status. Regular. Migrant.

Migration. Uncommon spring and fall migrant throughout the state. Occasionally common with peak counts of twenty-five to fifty birds. *Spring migration period:* Mid-April through mid-June with the bulk of the migration in May. Earliest dates: SOUTH, April 9, 14, 16, 17; NORTH, April 21, May 7, 8. Latest dates: SOUTH, June 6, 7, 17; NORTH, June 14, 15, 16, 21, 30. *Fall migration period:* Mid-July through early October with the bulk of the migration from mid-August through early September. Earliest dates: NORTH, July 4, 16, 20, 21; SOUTH, July 2, 14, 16, 18. Latest dates: NORTH, September 20, 23, 29; SOUTH, October 5, 6, 8.

PIPING PLOVER *Charadrius melodus*

Minnesota status. Regular. Migrant and summer resident.
Migration. Rare spring migrant throughout most of the state; uncommon near Duluth and possibly Lake of the Woods. Except in nesting locations the species is seen less often in the fall than in the spring. Peak spring daily counts at Duluth of eight to twelve birds. *Spring migration period:* Late April through late May with a peak in early and mid-May. Earliest dates: SOUTH, April 23, 28, May 2; NORTH, April 23, 26, 30. Latest dates: SOUTH, May 27, 28, June 2, 10; NORTH, none can be given because of breeding birds.
Fall migration period: Late July through early September. Earliest dates: NORTH, none can be given because of breeding birds; SOUTH, no data. Latest dates: NORTH, August 30, September 3, 7, 13; SOUTH, September 1, 28 (only dates).
Summer. Resident in a few areas of suitable habitat in the northern half of the state. Breeding patterns in the state are best known from the Duluth area where nests have been found sporadically since 1936, but the first nests in the state were found on Pine and Currey islands in Lake of the Woods in 1932. The most recent nesting report from Lake of the Woods was in 1941, but the birds undoubtedly still nest on the undisturbed beaches there. Breeding records have also been obtained from Otter Tail County (no location given, 1933), Douglas County (Lake Ida, 1936; Lake Carlos, 1936; Lake Alexander, 1937), and Mille Lacs Lake (Garrison, 1938). There are single summer observations from Cormorant Lake, Becker County; Salt Lake, Lac qui Parle County; and Stevens County.

KILLDEER *Charadrius vociferus*

Minnesota status. Regular. Migrant and summer resident; casual in winter.
Migration. Common spring and fall migrant throughout the state. Peak spring flocks of twenty-five to thirty birds, and peak fall flocks of fifty to sixty birds. *Spring migration period:* Mid-March through late April with a peak in early

and mid-April. Earliest dates: SOUTH, February 22, March *1*, *2*, 7, 9, 10; NORTH, March *8*, 17, 20, 21. *Fall migration period:* Mid-August through early December with the bulk of the migration from late September through mid-November. Latest dates: NORTH, November 3, 12, 14; SOUTH, none can be given because of wintering birds.

Summer. Resident; widespread and numerous throughout the state wherever suitable habitat exists.

Winter. From the Twin Cities area southeastward stragglers are observed in December and January. Over-wintering birds have been reported from Winona.

AMERICAN GOLDEN PLOVER
Pluvialis dominica

Minnesota status. Regular. Migrant; casual summer visitant.

Migration. Common spring and fall migrant in the central and western two-thirds of the state, becoming occasionally abundant along the western margin. Rare in the spring and uncommon in the fall in the eastern one-third of the state; rare in the southeastern region at any season. The peak flock size is usually twenty to fifty birds, but occasionally peak flocks may contain two hundred to five hundred birds. Daily counts of two thousand to four thousand birds are possible in the southwestern and west central regions. *Spring migration period:* Mid-April through early June with a peak in early and mid-May. Earliest dates: SOUTH, March 27, *30*, April *4*, 18, 21; NORTH, April *20*, *21*, 29, May 6, 7. Latest dates: SOUTH, June 6, 8, *19*; NORTH, June 4, 10. *Fall migration period:* Late August through mid-November with the bulk of the migration from mid-September through late October. Earliest dates: NORTH, July *31*, August *8*, *13*, 20, 22, 23; SOUTH, August *3*, *11*, 24, September 5, 7. Latest dates: NORTH, November 1, 5, 6; *17*; SOUTH, November 15, 16, 17.

Summer. Casual summer visitant in the west central region. There are records from mid-June through late July in three different summers in Lac qui Parle and Stevens counties; a continuous record was obtained during the summer of 1966 when two to eight birds were observed in Stevens County on seven occasions from early June through mid-July.

BLACK-BELLIED PLOVER *Pluvialis squatarola*

Minnesota status. Regular. Migrant.

Migration. Uncommon spring and fall migrant throughout the state; locally common, especially at Duluth. Peak flock size near Duluth is usually twenty to forty birds, but flocks of up to a hundred birds have been seen. *Spring migration pe-*

riod: Late April through early June with the bulk of the migration in May. Earliest dates: SOUTH, April *11*, 16, 19, 21; NORTH, May 8, 9, 16. Latest dates: SOUTH, June 3, 6, 9; NORTH, June 13, 15, 17, *25*. *Fall migration period:* Mid-August through mid-November with the bulk of the migration from mid-September through early October. Earliest dates: NORTH, July *31*, August 8, 13, 14; SOUTH, August *3*, 9, 14, 16, 17. Latest dates: NORTH, November 5, 7, 11, *16*, *22*; SOUTH, November 16, 17, 19.

RUDDY TURNSTONE *Arenaria interpres*

Minnesota status. Regular. Migrant.

Migration. Uncommon spring migrant throughout most of the state; common to occasionally abundant at Duluth. Peak flock size at Duluth is usually fifty to one hundred birds, but flocks of up to three hundred birds have been seen. Rare throughout most of the state in the fall; uncommon to occasionally common at Duluth. *Spring migration period:* Early May through mid-June with a peak in late May. Earliest dates: SOUTH, May 4, 5; NORTH, May *3*, 9, 12. Latest dates: SOUTH, May 30, 31, June *9*, *21*; NORTH, June 11, 14, 16, *19*, *22*. *Fall migration period:* Late July through late September with a peak in early September. Earliest dates: NORTH, July *4*, *11*, 27, 29, 30; SOUTH, July *6*, August 1, 16, 23. Latest dates: NORTH, September 15, 21, 26, October *5*, November *2*; SOUTH, September 12, 25, 29.

Family SCOLOPACIDAE: Woodcock, Snipe, and Sandpipers

AMERICAN WOODCOCK *Philohela minor*

Minnesota status. Regular. Migrant and summer resident.

Migration. Common to uncommon spring and fall migrant in the east central, central, north central, and northeastern regions; rare to uncommon elsewhere in the state. During the period of peak concentrations in the fall thirty to fifty birds can occasionally be found in good habitat. *Spring migration period:* Late March through early May with a peak in mid-April. Earliest dates: SOUTH, March 19, 21, 24; NORTH, March *20*, 28, 29, 30. *Fall migration period:* Early September through early November with a peak in late September. Latest dates: NORTH, October 22, 23, November *5*, *9*, *19*; SOUTH, November 7, 9, 19, December *3*, *29*.

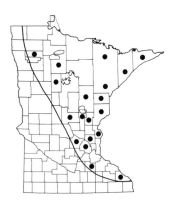

36. American Woodcock

Summer. Resident primarily in the northeastern, north central, central, and east central regions and in a few adjacent counties to the southeast and northwest (see map 36). Outside the map area there is one summer observation from Glacial Lakes State Park, Pope County (1972).

COMMON SNIPE *Capella gallinago*

Minnesota status. Regular. Migrant and summer resident; regular in winter.

Migration. Common spring and fall migrant throughout the state. Peak spring daily counts usually of twelve to fifteen birds, rarely thirty to fifty birds; peak fall daily counts usually of twenty-five to fifty birds, rarely up to a hundred birds. *Spring migration period:* Mid-March through mid-May with a peak in mid- and late April. Earliest dates: SOUTH, none can be given because of wintering birds; NORTH, March *15, 25, 26,* April 5, 6, 7. *Fall migration period:* Flocking begins in mid-July with migration from early September through mid-November; the bulk of the migration is from late September through late October. Latest dates: NORTH, November 6, 8, *17;* SOUTH, none can be given because of wintering birds.

Summer. Resident throughout the state. Most numerous in the north central region and adjacent counties in the northeastern region; least numerous in the southwestern and southeastern regions. There are breeding records from Polk, Aitkin, Mille Lacs, Sherburne, Anoka, Ramsey, Hennepin, McLeod, Nicollet, Martin, and Winona counties.

Winter. Uncommon in winter in the southeastern quarter of the state; no records outside this area. Congregations of fifteen to thirty birds have been observed during the first half of the winter.

LONG-BILLED CURLEW *Numenius americanus*

Minnesota status. Casual. Migrant. Summer resident in the nineteenth century.

Records. Twentieth-century records indicate that this species is primarily a casual spring migrant in the central part of the state from Duluth to Lac qui Parle County. There are spring records from the following counties: Douglas, St. Louis, Aitkin, Wilkin, McLeod (three records), Meeker, Kandiyohi, Hennepin, and Lac qui Parle. In addition, there are two fall records from Stearns County. *Spring migration period:* No regular migration periods can be defined from the few dates available. Earliest dates: April *10,* 20, 24, 25. Latest dates: May 24, 26, 28. *Fall migration period:* September 27, October 28 (only dates).

Former status. In the nineteenth century the species was more numerous as a migrant, and it bred on the prairie both south and west of the deciduous forests. Roberts (1932) cited breeding evidence from Jackson, Lac qui Parle, and Polk counties and stated that the species was especially numerous on the western prairies from the Iowa line northward, preferring in the northwest the sandy ridges or old beaches that border the Red River Valley on the east. There are three specimens (MMNH #3490, #3903, #8832) from this period.

WHIMBREL *Numenius phaeopus*

Minnesota status. Regular. Migrant; casual summer visitant.

Migration. Uncommon spring migrant and a rare fall migrant along the North Shore of Lake Superior. Usually only one to five birds are seen, but there are a few spring records of flocks of twenty to thirty birds. Casual elsewhere in the state at both seasons with records from Goodhue, Olmsted, Renville, Marshall, Aitkin, and Cass counties. *Spring migration period:* Mid-May through mid-June with a peak between May 20 and May 25. Earliest dates: April *23*, May 12, 18. Latest dates: June 17, 19, 23. *Fall migration period:* Poorly known but probably late August through late September. Earliest date: August 28 (only date). Latest dates: September 19, 22, 25, October *18*.

Summer. Records of observations on Minnesota Point, Duluth, in late June and July in three separate years: June 29 (three birds) and July 1 (two birds), 1969; July 7, July 28, and August 1, 1943; and July 18, 1937. Because of the infrequency of the records and the lack of records for consecutive years, it is impossible to determine whether these birds were migrants or summering individuals.

ESKIMO CURLEW *Numenius borealis*

Minnesota status. Extirpated. Regular migrant in the nineteenth century. .

Former status. Roberts (1932) summarized all that is known about this species: "The Eskimo Curlew, now long since absent from Minnesota, formerly passed northward in the spring in great numbers through the western part of the Mississippi and Missouri valleys. . . . It is evident that it disappeared from the western part of the state, where it was without doubt once abundant as a spring migrant, before that region was explored to any extent by bird-students. No Minnesota specimens are known." The few hearsay records that he cites are from the 1880s.

UPLAND SANDPIPER (Upland Plover)
Bartramia longicauda

Minnesota status. Regular. Migrant and summer resident.

Migration. Uncommon spring and fall migrant throughout most of the state; local and rare in the north central and northeastern regions (known from a few breeding locations in Clearwater, Aitkin, and St. Louis counties). Usually seen as individuals or in small groups of two to five birds, occasionally in concentrations of up to fifteen birds, especially in the fall. *Spring migration period:* Mid-April through late May with a peak in early May. Earliest dates: SOUTH, April 7, 17, 18, 20; NORTH, April 20, 25, 28. *Fall migration period:* Early July through late August; there is a gradual exodus from the state with most birds departing by early August. Latest dates: NORTH, August 6, 10, 11, *31*, October *19*; SOUTH, August 12, 15, 25, September *11*, *14*, October *4*, *26*.

Summer. Resident throughout most of the state; very scarce in the north central and northeastern regions and in adjacent Pine, Kanabec, and Mille Lacs counties. In the north central and northeastern regions there are breeding records from Clearwater County, Aitkin County, and St. Louis County (Duluth and Hibbing), and a few other summer observations. The species is not known to occur in Cook, Lake, Koochiching, Itasca, and Lake of the Woods counties. In the northwestern region there are breeding records as far north as Pennington County and summer observations from Roseau and Marshall counties.

SPOTTED SANDPIPER *Actitis macularia*

Minnesota status. Regular. Migrant and summer resident.
Migration. Common spring and fall migrant throughout the state. Normally encountered as individuals or in small groups of two or three birds, but occasionally congregations of ten to twenty-five birds are seen, especially in the spring. *Spring migration period:* Mid-April through late May with a peak in mid-May. Earliest dates: SOUTH, April 11, 14, 15; NORTH, April 22, 25, 28. *Fall migration period:* Mid-August through late October; no peak period has been noted; most birds leave by late September. Latest dates: NORTH, October 8, 14, 15, *28*; SOUTH, October 19, 22, 23, November *2*.
Summer. Resident, breeding throughout the state. Most numerous near the lakes in northern Minnesota and along the Mississippi River.

SOLITARY SANDPIPER *Tringa solitaria*

Minnesota status. Regular. Migrant; accidental summer resident.
Migration. Uncommon spring and fall migrant throughout the state; most often seen in the eastern and central regions, less frequently seen in the western regions. Although most records are of individual birds, flocks of two to six birds and peak aggregations of ten to twelve birds are occasionally

reported. *Spring migration period:* Mid-April through late May with a peak in early and mid-May. Earliest dates: SOUTH, April 7, 8, 12, 15, 16; NORTH, April *19, 20*, 28, May 3, 4. Latest dates: SOUTH, May 24, 25, 29, June *2*; NORTH, May 24, 25, June 2, *9*. *Fall migration period:* Very late June through mid-October with no peak period noted. Earliest dates: NORTH, June 26, 27, 28; SOUTH, June *26*, 30, July 1, 2. Latest dates: NORTH, October 13, 15, 17, *26*; SOUTH, October 7, 10, *26*.

Summer. On July 11, 1973, a pair and one half-grown young bird were found along the Mississippi River in Verdon Township, Aitkin County (*Loon* 45:96).

GREATER YELLOWLEGS *Tringa melanoleucus*

Minnesota status. Regular. Migrant.

Migration. Uncommon spring and fall migrant throughout the state. Usually found in small groups of one to five birds, but occasionally concentrations of twenty-five to thirty-five birds are seen. *Spring migration period*: Late March through late May with a peak in mid- and late April. Earliest dates: SOUTH, March 22, 24, 28; NORTH, March *31*, April 7, 8, 11. Latest dates: SOUTH, May 23, 27, 30, June *6*; NORTH, May 26, 27, 29. *Fall migration period:* Possibly very late June through mid-November; migration usually does not start until mid-July. Earliest dates: NORTH, July 1, 10; SOUTH, June 27, 30, July 1. Latest dates: NORTH, November 5, 6, *14*; SOUTH, November 16, 17, *22*.

Summer. A few observations between June 7 and June 26 may be classified as reports of either summering birds or migrants: June 13, 1966 (Lac qui Parle County); June 18, 1970 (Traverse County); June 20, 1894; and June 22, 1895 (Jackson County).

LESSER YELLOWLEGS *Tringa flavipes*

Minnesota status. Regular. Migrant.

Migration. Common spring and fall migrant throughout the state. The species is usually encountered in groups of five to twenty-five birds, but large aggregations of up to six hundred birds are occasionally found. *Spring migration period:* Late March through early June with the bulk of the migration from mid-April through mid-May. Earliest dates: SOUTH, March *17, 18*, 23, 24; NORTH, April *2*, 11, 13. Latest dates: SOUTH, May 29, 30, June 2, *6*; NORTH, May 26, 31, June 2, *8, 9*. *Fall migration period:* Very late June through mid-November with the bulk of the migration from early July through early September. Earliest dates: NORTH, June 28, July 1; SOUTH, June 26, July 1, 2. Latest dates: NORTH, October 22, 23, 27, November *12*; SOUTH, November 17, 18, 19.

Summer. Observations have been recorded between June 15 and June 24 in eight different years; it is not known whether the birds were migrants or summer visitants. All but one of the records are from the western margin of the state.

WILLET *Catoptrophorus semipalmatus*

Minnesota status. Regular. Migrant; casual summer resident.

Migration. Uncommon spring migrant throughout most of the state; rare in the north central and northeastern regions (excluding Duluth). Rare fall migrant everywhere. Peak flock size is usually six to eight birds, but there are a few records of twenty birds in a flock. *Spring migration period:* Mid-April through late May with a peak in late April. Earliest dates: SOUTH, March *21*, April 10, 13, 24; NORTH, April 26, 28, 30. Latest dates (beyond breeding areas): SOUTH, May 14, 15; NORTH, May 24, 25, 26. *Fall migration period:* Early August through mid-October with no peak noted. Earliest dates (beyond breeding areas): NORTH, August 12 (only date); SOUTH, August 3, 8, 10. Latest dates: NORTH, September 26, October *19* (only dates); SOUTH, September 13, 20, October *11*.

Summer. The status of this species both historically and at present is very poorly known. The only information available for the nineteenth century is from Roberts (1932), who found that the species bred commonly in Grant and Traverse counties in 1879 and that it was numerous in Lac qui Parle County in 1889. It seems to have been only a casual resident since the beginning of the twentieth century. The only breeding evidence is from the Pomme de Terre River, Swift County, where broods were seen in 1931 and 1932. Recent summer observations: Scott County (three adults, 1961), Lac qui Parle County (several sightings, includings a courting pair in 1962), Stevens County (1964), Clay County (1966), Traverse County (two adults, 1970), McLeod County (1971), and Marshall County (1971).

RED KNOT (Knot) *Calidris canutus*

Minnesota status. Regular. Migrant.

Migration. Very rare spring and fall migrant throughout the state. Most numerous in the eastern regions, especially at Duluth where the largest counts (eight to fifteen birds) have been made. *Spring migration period:* Late May through mid-June. Earliest dates: SOUTH, May *9*, 20, 22; NORTH, May *16*, 21, 22, 24. Latest dates: SOUTH, May 30, June 6 (only dates); NORTH, June 11, 14. *Fall migration period:* Late July through mid-September with the bulk of the migration from mid-August through late September.

Earliest dates: NORTH, July 19, 28 (only dates); SOUTH, July 27 (only date). Latest dates: NORTH, September 17, 18, 24; SOUTH, September 14, 15, 26.

PURPLE SANDPIPER *Calidris maritima*

Minnesota status. Accidental. One winter record.
Records. A single bird was found at the harbor in Grand Marais, Cook County, on December 17, 1966 (*Loon* 39:64), and was collected on December 20, 1966 (MMNH #22252).

PECTORAL SANDPIPER *Calidris melanotos*

Minnesota status. Regular. Migrant; casual summer visitant.
Migration. Common spring and fall migrant throughout most of the state; uncommon in both seasons in the northeastern region. Normal flock size varies from five or ten birds up to fifty birds; occasionally aggregations of one hundred to five hundred birds are found. *Spring migration period:* Very late March through early June with the bulk of the migration occurring from late April through mid-May. Earliest dates: SOUTH, March *23*, *26*, 30, 31; NORTH, March *31*, April 16, 17, 21. Latest dates: SOUTH, May 27, 28, June *4*, *6*, *7*; NORTH, June 2, 7, *12*. *Fall migration period:* Early July through mid-November with the bulk of the migration occurring from mid-August through late September. Earliest dates: NORTH, July 9, 15, 17; SOUTH, July 5, 6, 8. Latest dates: NORTH, October 25, 28, 31, November *17*; SOUTH, November 12, 16, 17.
Summer. There are ten records from mid-June and late June, mostly from the northern half of the state, representing either migrants or summering birds. In addition, birds were seen regularly in Stevens County from June 6 to June 28 in 1964.

WHITE-RUMPED SANDPIPER
Calidris fuscicollis

Minnesota status. Regular. Migrant.
Migration. Uncommon spring migrant throughout most of the state; common in the western regions. Rare fall migrant throughout most of the state; casual in the northeastern region. Normal flock size is three to ten birds, but occasionally flocks of twenty to fifty birds are encountered. At the peak of the spring migration daily counts of two hundred to four hundred birds can be made at localities along the western margin of the state. *Spring migration period:* Early May through mid-June with a peak in late May. Earliest dates: SOUTH, April *27*, May 1, 3, 4; NORTH, April *27*, May 15,

16, 19. Latest dates: SOUTH, June 13, 14, 17; NORTH, June 12, 13, 14. *Fall migration period:* Mid-July through late September; no peak noted. Earliest dates: NORTH, July 21 (only date); SOUTH, July 16, 18 (only dates). Latest dates: NORTH, September 2, 13 (only dates), October *16*; SOUTH, September 6, 14, 26, October *9, 14*.

Summer. There are à few records from mid-June through early July: June 19–28, 1972 (Aitkin County); June 27, 1942 (Duluth); July 1, 1894 (Jackson County); July 6, 1966 (Traverse County).

BAIRD'S SANDPIPER *Calidris bairdii*

Minnesota status. Regular. Migrant.

Migration. Uncommon spring and fall migrant throughout most of the state; rare in the spring and uncommon in the fall in the northeastern region. Normal flock size is three to ten birds; flocks of twenty-five to a hundred birds are very unusual. *Spring migration period:* Very late March through early June; the bulk of the migration begins in late April and reaches a peak in early and mid-May. Earliest dates: SOUTH, March *20*, 28, 29, 31; NORTH, March *31*, April 15, 16, 25. Latest dates: SOUTH, May 30, 31, June *6*; NORTH, June 3, 8, 11. *Fall migration period:* Mid-July through late October with a peak in late August and early September. Earliest dates: NORTH, July *4*, 15, 16; SOUTH, July *6*, 16, 31 (only dates). Latest dates: NORTH, September 29, October 16, 23, November *6, 9*; SOUTH, October 29, 31, November 1, *6*.

Summer. Two June dates from the northern half of the state: June 19 and June 28, 1972 (Aitkin County); June 20, 1938 (Duluth).

LEAST SANDPIPER *Calidris minutilla*

Minnesota status. Regular. Migrant.

Migration. Common spring and fall migrant throughout most of the state; uncommon in the spring in the north central and northeastern regions. Normal flock size is five to twenty birds, but occasionally congregations of fifty to a hundred birds are seen. *Spring migration period:* Early April through early June; the bulk of the migration begins in late April and reaches a peak in May. Earliest dates: SOUTH, March *30*, April 4, 6, 9; NORTH, April *9, 16*, May 7, 8. Latest dates: SOUTH, May 31, June 6, *10, 12*; NORTH, June 1, 3, 9, *14*, 20. *Fall migration period:* Early July through mid-October. Earliest dates: NORTH, July 1, 2; SOUTH, June *25, 28*, July 4, 6. Latest dates: NORTH, October 11, 14, 15, *29*; SOUTH, October 11, 13, 16, November *9*.

DUNLIN *Calidris alpina*

Minnesota status. Regular. Migrant.

Migration. Uncommon to locally common spring migrant; common to abundant at Duluth at the migration peak. Rare fall migrant; uncommon to occasionally common at Duluth. Normal flock size is five to fifteen birds with peak daily counts at Duluth of up to three hundred birds. *Spring migration period:* Early May through mid-June with a peak in late May. Earliest dates: SOUTH, April *11*, *17*, *18*, *22*, 29, May 2, 3; NORTH, April *25*, May 7, 9, 12. Latest dates: SOUTH, June 10, 11, 13; NORTH, June 11, 12, 13, *17*. *Fall migration period:* From sometime in July through early November. Earliest dates: NORTH, July *3*, 18, 23 (only dates); SOUTH, July *6*, *10*, 24 (only dates). Latest dates: NORTH, October 28, 31, November 2, *9*; SOUTH, November 9, 10, 11, *17*.

SEMIPALMATED SANDPIPER *Calidris pusillus*

Minnesota status. Regular. Migrant.

Migration. Common spring and fall migrant throughout the state, locally abundant (especially at Duluth). Normal flock size is twenty to a hundred birds, and large concentrations of four hundred to five hundred birds are seen. *Spring migration period:* Mid-April through mid-June with a peak in late May and early June. Earliest dates: SOUTH, April *1*, *8*, 14, 15, 18; NORTH, May 7, 8. Latest dates: SOUTH, June 10, 11, 12, *19*, *17–28*; NORTH, June 12, 15, *20*, *23*, *24*, *28*. *Fall migration period:* Early July through mid-October with the bulk of the migration from mid-August through mid-September. Earliest dates: NORTH, July 2, 18, 20; SOUTH, July 2, 5, 6. Latest dates: NORTH, October 10, 11, *17*; SOUTH, October 18, 20, 22, *27*, *30*.

WESTERN SANDPIPER *Calidris mauri*

Minnesota status. Regular. Migrant.

Migration. Rare to uncommon migrant in the southern half of the state; rare to casual migrant (especially at Duluth in the spring) in the northern half. Largest flocks (five to eight birds) are reported in the southwestern region. The species was added to the state list for the first time in 1960, but it probably was present earlier. *Spring migration period:* Mid-May through early June. Earliest dates: SOUTH, April *25*, May 2, 12, 17; NORTH, May 26 (only date). Latest dates: SOUTH, May 31, June 4, 6; NORTH, June 1 (two dates). *Fall migration period:* July through September. Earliest dates: NORTH, July 31, August 10, 18; SOUTH, July 2, 14, 17. Latest dates: NORTH, September 6, 19, 27; SOUTH, September 10, 16, 25.

SANDERLING *Calidris alba*

Minnesota status. Regular. Migrant.

Migration. Common spring and fall migrant in the eastern half of the state; locally abundant, especially at Duluth. Uncommon spring and fall migrant in the western half of the state. Flocks frequently contain ten to a hundred birds with peak daily counts at Duluth of two hundred to five hundred birds. *Spring migration period:* Late April through mid-June with a peak in late May and early June. Earliest dates: SOUTH, April *18*, 24, 25, 27; NORTH, April *30*, May 5, 7, 9. Latest dates: SOUTH, June 3, 4, 6; NORTH, June 15, 16, *20*, *24*, *28*, *29*. *Fall migration period:* Mid-July through late October with the bulk of the migration in September. Earliest dates: NORTH, July *11*, 18, 19; SOUTH, July 2, *10*, *11*, August 4, 7, 10. Latest dates: NORTH, October 25, 28; SOUTH, October 26, 27, 28, November *9*.

SHORT-BILLED DOWITCHER
Limnodromus griseus

Minnesota status. Regular. Migrant.

Migration. Rare spring and fall migrant throughout the state. The largest concentration on record is an unusually large flock of 259 birds on August 23, 1966, in Jackson County; the next largest concentration on record is a flock of 20 birds. Since little attention has been paid to the separation in the field of the two dowitcher species, the migration of the Short-billed Dowitcher is poorly known. *Spring migration period:* Early May through early June. Earliest dates: SOUTH, April *14*, *25*, May 2, 3; NORTH, May 19, 20 (only dates). Latest dates: SOUTH, May 23, 24, 30; NORTH, May 27, June 1, 2, *10*. *Fall migration period:* Early July through early September. This species apparently leaves the state earlier in the fall than the Long-billed Dowitcher does. Earliest dates: NORTH, June 30, July 4 (only dates); SOUTH, July 6, 10, 11. Latest dates: NORTH, no data; SOUTH, September 2, 4, *26*.

LONG-BILLED DOWITCHER *Limnodromus scolopaceus*

Minnesota status. Regular. Migrant.

Migration. Uncommon spring and fall migrant throughout most of the state; rare, especially in the fall, in the north central and northeastern regions. Normal flock size is five to thirty birds; larger flocks, up to two hundred birds, occasionally occur. The migration patterns of the two dowitcher species are not known very well because of the difficulty of separating the two species in the field. The problem is acute in late spring (May and June) and early fall (July and August) when the two species occur together, and there is the possibility that some of the following records may include both species. *Spring migration period:* Late April through late May. Earliest dates: SOUTH, April *13, 16*, 24, 27, 29; NORTH, May 10, 13, 14. Latest dates: SOUTH, May 22, 23, 28, June *5*; NORTH, May 25, 29, June 2, *8, 10, 13*. *Fall migration period:* Early July through early November with a peak in early and mid-October. Earliest dates: NORTH, July 9, 14, 23; SOUTH, June *26, 28*, July 2, 3, 6. Latest dates: NORTH, September 21, October 12, 27; SOUTH, November 2, 7, 9.

STILT SANDPIPER *Micropalama himantopus*

Minnesota status. Regular. Migrant.
Migration. Uncommon spring and fall migrant throughout most of the state; casual in the spring and rare in the fall in the north central and northeastern regions. Normal flock size is two to twenty birds; larger flocks usually number around a hundred birds, but one concentration of a thousand birds was seen in Lyon County on August 22, 1971. *Spring migration period:* Early May through early June with a peak in mid-May and late May. Earliest dates: SOUTH, April *18*, May 1, 6; NORTH, May 23 (only date). Latest dates: SOUTH, June 5, 6, 10, *13*; NORTH, June 13 (only date). *Fall migration period:* Early July through early October with a peak from late August through mid-September. Earliest dates: NORTH, July 9, 11, 15; SOUTH, July 1, 4, 6. Latest dates: NORTH, September 25, 28, October 14 (only dates); SOUTH, October 9, 10, 17.

BUFF-BREASTED SANDPIPER *Tryngites subruficollis*

Minnesota status. Regular. Migrant.
Migration. Rare spring migrant in the western regions; casual elsewhere. Uncommon fall migrant in the western regions and at Duluth; rare elsewhere. Normal flock size is two to ten birds; occasionally flocks of twenty-five to fifty birds are encountered. *Spring migration period:* Throughout the month of May. Earliest dates: SOUTH, April *26*, May 5, 6, 12; NORTH, May 18 (only date). *Fall migration period:* Late July through late September with a peak in late August and early September. Earliest dates: NORTH, July 26, 28, 29; SOUTH, July *31*, August 6, 8, 9. Latest dates: NORTH, September 21, 23, 27; SOUTH, September 10, 23, October 1.

MARBLED GODWIT *Limosa fedoa*

Minnesota status. Regular. Migrant and summer resident.
Migration. Common to locally abundant spring migrant in

the western regions and the prairie portions of the central region; rare elsewhere in the state. Uncommon fall migrant in the western regions and the central prairie; accidental elsewhere. At the spring migration peak on the western prairies flocks of fifty to two hundred birds are seen. *Spring migration period:* Mid-April through late May with the bulk of the migration from late April through mid-May. Earliest dates: SOUTH, April 8, 9, 10; NORTH, April *9*, *11*, 15, 17. Latest dates (beyond breeding areas): SOUTH (below the Minnesota River), May 20, 23, June 1; NORTH (northeast and north central regions), May 23, 24, 27. *Fall migration period:* Late June through late August with the bulk of the migration in July; most birds leave by early August. Earliest dates (beyond breeding areas): No data. Latest dates: NORTH, August 2 (only date); SOUTH, August 20, 21, 29, September *26*.

37. Marbled Godwit (1930)

Summer. Resident primarily in the northwestern region (see map 37). Although there is only one recent breeding record (Big Stone County, 1973) from the prairie in the west central and central regions, a number of observations (particularly in Stevens, Swift, Kandiyohi, and Stearns counties) indicate that a sparse breeding population exists there. Formerly the breeding territory was more widespread. Roberts stated that the species was a summer resident throughout the prairie region in the nineteenth century, although there are no data from south of the Minnesota River.

HUDSONIAN GODWIT *Limosa haemastica*

Minnesota status. Regular. Migrant.
Migration. Uncommon spring migrant in the western regions; rare in the central and eastern regions. Casual fall migrant throughout the state. Spring flock size is usually two to ten birds, but occasional concentrations of twenty-five to thirty birds are seen. *Spring migration period:* Late April through early June with a peak in mid-May. Earliest dates: SOUTH, April *10*, *13*, 19, 20, 22; NORTH, April *25*, May 8, 11. Latest dates: SOUTH, May 25, 29, June 1, 7; NORTH, May 27, June 4, 6. *Fall migration period:* August and September. Earliest dates: NORTH, August 8, 12 (only dates); SOUTH, no data. Latest dates: NORTH, September 15 (only date); SOUTH, October 29 (only date).

RUFF *Philomachus pugnax*

Minnesota status. Accidental. Three spring records.
Records. One bird was seen by many people from April 26 through May 2, 1971, near Green Isle, Sibley County (*Loon* 43:93). On May 13, 1973, one bird was seen near

Lastrup, Morrison County (*Loon* 45:63). One bird was seen and photographed between May 23 and May 31, 1964, in a slough near Alberta, Stevens County (*Loon* 32:44–45, 53–55).

Family RECURVIROSTRIDAE: Avocets
AMERICAN AVOCET *Recurvirostra americana*

Minnesota status. Regular. Migrant; irregular summer resident.

Migration. Uncommon spring migrant in the western regions; casual elsewhere. Rare fall migrant in the western regions; accidental elsewhere. Normal flock size is five to ten birds with occasional peak counts of twenty to thirty birds. Before the 1950s this species was only a casual migrant. *Spring migration period:* Mid-April through mid-May. Earliest dates: SOUTH, April 15, 17, 20; NORTH, April 19, 22 (only dates). Latest dates (beyond breeding areas): SOUTH, May 13, 16 (only dates); NORTH, no data. *Fall migration period:* Very poorly known; possibly August through October. Earliest dates (beyond breeding areas): No data. Latest dates: NORTH, August 9, October *31* (only dates); SOUTH, September 20, October 7, third week of October, November *1*.

Summer. Between 1956 and 1964 this species was found nesting in a few counties in the western part of the state: Lyon County (near Balaton, 1956); Stevens County (near Alberta, 1959); Otter Tail County (Orwell Refuge, 1959); Lac qui Parle County (near Madison, 1959; Salt Lake, 1961, 1962, 1964). In 1973 downy young were found north of Ortonville, Big Stone County. These reports are the only evidence that the species breeds in Minnesota, although some birds collected near Brown's Valley, Traverse County, between June 21 and July 8, 1887, were presumed to have been nesting. There are no other summer observations.

Family PHALAROPODIDAE: Phalaropes
RED PHALAROPE *Phalaropus fulicarius*

Minnesota status. Accidental. One fall record.

Records. The only record is of a bird seen and photographed on November 17, 1963, at Knife River, Lake County (*Loon* 36:25).

WILSON'S PHALAROPE *Steganopus tricolor*

Minnesota status. Regular. Migrant and summer resident.

Migration. Common to locally abundant migrant in the

western regions; more numerous in the spring than in the fall. In the eastern parts of the range the species is less numerous, becoming an uncommon migrant in the east central and southeastern regions and a rare to casual migrant in the northeastern region. The species is normally encountered as individuals or in small flocks of two to ten birds, but concentrations of one hundred to four hundred birds are common at the spring migration peak in the western regions. *Spring migration period:* Late April through late May with a peak in early May. Earliest dates: SOUTH, April 20, 21; NORTH, April 27, May 6, 7, 8. *Fall migration period:* Late July through late September; there is a gradual exodus from the state with no noticeable peak. Latest dates: NORTH, September 17, 24, 26; SOUTH, September 16, 20, 28, October 9.

38. Wilson's Phalarope (1900)

Summer. Resident throughout much of the central and western part of the state (see map 38) but very scarce in many areas. Most numerous in the northwestern region, especially in the southern counties. In 1971 and 1972 the species was found nesting in rice paddies in Aitkin County. South of the Minnesota River its status is poorly known; the most recent breeding data (1947, 1948) in this area are from Lac qui Parle County. There have been no breeding season observations during this century in the southwestern or south central regions, although the species formerly occurred there in good numbers.

NORTHERN PHALAROPE *Lobipes lobatus*

Minnesota status. Regular. Migrant.

Migration. Common spring and fall migrant in the southwestern and west central regions; casual in the north central and northeastern regions; uncommon migrant throughout the rest of the state. Normal flock size is two to fifteen birds, and peak flock size is usually thirty to fifty birds, but a few concentrations of one hundred to two hundred birds have been reported. *Spring migration period:* Early May through mid-June with a peak in late May. Earliest dates: SOUTH, May 4, 5, 8; NORTH, May 15 (only date). Latest dates: SOUTH, June 11, 12, *27–July 1*; NORTH, June 12 (two dates). *Fall migration period:* Late July through early September. Earliest dates: NORTH, July 16, 25 (only dates); SOUTH, July 31, August 2, 4. Latest dates: NORTH, September 28, 29, October 8; SOUTH, October 1, 6, *18, 28.*

Family STERCORARIIDAE: Jaegers

POMARINE JAEGER *Stercorarius pomarinus*

Minnesota status. Accidental. Four fall records.

Records. One bird was seen on Minnesota Point, Duluth,

on August 5, 1973 (*Loon* 45:136–137). Another bird was seen and photographed in the same area on August 15, 1972 (*Loon* 44:88–89, cover). On September 16, 1973, one bird was observed on the shore of Lake Superior off Stony Point, St. Louis County (*Loon* 46:40–41). The latest fall date is for a single bird seen on October 11, 1970, at Minnesota Point (*Loon* 43:95).

PARASITIC JAEGER *Stercorarius parasiticus*

Minnesota status. Regular. Migrant

Migration. Very rare fall migrant on Lake Superior, particularly at Duluth; casual elsewhere (specimens from Jackson and Pipestone counties; observations from Ramsey, Roseau, and Wabasha counties). Casual spring migrant at Duluth; unknown elsewhere. Usually only single birds have been observed, but on five occasions at Duluth two or three birds were seen together. Earliest dates: NORTH, August 22, 28, 30; SOUTH, September 8, 15 (only dates). Latest dates: SOUTH, September 15, 19 (only dates); NORTH, September 18, 19, 21. There are two early October observations of jaegers (either Parasitic Jaegers or Long-tailed Jaegers), one from Duluth and one from Mille Lacs County. *Spring migration period:* Late May. Only three records: Single birds were seen at Duluth on May 21, 1949, and May 25, 1958, and a very dessicated bird was picked up on Minnesota Point, Duluth, on June 1, 1969.

LONG-TAILED JAEGER
Stercorarius longicaudus

Minnesota status. Accidental. One spring record, one summer record, and two fall records.

Records. One adult was observed on April 21, 1962, on the Crow Wing River, Wadena County (*Flicker* 34:54). On July 1, 1898, a single bird was collected near Warren, Marshall County (MMNH #8476). The fall records include an immature female collected on October 4, 1942, at Heron Lake, Jackson County (MMNH #8749), and an observation of an adult on November 16 or 17, 1934, at Dyers Lake, Cook County (Roberts, 1936).

Family LARIDAE: Gulls and Terns

GLAUCOUS GULL *Larus hyperboreus*

Minnesota status. Regular. Migrant and winter visitant.

Migration. Uncommon migrant along the shore of Lake Superior and at the gull concentration areas near Duluth. Casual elsewhere with records from the Twin Cities area (Hennepin, Ramsey, Washington, Dakota, and Goodhue counties — a total of nine records), and from Roseau and Kandiyohi counties (one record each). *Fall migration period:* Mid-November through mid-December with a peak in very late November. Immature birds arrive first; adults do not usually appear until early December (earliest dates: November 19, 23, 30). Earliest dates: NORTH, November *1*, *7*, 12, 13, 14; SOUTH, November *21*, December 4, 9, 11. *Spring migration period:* Mid-March through late May with no peak noted. Adults depart first (latest dates: April 5, 6, 8, *15*); although almost all immatures leave by late April, a few linger throughout May. Latest dates: SOUTH, April 18, 20, 22, *28*; NORTH, May 21, 23, 24, June *1*, *3*.

Winter. Uncommon winter visitant along the shore of Lake Superior. Peak concentrations occur at the western tip of Lake Superior (Duluth and Two Harbors); flocks usually contain ten to fifteen birds (with one record of a flock of twenty birds). Accidental in winter away from Duluth and the North Shore. Only one winter record (January 1, 1969, Black Dog Lake, Dakota County); all the other inland records are from the migration period.

ICELAND GULL *Larus glaucoides*

Minnesota status. Casual. Winter visitant.

Records. Only one specimen (MMNH #10539), an immature bird collected on Lake Superior at Duluth on February 25, 1951, is available. An earlier specimen (MMNH #7755) collected on August 10, 1931, in Cook County was originally identified as an Iceland Gull but has recently been identified as an albino Herring Gull (G. McCaskie, personal communication, December, 1973). The identification of two birds was substantiated by photographs: a first-year immature at Knife River, Lake County, on January 10, 1968 (*Loon* 41:26–27), and an all-white immature at Two Harbors, Lake County, on February 28, 1967 (*Loon* 39:48; National Photoduplicate File #43-2Ta and #43-2Tb). There are a number of other observations of immature birds, most of them discussed in an article in 1967 (*Loon* 39:44–48). The article deals with the problem of separating Iceland Gulls from small Glaucous Gulls; the possibility that these species may be confused with the Thayer's Gull is not considered. Subsequent observations have established the presence of small numbers of Thayer's Gulls on Lake Superior in the winter, and many earlier sightings of Iceland Gulls have been discarded because the reports were not sufficiently detailed to rule out the possibility that the birds were Thayer's Gulls. Three sightings, all from Lake Superior in Lake County, are thought to be valid: January

15, 1967 (*Loon* 39:47); February 2, 1967 (*Loon* 39:47–48); April 5, 1971 (J. C. Green).

GREAT BLACK-BACKED GULL *Larus marinus*

Minnesota status. Accidental. One spring record and one fall record.

Records. One adult was seen at Duluth on April 30, 1962 (*Flicker* 34:99–100), and one adult was photographed from a fishing boat on the western end of Lake Superior (in St. Louis County) on November 23, 1948 (*Flicker* 21:63–64).

HERRING GULL *Larus argentatus*

Minnesota status. Regular. Migrant, summer resident, summer visitant, and winter visitant.

Migration. Common migrant throughout the state, becoming locally abundant around large lakes and rivers. Peak numbers occur at the western end of Lake Superior in the fall (one thousand to three thousand birds in November) and along the lower Mississippi River at the time of the fall freeze-up and the spring thaw (one thousand to five thousand birds). *Spring migration period:* Mid-February through late May with the bulk of the migration from mid-March through late April. Earliest dates: SOUTH, February *13*, 19, 20, 24; NORTH (inland from Lake Superior), February *26*, March *5*, 13, 14, 16. *Fall migration period:* Probably September through December with the bulk of the migration in October and November. Latest dates: NORTH (inland from Lake Superior), November 23, 27, 29; SOUTH, no dates can be given because birds linger until the fall freeze-up with some stragglers staying until mid-January.

Summer. Summer resident on Lake Superior, along the border lakes from Lake of the Woods to Cook County, and also sparingly on Mille Lacs Lake. The colonies on Lake Superior vary from one hundred to three hundred nests on large rocky islands to isolated pairs and small colonies on the mainland cliffs. The large lakes along the Canadian border as well as Lake Vermilion, St. Louis County, may support colonies of a hundred pairs or more, but the usual population on smaller lakes is one to five pairs. A few nests (under five) were found in the Ring-billed Gull colony on Hennepin Island, Mille Lacs Lake, in 1968, 1969, and 1970. Summer visitant throughout the state near large bodies of water.

Winter. Abundant winter visitant on Lake Superior. Concentrations vary from five hundred to one thousand birds early in the winter to one hundred to three hundred birds in February when the lake may be almost completely frozen over. From mid-January through mid-February the species is found only near Lake Superior.

THAYER'S GULL *Larus thayeri*

Minnesota status. Casual. Winter visitant.

Records. In the winters of 1970–1971 and 1971–1972 at sites of gull concentrations between Duluth and Two Harbors, Green observed seventeen immature birds that did not belong to the gull species commonly found in the area in the winter (Herring Gulls, Glaucous Gulls, and Iceland Gulls) and deduced that the birds were Thayer's Gulls. (At the time the benefit of personal experience from observers in areas where the species is known to occur was not available; in addition, the literature on the identification of immature Thayer's Gulls is scanty.) Photographs were taken of three birds: January 1, 1971, Knife River; January 17, 1971, Knife River; February 8–9, 1972, Duluth dump. These have been viewed by Guy McCaskie (December, 1973) and Joseph R. Jehl, Jr. (January, 1974) who agreed that the birds were Thayer's Gulls. Allowing for the fact that individual birds may have been observed more than once (two birds were seen together several times), about five birds were seen from November 15, 1970, through May 3, 1971, and about three birds were seen from November 19, 1971, through March 26, 1972. In addition, Green's unpublished field notes on the plumage of immature gulls previously identified as Iceland Gulls reveal the probability of several other records of Thayer's Gulls from the Duluth–Two Harbors area: November 14, 1964; December 27, 1964; April 24, 1968; May 6, 1970. In addition, one adult bird was seen on December 23, 1973, and described by G. McCaskie at Duluth.

RING-BILLED GULL *Larus delawarensis*

Minnesota status. Regular. Migrant, summer resident, and summer visitant; accidental in late winter.

Migration. Abundant migrant throughout the state in both seasons. Flocks usually contain three hundred to eight hundred birds, but in the fall peak daily counts of several thousand birds are sometimes obtained. *Spring migration period:* Mid-March through late May with the bulk of the migration in April (adults) and in May (immature birds). Earliest dates: SOUTH, March *3*, 8, 11, 12; NORTH, March 28, 29, April 1. *Fall migration period:* Mid-August through late December with the bulk of the migration from mid-September through mid-October. Latest dates: NORTH, November 28, December 2, 6, *13*; SOUTH, January 2, 3.

Summer. Resident primarily at Mille Lacs Lake (fifty to

ninety nests, 1966–1972) with a few birds nesting on Leech
Lake (one pair in 1960, six pairs in 1971), and sporadic but
mostly unsuccessful nesting in the Duluth-Superior harbor
(1957, 1973). Summer visitant around large lakes throughout the state.

Winter. The only record of an overwintering bird was one
at Black Dog Lake, Dakota County, in 1970–1971.

FRANKLIN'S GULL *Larus pipixcan*

39. Franklin's Gull

Minnesota status. Regular. Migrant and summer resident.
Migration. Common spring migrant throughout the southwestern quarter of the state and the northwestern region;
rare elsewhere. Common to locally abundant fall migrant
throughout most of the state; uncommon in the southeastern
region; rare in the north central and northeastern regions. At
the migration peak it is not unusual to see thousands of birds
in the western and central parts of the state. *Spring migration period:* Mid-March through early June with the bulk of
the migration from mid-April through mid-May. Earliest
dates: SOUTH, March 13, 14, 15; NORTH, April 5, 6. Latest
date (northeastern region): June 6. *Fall migration period:*
Late July through late November with the bulk of the migration from late September through late October. Earliest
dates (north central region): July 31, August 2. Latest dates:
NORTH, October 31, November 4 (only dates); SOUTH,
November 23, 25, 27.

Summer. Resident primarily in the western regions (see
map 39), breeding in large colonies that shift location from
year to year. The largest reported colonies have been from
Heron Lake, Jackson County (fifty thousand nests in 1916,
one hundred thousand nests in 1937). Since the mid-1960s
there have been colonies at Lake Osakis, Todd County, and
at Agassiz National Wildlife Refuge, Marshall County.
During the summer the birds range throughout the western
and central regions of the state.

BONAPARTE'S GULL *Larus philadelphia*

Minnesota status. Regular. Migrant and summer visitant.
Migration. Common to occasionally abundant migrant in
the central and northern wooded regions; uncommon to rare
on the prairie and in the southeastern region. Concentrations occur regularly at Duluth in the spring (one thousand
to three thousand birds) and at Mille Lacs Lake in the fall
(two hundred to five hundred birds). *Spring migration
period:* Early April through early June with a peak in early
and mid-May. Earliest dates: SOUTH, April 4, 6; NORTH,
April 18, 19. Latest dates: SOUTH, May 31 (only date);
NORTH, none can be given because of summering birds.

Fall migration period: Late July through late November with the bulk of the migration from mid-September through early November. Earliest dates: NORTH, none can be given because of summering birds; SOUTH, July 23, August 11 (only dates). Latest dates: NORTH, November 18, 22, 23; SOUTH, November 16, 21, 27.

Summer. Rare visitant on large lakes in the northern half of the state. Immature birds linger regularly until late June and appear in late July in many locations, but midsummer records (from June 20 to July 20) are available only from Lake of the Woods, Leech Lake, and Duluth. There is only one record of adults in midsummer. One summer record exists for the southern half of the state: one immature bird seen on June 23, 1963, at Grass Lake, Hennepin County.

LITTLE GULL *Larus minutus*

Minnesota status. Accidental. Two spring records.

Records. The first record was of two adults seen on Lake Pepin, Goodhue County, on March 25, 1972 (*Loon* 44:56). The second record was of three adults and four immatures seen by many people and photographed at Duluth on May 27, 1973 (J. C. Green *et al.*; *American Birds* 27:776).

IVORY GULL *Pagophila eburnea*

Minnesota status. Accidental. Four winter records.

Records. All the records for this species are observations from Lake Superior. One immature bird was seen at French River, St. Louis County, on December 27, 1948 (*Flicker* 21:21). From late December, 1966, until late January, 1967, one immature bird remained at a fishing station near Grand Portage, Cook County (*Loon* 39:61). One bird was seen in early January, 1956, at Two Harbors, Lake County (Mr. and Mrs. R. B. Evans; notes in MMNH file). During the winter of 1970–1971 there were detailed observations of single adults from three localities: October 28, 1970, mouth of Onion River, Cook County; February 17, 1971, Duluth city dump; March 14, 1971, Knife River, Lake County. The last two records are probably sightings of the same bird because winter gull flocks frequently range between these points.

BLACK-LEGGED KITTIWAKE *Rissa tridactyla*

Minnesota status. Accidental. One winter record.

Records. A single immature bird was present at Knife River, Lake County, on December 15–16, 1964, and was photographed when first discovered (*Loon* 37:59–60 and cover; National Photoduplicate File #40-1B).

SABINE'S GULL *Xema sabini*

Minnesota status. Hypothetical.

Records. There is a single observation of an immature bird on October 1, 1944, on the St. Croix River at Stillwater, Washington County (*Auk* 64:146–147).

FORSTER'S TERN *Sterna forsteri*

Minnesota status. Regular. Migrant and summer resident.
Migration. Common spring migrant throughout the prairie and in the central part of the state west of the Mississippi River; elsewhere rare to casual. In the fall uncommon in the breeding range and casual elsewhere. No peak concentrations have been reported. *Spring migration period:* Early April through late May with no peak noted; most first arrivals are in mid-April and late April. Earliest dates: SOUTH, April 2, 4, 6; NORTH, April 16, 17, 20. *Fall migration period:* Mid-July through early October; almost all birds depart by late September. Latest dates: NORTH, September 30, October 8, 9, *24*; SOUTH, September 30, October 2, 3, *14*.

Summer. Resident in the western regions and in the central part of the state north of the Minnesota River and west of the Mississippi River (see map 40). The species was not found breeding in the Twin Cities area until the 1940s, but it has nested there ever since. The birds are usually found in small colonies; larger groups (hundreds of pairs) have been reported from Heron Lake, Jackson County, and Clearwater Lake, Wright County.

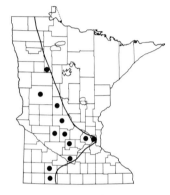

40. Forster's Tern

COMMON TERN *Sterna hirundo*

Minnesota status. Regular. Migrant and summer resident.
Migration. Common spring migrant in the eastern regions (abundant at Duluth); uncommon to rare in the western regions. The exact status of the species is uncertain in areas where the Forster's Tern breeds because observers are often not careful to distinguish the two species in the field. At the migration peak (May 15 to May 25) at Duluth several thousand birds can be seen. In the fall the species is rare to uncommon, and most observations occur near breeding localities. *Spring migration period:* Mid-April through early June with a peak between May 15 and May 25. Earliest dates: SOUTH, April 16, 17, 18; NORTH, May 1, 2, 3. *Fall migration period:* Early August through very early October with a peak in early September. Latest dates: NORTH, September 30, October 3, 6, *23*; SOUTH, September 26, 29, October 2, *11*, *13*.

Summer. Resident primarily in colonies on large lakes in the north central and northeastern regions (see map 41). The

41. Common Tern

biggest colonies (five hundred to a thousand pairs) are on Lake of the Woods, Leech Lake, and Mille Lacs Lake. The only breeding record from outside the northeastern and north central regions is from Cotton Lake, Becker County (1963). The Common Tern is a summer visitant in other regions of the state, but its status is poorly known because of confusion with the Forster's Tern.

ARCTIC TERN *Sterna paradisaea*

Minnesota status. Accidental. One spring record.
Records. On May 27, 1973, three birds of this species were identified in a flock of gulls and terns resting on an asphalt runway on Minnesota Point, Duluth (J. C. Green *et al.*); good photographs were also obtained (M. M. Carr; *American Birds* 27:776).

LEAST TERN *Sterna albifrons*

Minnesota status. Accidental. One spring record, one summer record, and two fall records.
Records. The details of two records are on file (MMNH), and reports of the other two have been published: May 19–26, 1951, flock, Mother's Lake, Hennepin County; June 18, 1955, Moore Lake, Anoka County; September 11, 1965, Hendricks, Lincoln County (*Loon* 38:40); September 26, 1970, Cottonwood, Lyon County (*Loon* 43:25).

CASPIAN TERN *Hydroprogne caspia*

Minnesota status. Regular. Migrant and summer visitant; casual summer resident.
Migration. Common spring and fall migrant from the Mississippi River northeastward; uncommon migrant farther west. Peak daily counts at large northern lakes or on the lower Mississippi River of thirty to sixty birds. *Spring migration period:* Late April through early June with a peak in late May. Earliest dates: SOUTH, April *19*, 25, 29, May 1; NORTH, April 30, May 2, 4. *Fall migration period:* Late July through mid-October; most birds leave by late September. Latest dates: NORTH, September 22, 26, October 1, *15*, *18*; SOUTH, October 11, 14, 17, *26*, *27*.
Summer. Rare to locally uncommon summer visitant around large lakes in the area north and east of a line from Wright County to Clearwater and Roseau counties. The only breeding record is of two nests found on Gull Island, Leech Lake, in 1969 (*Loon* 41:83–84).

BLACK TERN *Chlidonias niger*

Minnesota status. Regular. Migrant and summer resident.
Migration. Abundant spring migrant throughout most of the

state; common at Duluth and uncommon elsewhere in the northeastern region. In the fall the numbers decrease, but the species is still common until most breeding birds have left the marshes. *Spring migration period:* Late April through early June with the bulk of the migration in the second half of May. Earliest dates: SOUTH, March *22*, *31*, April 23, 25; NORTH, April *20*, May 2, 8. *Fall migration period:* Mid-July through early October; most birds leave by mid-September. Latest dates: NORTH, September 24, October 1, 6, *28*; SOUTH, October 8, 10, 12, *27*, November 7, *11*.

Summer. Summer resident throughout the state except in parts of the northeastern region where marshy lakes are rare. The species is not known to breed in Lake and Cook counties.

Family ALCIDAE: Auks and Murres

DOVEKIE *Alle alle*

Minnesota status. Accidental. Two fall records.
Records. Two birds were found in November, a time of severe storms along the coastal migration route: November 5, 1962, near Grand Rapids, Itasca County (MMNH #18603); November 13, 1931, Lake of the Woods (MMNH #7820).

ANCIENT MURRELET *Synthliboramphus antiquus*

Minnesota status. Accidental. Four fall records and one winter record.
Records. One bird was shot on Lake Kabetogama, St. Louis County, in October, 1970 (MMNH #27116). Three other fall records: November 5, 1905, Lake Hook, McLeod County (MMNH #5947); November 14, 1961, Pelican Lake, Crow Wing County (MMNH #17658); November 22, 1950, Cutfoot Sioux Lake, Itasca County (MMNH #9639). One bird was found dead on a highway near Fort Ripley, Crow Wing County, on February 28, 1969 (*Loon* 41:57).

Family COLUMBIDAE: Pigeons and Doves

BAND-TAILED PIGEON *Columba fasciata*

Minnesota status. Accidental. Two summer records.
Records. One bird was seen on June 12, 1971, in Sand Dunes State Forest, Sherburne County (*Loon* 43:57). Another bird was present through most of July, 1969, near

Morris, Stevens County (photograph by E. H. Strubbe; *Loon* 41:68–69).

ROCK DOVE *Columba livia*

Minnesota status. Regular. Permanent resident.
Distribution. The original stock of this species consisted of domesticated birds introduced from Europe, and their wild and semiwild descendants are found in cities and towns and around farm buildings throughout the state.

MOURNING DOVE *Zenaida macroura*

Minnesota status. Regular. Migrant and summer resident; regular in winter.
Migration. Abundant migrant; uncommon to rare in the northeastern region and in the adjacent parts of the north central region. *Spring migration period:* Early March through late April with a peak from late March through early April. Earliest dates: SOUTH, none can be given because of wintering birds; NORTH, March 25, 27, 30. *Fall migration period:* Mid-September through late November with the bulk of the migration in October. Latest dates: NORTH, November 20, 22, 29, December *10*; SOUTH, none can be given because of wintering birds.
Summer. Resident throughout the state except in Lake and Cook counties and in the heavily wooded parts of St. Louis, Koochiching, and Itasca counties. The species reaches its greatest abundance in wooded areas on the prairie.
Winter. Regular visitant (uncommon in some winters) in the southern half of the state; the numbers are usually reduced by late winter. It is not known whether the birds present in winter are also local summer residents. The very rare attempts to overwinter in the northern half of the state are usually unsuccessful.

PASSENGER PIGEON *Ectopistes migratorius*

Minnesota status. Extinct.
Discussion. The demise of this species is too well known to need lengthy retelling here — the last bird died in the Cincinnati Zoological Gardens in 1914. Roberts (1932) summarized the Minnesota information as follows: "An abundant summer resident throughout the state, breeding both irregularly in large colonies and regularly in isolated pairs in all wooded regions. The large spring flocks ceased arriving about 1880 and after that date [the species] diminished rapidly in numbers. There are no reliable records for the state since 1895." There are eight specimens from Minnesota in the Bell Museum of Natural History.

Family CUCULIDAE: Cuckoos and Anis

YELLOW-BILLED CUCKOO
Coccyzus americanus

Minnesota status. Regular. Migrant and summer resident.
Migration. Uncommon spring migrant in the southern half of the state and rare to casual in the northern half; in the fall less numerous throughout the state. *Spring migration period:* Early May through early June. Earliest dates: SOUTH, May 6, 8; NORTH, May 28, June 6 (only dates). *Fall migration period:* August and September. Latest dates: NORTH, September 18, 22, 24, October *4*; SOUTH, September 27, 29, October 1, *18, 21*.
Summer. Resident throughout most of the state; casual in the northeastern region and in the adjacent counties in the north central region. The species is most numerous in the southeastern region. All the nesting records are from the southern half of the state, but other breeding evidence has been reported from Clearwater, Wadena, and Pine counties.

BLACK-BILLED CUCKOO
Coccyzus erythropthalmus

Minnesota status. Regular. Migrant and summer resident.
Migration. Uncommon to occasionally common migrant throughout the state. *Spring migration period:* Early May through early June; most of the migration takes place during the second half of May. Earliest dates: SOUTH, April *13*, May 1, 4, 5; NORTH, May *9*, 18, 20, 21. *Fall migration period:* Probably from sometime in August through early October. Latest dates: NORTH, September 20, 29, October 2; SOUTH, October 2, 3, *22*.
Summer. Resident throughout the state. The numbers present vary from year to year, particularly in the northern regions where the species becomes numerous during outbreaks of tent caterpillars.

GROOVE-BILLED ANI *Crotophaga sulcirostris*

Minnesota status. Accidental. Four fall records.
Records. Roberts (1932) mentioned that one bird was collected along the Mississippi River near Red Wing (MMNH #8478), but it was subsequently discovered that the bird was shot on the Wisconsin side of the river and thus could not be regarded as a Minnesota record (*Passenger Pigeon* 26:26–28). There are four state records: one bird (MMNH #15765) was trapped on September 17, 1959, near Ortonville, Big Stone County. An immature bird was recorded (probably on the basis of a sighting) on October 5, 1973, at

the Roseau River Wildlife Area, Roseau County (*Loon* 46:34; 92–93). Two birds were found dead, one on October 20, 1958, in Lac qui Parle County (*Flicker* 31:60) and another on October 20, 1968, in Washington County (*Loon* 41:54).

Family TYTONIDAE: Barn Owls

BARN OWL *Tyto alba*

Minnesota status. Casual. The species occurs in all seasons and has bred in the state; it was formerly more regular in occurrence.

Discussion. Casual permanent resident in the southern half of the state; accidental elsewhere. Only one record (Nobles County) since 1965. In the early 1960s there were several reports from the southwestern and south central regions, including a breeding record from Martin County (*Loon* 36:6–7). Since the reports before 1960 are not continuous, it is not certain whether this species has always been casual with erratic periods of abundance or whether it was at one time a rare but regular permanent resident south of a line between Lac qui Parle and Hennepin counties (excluding the southeastern region where it has never been reported). Earlier nesting records are from Martin (1924) and Rice (1891) counties. Northern breeding season observations include a family near Park Rapids, Hubbard County (1944), and a pair at Lutsen, Cook County (1953). All other northern reports are from fall and winter (several in the late 1920s from Douglas to Roseau counties, and one in 1960 from Duluth). There are five specimens in the Bell Museum of Natural History from the period 1915–1955.

Family STRIGIDAE: Typical Owls

SCREECH OWL *Otus asio*

Minnesota status. Regular. Permanent resident.

Distribution. Permanent resident throughout most of the state except in the northeastern region and in the adjacent counties in the north central region. Breeding has been confirmed as far north as Polk County in the west and Morrison County in the east. Several records (all seasons) are available from areas farther north; the species is probably a rare resident from Roseau to Carlton counties. There are three records from the southern one-third of St. Louis County, although the species is not known to occur elsewhere in the county. The species is absent from Cook,

Lake, Koochiching, and Itasca counties. The abundance of the species has declined since the early 1960s.

GREAT HORNED OWL *Bubo virginianus*

Minnesota status. Regular. Primarily permanent resident; also winter visitant.

Distribution. Permanent resident throughout the state. Banding data indicate that the population in the southern and central regions of the state is more sedentary than that in the northern regions. Birds released from banding locations in the northern one-third of the state have been recovered up to five hundred miles away. There are also occasional influxes of this species in winter in the context of sharp increases in the total number of owls seen. These influxes have occurred in all parts of the state.

SNOWY OWL *Nyctea scandiaca*

Minnesota status. Regular. Migrant and winter visitant; accidental in summer.

Migration. Rare to uncommon fall migrant throughout the state, usually more numerous in the northern half; in the spring usually rare everywhere. Numbers vary sharply from year to year. In invasion years the species usually arrives earlier in the fall and lingers longer into the spring than in normal years. *Fall migration period:* Mid-October through late December. Earliest dates: NORTH, October *4*, *5*, *10*, 17, 19, 21; SOUTH, October *16*, *23*, 29, 30. *Spring migration period:* Mid-February (possibly earlier in the south) through mid-April with stragglers into May. Latest dates: SOUTH, April 11, 13, 14, May *3*; NORTH, May 5, 6, 9, *16*, *28*.

Winter. Rare to uncommon visitant throughout the state, becoming less numerous in the south. Abundance varies from year to year and from place to place. Invasions may be statewide or more localized and usually occur two or three times a decade. Winter hunting territories are established where there is a good food supply. Concentrations of five to fifteen birds are found around the Duluth harbor.

Summer. The only reports for this season are given in Roberts (1932): June 3, 1890, Meeker County; early August, 1927, Washington County.

HAWK OWL *Surnia ulula*

Minnesota status. Regular. Winter visitant; casual summer resident.

Migration. Rare in the northern regions (uncommon in invasion years); accidental in the southern regions. In the central regions the species occurs as a casual migrant only in invasion years. More numerous in the fall than in the spring. *Fall migration period:* Mid-October through late November with exceptionally early arrivals in invasion years. Earliest dates: NORTH, September *15, 23, 25*, October 6, 9, 10; SOUTH, October *12*, 20, 27, 31. *Spring migration period:* Probably late February through early April with stragglers present in May in invasion years. Latest dates: SOUTH, March 22, May *21* (only dates); NORTH, April 28, May 2, 4, *27*.

Winter. Rare but regular visitant in the wooded portions of the northern regions. Casual in the central regions and accidental in the southern regions, occurring usually only in invasion years. During invasion years (about once a decade) the species becomes uncommon in its normal winter range and may be common in favorable habitats such as the muskeg formed on the beds of Glacial Lake Agassiz, Glacial Lake Upham, and Glacial Lake Aitkin.

Summer. After major invasions a few birds remain during the summer, and breeding has been reported in Norman County (1885), Roseau County (1906 or 1907), and St. Louis County (1963; *Flicker* 35:129–134).

BURROWING OWL *Speotyto cunicularia*

Minnesota status. Regular. Migrant and summer resident.

Migration. Rare migrant on the prairie; casual to accidental elsewhere. Most birds at any season are observed on breeding territories. *Spring migration period:* Early April through late May with most first arrivals in late April. Earliest dates: SOUTH, March *26*, April 5, 7, 9; NORTH, no data. *Fall migration period:* Probably from sometime in August through mid-October; most birds leave by late September. Latest dates: SOUTH, September 27, October 7, 14; NORTH, no data.

Summer. Resident on the prairie along the western margin of the state. Breeding has been recorded as far east as Mahnomen County in the north and Jackson County in the south. The abundance of the species has been much reduced since the 1940s. A study in the early 1960s in west central Minnesota by R. A. Grant (*Loon* 37:2–17) indicates that the species selects farmland habitats made up of short-cropped pastures populated by colonies of Richardson's Ground Squirrels. Intensive farming practices have reduced this habitat, and it is possible that the species no longer breeds in the state.

Winter. One record: December 14, 1893, Lac qui Parle County (Roberts, 1932).

BARRED OWL *Strix varia*

Minnesota status. Regular. Permanent resident.

Distribution. Permanent resident throughout the state. Least numerous in the prairie regions. It is assumed that the species breeds in the wooded areas adjacent to lakes and rivers on the prairie, but no nests have been reported. There are breeding records for the rest of the state. Winter influxes have occasionally occurred, especially in the north.

GREAT GRAY OWL *Strix nebulosa*

Minnesota status. Regular. Winter visitant; casual summer resident.

Migration and winter. Rare winter visitant in the northern half of the state; casual or accidental in the southern half. Most regular within a hundred miles of the Canadian border. Invasions, during which the species becomes uncommon, occur at irregular intervals and are usually localized. Recent examples: 1965–1966, northeastern region, *Loon* 38:44–45; 1968–1969, northeastern and east central regions, *Loon* 41:36–39. The occurrence of the species in the southern half of the state is not necessarily correlated with invasions. Unlike some other winter owls this species has no regular fall migration; invasions may begin any time from October through December. *Fall:* Most birds do not arrive until late October. Earliest dates: NORTH, September *12*, *17*, October *4*, 15, 20, 21; SOUTH, winter. *Spring:* Most birds leave by mid-March; birds present in late April and May are considered residents. Latest dates: SOUTH, March 5, 15, 23; NORTH, March 26, April 4, 11.

Summer. Casual summer resident in Roseau County. Nests were found in Roseau County in 1935 (*Flicker* 7:17) and 1970 (*Loon* 42:88–93). There are also breeding season observations from Cook, Lake, St. Louis, Itasca, Aitkin, Clearwater, and Lake of the Woods counties.

LONG-EARED OWL *Asio otus*

Minnesota status. Regular. Migrant, summer resident, and winter visitant.

Migration. Rare migrant throughout the state in both seasons. *Spring migration period:* From sometime in March through late April. Earliest dates: SOUTH, none can be given because of wintering birds; NORTH, April 2, 11, 14. *Fall migration period:* Late September through late November with stragglers into early winter. Latest dates: NORTH, December 3, 11, 12; SOUTH, none can be given because of wintering birds.

Summer. Resident throughout the wooded portions of the state. The species is not known to nest on the prairie, even in the wooded valleys, except in the northwestern region (Ada, Crookston).

Winter. Regular but rare in winter in the southern half of the state. It is not known whether the birds are local residents or visitants from farther north; those on the prairie are probably visitants. In the northern half of the state the few winter records that exist are from Duluth and Fargo-Moorhead, and they indicate the presence of the species only through early January.

SHORT-EARED OWL *Asio flammeus*

Minnesota status. Regular. Migrant, summer resident, and winter visitant.

Migration. Uncommon migrant throughout most of the state; rare in the northeastern and southeastern regions. *Spring migration period:* Early March through late April with a peak in mid-April. Earliest dates: SOUTH, none can be given because of wintering birds; NORTH, March 2, 12, 15, 16. *Fall migration period:* Late September through early December with the bulk of the migration in October. Latest dates: NORTH, November 30, December 4, 6; SOUTH, none can be given because of wintering birds.

Summer. Resident throughout most of the state. Most numerous in the northwestern and west central regions. No breeding season reports exist for the Twin Cities area or the southeastern region. The abundance of the species appears to have been reduced in recent years, probably owing to the loss of habitat.

Winter. Regular in winter in the southern half of the state. The numbers vary from rare to uncommon, depending upon the snow conditions and the food supply, and usually decrease by late winter. In the northern half of the state, if conditions are favorable, individuals may winter in the northwestern region. There are also two January records from southern St. Louis County.

BOREAL OWL *Aegolius funereus*

Minnesota status. Regular. Winter visitant.

Migration and winter. Regular but very rare winter visitant in the northern regions; casual in the central regions; accidental in the southern regions and in prairie counties. Invasions occur at irregular intervals, most frequently in the northern regions but also in the central and east central regions; the invasions usually take place in late winter (mid-January through March), and many birds are found dead or starving. The species is rare, even in invasion years. *Fall:* Not usually seen until December; all earlier dates are listed. Earliest dates: SOUTH, October 20, November 18;

NORTH, November *4*, *9*, 21, 27, December 9. *Spring:* Usually gone by late March. Latest dates: SOUTH, March 1, 4, April *21*; NORTH, April 6, 10, 13, May *17*.

Summer. There are no records. One published account (*Auk* 43:544) of a bird heard "singing" in May was regarded by Roberts (1932) as evidence that the species may breed in the state, but the details of the account do not preclude the possibility of confusion with the Saw-whet Owl.

SAW-WHET OWL *Aegolius acadicus*

Minnesota status. Regular. Migrant, summer resident, and winter visitant.

Migration. Rare migrant throughout the state. Most numerous in the wooded portion of the state. The increase in the number of observations of this bird in late fall and early spring and the data from banding stations indicate regular migration peaks. Extreme dates cannot be given because the species occurs throughout most of the state in summer and winter. *Spring migration period:* Probably late February (south) through early May (north) with a peak in late March and early April. *Fall migration period:* Late September through late November with a peak in October.

Summer. Resident throughout the wooded portion of the state as far south as the Twin Cities area. Nesting records exist for Hennepin, Sherburne, Wadena, and Kittson counties. At one time the species was probably a resident in the southeastern region, but there have been no twentieth-century observations of it. More numerous in the northern regions than in the central regions. Roberts (1932) described this owl as breeding throughout the state, but no old or modern summer records exist for the west central, southwestern, or south central regions.

Winter. Rare throughout the wooded portion of the state; casual in the prairie counties. It is not known whether the breeding birds remain in the same locality all year.

Family CAPRIMULGIDAE: Goatsuckers

WHIP-POOR-WILL *Caprimulgus vociferus*

Minnesota status. Regular. Migrant and summer resident.

Migration. Rare spring migrant throughout the wooded portion of the state; casual on the prairie. Most birds reported in the spring are probably on breeding territories. The fall status is unknown; the species is almost never reported at this season because the birds are usually silent. *Spring migration period:* Late April through late May with a peak in early May. Earliest dates: SOUTH, April *17*, 22,

25; NORTH, April *12*, *22*, May 2, 3. *Fall migration period:* Early August through late September. Latest dates: NORTH, September 13, 15; SOUTH, September 25, 26, 28, October 2.

Summer. Resident throughout the wooded portion of the state; very scarce in the northeastern region and in adjacent Koochiching and Itasca counties (no nesting records from these areas). Most numerous in the southeastern region and in parts of the northwestern and north central regions (Roseau, Lake of the Woods, Marshall, Beltrami, and Clearwater counties). Not known on the prairie.

POOR-WILL *Phalaenoptilus nuttallii*

Minnesota status. Accidental. One spring record.
Records. One bird was found almost dead on April 16, 1963, in Swift County (*Flicker* 35:65–66) and subsequently was given to the Bell Museum of Natural History (MMNH #18903).

COMMON NIGHTHAWK *Chordeiles minor*

Minnesota status. Regular. Migrant and summer resident.
Migration. Abundant migrant throughout the state in spring and fall. The largest migration flights occur in the fall, especially at Duluth where in late afternoon a thousand birds per hour may be observed between August 18 and August 25. *Spring migration period:* Late April through late May with the bulk of the migration in the second half of May. Earliest dates: SOUTH, April *10*, *15*, 21, 24, 26; NORTH, May 2, 3, 7. *Fall migration period:* Late July (north) through mid-October (south) with a peak in the last half of August. Latest dates: NORTH, September 16, 17, 19, *24*; SOUTH, October 8, 9, 12, *22*.

Summer. Resident throughout the state. The species is numerous in wild habitats from the prairie to the northern coniferous forests, nesting in rocky openings in the woods. In towns and cities the species nests on flat roofs.

Family APODIDAE: Swifts

CHIMNEY SWIFT *Chaetura pelagica*

Minnesota status. Regular. Migrant and summer resident.
Migration. Abundant migrant throughout the state in both seasons. In spring and fall roosts of several hundred to over a thousand birds are found in large chimneys in urban areas. Banding records indicate that both migrant and resident birds are involved in these concentrations (H. H. Goehring, personal communication). *Spring migration period:* Mid-April through early June (north). Earliest dates: SOUTH,

April *11*, 16, 17, 19; NORTH, April *26*, 29, May 1, 2. *Fall migration period:* Mid-August through early October with a peak in late August and early September. Latest dates: NORTH, September 13, 14, 21, October *23*, *26*; SOUTH, October 5, 13, 17, *26*.

Summer. Resident throughout the state. The species is most numerous around human habitations because it nests in chimneys and abandoned buildings, but it also is found in heavily forested areas, following its natural pattern of nesting in hollow trees.

Family TROCHILIDAE: Hummingbirds

RUBY-THROATED HUMMINGBIRD
Archilochus colubris

Minnesota status. Regular. Migrant and summer resident.
Migration. Common migrant throughout the state in spring and fall. *Spring migration period:* Very late April through early June, with the bulk of the migration in the second half of May. Earliest dates: SOUTH, April *14*, *23*, 27, 30; NORTH, April *30*, May 4, 7, 8. *Fall migration period:* Early August through early October, with the bulk of the migration in late August and early September. Latest dates: NORTH, October 1, 2, *6*, *9*; SOUTH, October 6, 7, 8, *28*.
Summer. Resident throughout the state, breeding in all regions.

Family ALCEDINIDAE: Kingfishers

BELTED KINGFISHER *Megaceryle alcyon*

Minnesota status. Regular . Migrant and summer resident; regular in winter.
Migration. A common migrant throughout the state in spring and fall. *Spring migration period:* Mid-March through early May, with the bulk of the migration in early and mid-April. Earliest dates: SOUTH, none can be given because of wintering birds; NORTH, March *30*, April *1*, 7, 8. *Fall migration period:* Probably from late August through late November. Latest dates: NORTH, October 26, 29, November 1, December *22*; SOUTH, none can be given because of wintering birds.
Summer. Resident throughout the state wherever there is suitable habitat.
Winter. Regular but uncommon in early winter from the Twin Cities area southward; rare after early January; casual in winter from the Twin Cities as far north as Stearns County. No overwintering records north of Stearns County.

Family PICIDAE: Woodpeckers

COMMON FLICKER (Yellow-shafted Flicker)
Colaptes auratus

Minnesota status. Regular. Migrant and summer resident; regular in winter.

Migration. Abundant spring and fall migrant throughout the state. Peak daily counts of five hundred to eight hundred birds are not unusual. *Spring migration period:* Early March through early May with a peak in the second half of April. Earliest dates: SOUTH, none can be given because of wintering birds; NORTH, March 30, 31, April 4. *Fall migration period:* Late August through early November with stragglers present throughout November and December; migration peak in September. Latest dates: None can be given because of stragglers and overwintering birds.

Summer. Resident throughout the state; widespread and numerous everywhere.

Winter. Regular but uncommon throughout the southern half of the state; in the northern half regular but rare from Duluth and Moorhead southward, casual farther north. The number of birds present declines after mid-January, but the species overwinters as far north as Cook County. It is not known whether the winter birds are lingering migrants or summer residents, but the former seems more likely.

Taxonomic note. There are many reports of flickers that have red or salmon-pink wing linings; most of the reports are from the western part of the state during migration or in winter. A few specimens of hybrid or introgressant flickers are available in the Bell Museum of Natural History. Only two reports of observations include enough details for positive identification of the Red-shafted Flicker, *C. a. cafer.*

PILEATED WOODPECKER *Dryocopus pileatus*

Minnesota status. Regular. Permanent resident.

Distribution. Permanent resident throughout the forested part of the state and the heavily timbered valleys and lakeshores of the prairie. In the area south of the Minnesota River valley and west of Blue Earth County the species is very rare, probably because sufficient habitat does not exist there.

RED-BELLIED WOODPECKER *Centurus carolinus*

Minnesota status. Regular. Permanent resident; casual migrant and winter visitant beyond the regular range.

Distribution. Permanent resident from Stearns County south and east; known to nest in the same area (see map 42). Roberts (1932) stated that the species had expanded its

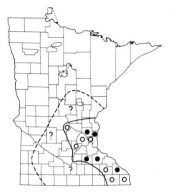

42. Red-bellied Woodpecker

range into Minnesota in the early part of the century and by 1930 was found breeding as far north and west as the Twin Cities. By 1970 the species was reported regularly in fall, winter, and spring as far north as Crow Wing County and as far west as the Des Moines River drainage, but no summer data or breeding records are available from this area. There are occasional reports from outside the suspected breeding range, mostly for fall and winter, as far north as Upper Red Lake, Grand Rapids, and Duluth. The extralimital spring records are all from the shore of Lake Superior from Duluth to Cook County.

RED-HEADED WOODPECKER
Melanerpes erythrocephalus

Minnesota status. Regular. Migrant and summer resident; regular in winter.

Migration. Common spring and fall migrant throughout most of the state; uncommon or rare in the heavily wooded northern regions. *Spring migration period:* Late March through late May; peak migration probably in early May. Earliest dates: SOUTH, none can be given because of wintering birds; NORTH (beyond winter range), April *10*, 24, 26, 28. *Fall migration period:* Early August through late October with a peak in late August. Latest dates: NORTH (beyond winter range), October 3, 4, 10; SOUTH, none can be given because of wintering birds.

Summer. Resident throughout the state. The species does not breed in the heavily wooded portions of the northern regions, but it does occur in areas where farms or towns have displaced the woodlands.

Winter. Regular in winter in the southeastern quarter of the state as far north as Mille Lacs Lake and as far west as Stearns County. The number of birds varies yearly, but the species is usually uncommon. Casual as far north as Duluth and Wadena County. No records from the western prairie. It is not known whether the winter birds are visitants or summer residents, but the latter seems more likely.

YELLOW-BELLIED SAPSUCKER
Sphyrapicus varius

Minnesota status. Regular. Migrant and summer resident; casual in winter.

Migration. Uncommon summer and winter migrant throughout the state; may be common briefly at the migration peak. *Spring migration period:* Late March through mid-May with a peak during the last three weeks of April. Earliest dates: SOUTH, March 22, 23, 25; NORTH, April 6, 7. *Fall migration period:* Late August through late October.

Latest dates: NORTH, October 19, 20, 23, *29*; SOUTH, none can be given because stragglers linger into early winter.

Summer. Resident throughout the forested parts of the state. No breeding records or modern summer records exist for areas south of the Minnesota River and west of Rice County.

Winter. In early winter rare from the Twin Cities southward and eastward; casual from the Twin Cities as far north as Stearns County. Casual throughout the state after early January.

WILLIAMSON'S SAPSUCKER
Sphyrapicus thyroideus

Minnesota status. Hypothetical.
Records. One observation was made in Worthington, Nobles County, on April 22, 1972 (*Loon* 44:52–53).

HAIRY WOODPECKER
Dendrocopos villosus

Minnesota status. Regular. Permanent resident.
Distribution. Permanent resident, breeding throughout the state.
Migration (winter). Specimens in the Bell Museum of Natural History indicate that the large northern race (*D. v. septentrionalis*) occurs as far south as the Twin Cities from early October through late April, but there are not enough specimens to suggest how regular and how extensive the migration movements are. If the published banding data indeed pertain to the resident subspecies (*D. v. villosus*), it appears that resident populations do not wander from their summer areas.

DOWNY WOODPECKER *Dendrocopos pubescens*

Minnesota status. Regular. Permanent resident.
Distribution. Permanent resident, breeding throughout the state.
Migration (winter). A northern race of the Downy Woodpecker (*D. p. nelsoni*) occurs in Minnesota in the winter, but some individuals of the local breeding race (*D. p. medianus*) show characters intermediate between *nelsoni* and *medianus*; as a result, it is difficult to delineate the movements of birds of the northern race, especially since few specimens are available.

BLACK-BACKED THREE-TOED
WOODPECKER *Picoïdes arcticus*

Minnesota status. Regular. Migrant, winter visitant, and summer resident.
Migration. Uncommon fall migrant along the shore of

43. Black-backed Three-toed
    Woodpecker (1900)

Lake Superior; rare to locally uncommon elsewhere in the northern regions in both seasons. Casual in the wooded areas elsewhere in the state; accidental on the prairie south of the Red River Valley. *Fall migration period:* Mid-September (north) through mid-November with a peak in late October. Earliest dates: NORTH, none can be given because of breeding birds; SOUTH, October 5, 25, 27, 28. *Spring migration period:* Probably from sometime in March through late April. Latest dates: SOUTH, April 20, 22, 26, May 4; NORTH, none can be given because of breeding birds.
Winter. Rare to locally uncommon winter visitant in the northern regions; casual in the wooded areas elsewhere in the state; accidental on the prairie south of the Red River Valley.
Summer. Resident throughout the coniferous forests in the northern regions (see map 43), with breeding records from as far west as Becker County (1887) and as far south as Nisswa, Crow Wing County; very scarce everywhere. (The species is found in the same areas in winter, but the winter population seems to be more numerous and more widespread than the breeding population.) Most numerous in northern Lake and Cook counties. One nineteenth-century breeding record outside this range was listed by Roberts (1932), but the record was not firsthand and the details are suspect.

NORTHERN THREE-TOED WOODPECKER
Picoïdes tridactylus

Minnesota status. Regular. Winter visitant and casual summer visitant.
Migration. Very rare winter visitant in the coniferous forests in the northern regions; casual farther south (to Stearns and Hennepin counties); unknown elsewhere. Earliest dates: NORTH, September 29, October 2, 14; SOUTH, November 26 (only date). Latest dates: SOUTH, March 10, 29 (only dates), May *12*; NORTH, March 30, April 5, 17, May *13*.
Summer. Reported occasionally within about fifty miles of the Canadian border from the Northwest Angle to Cook County and in Itasca State Park. No nests have been found, and the only evidence of breeding is a family group found at Itasca State Park in 1902 (Roberts, 1932).

Family TYRANNIDAE:
Tyrant Flycatchers

EASTERN KINGBIRD *Tyrannus tyrannus*

Minnesota status. Regular. Migrant and summer resident.
Migration. Common migrant throughout the state in both

seasons. *Spring migration period:* Mid-April through early June with the bulk of the migration during the last three weeks of May; arrivals before late April are unusual. Earliest dates: SOUTH, April 7, 15, 16, 18; NORTH, April *30*, May 5, 6. *Fall migration period:* Early August through late September with a peak in late August and early September. Latest dates: NORTH, September 16, 17, *22*, October *15*; SOUTH, September 20, 23, 26.
Summer. Resident throughout the state, breeding in all regions.

WESTERN KINGBIRD *Tyrannus verticalis*

Minnesota status. Regular. Migrant and summer resident.
Migration. Uncommon migrant throughout most of the state; casual in the northeastern region and in the adjacent counties in the north central region. *Spring migration period:* Early May through early June. Earliest dates: SOUTH, April *26*, May 3, 4, 5; NORTH, May 5, 6, 11. *Fall migration period:* Early August through mid-September. Latest dates: NORTH, September 4, 8, *28*; SOUTH, September 12, 14, 17.
Summer. Resident throughout most of the state except the southeastern region, most of the south central region, the northeastern region, and most of the north central region. There are breeding records for the northern regions as far east as Hackensack, Cass County; for the central regions as far east as Granite Township, Morrison County, and Langdon, Washington County; and for the southern regions as far east as Jackson and LeSueur counties (see map 44). Roberts (1932) discussed the spread of this species into Minnesota from the west between 1880 and 1930. The range in the state has not changed much since Roberts wrote, but the species is less numerous in the prairie regions now than it was in the 1920s.

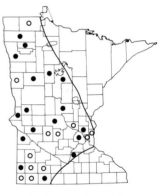

44. Western Kingbird

SCISSOR-TAILED FLYCATCHER
Muscivora forficata

Minnesota status. Casual. Spring migrant and summer visitant; three fall records.
Records. Almost all the records of this species are from mid-May through early July with half of them in June. Earliest dates: May 14, 16, 24. Latest dates: June 10, 14, 19, July 3–7. These records are scattered throughout the state from Lake of the Woods and Lake counties to Jackson and Winona counties. There are only three fall records: August 10, 1963, Hennepin County (*Flicker* 35:107); October 12, 1973, Duluth (J. C. Green); October 23, 1958, Carlton County (MMNH #14562; the only specimen).

GREAT CRESTED FLYCATCHER
Myiarchus crinitus

Minnesota status. Regular. Migrant and summer resident.
Migration. Uncommon spring migrant throughout the state; most observations are of birds on breeding territories. Less numerous in the fall with a gradual exodus from breeding territories. *Spring migration period:* Early to late May. Earliest dates: SOUTH, April *25*, May 1, 3, 4; NORTH, May 8, 12, 14. *Fall migration period:* Probably early August through late September. Latest dates: NORTH, September 25, 27, 30, October *5*, *26*; SOUTH, September 20, 23, 27, October *10*, *16*.
Summer. Resident throughout the state; scarce in Lake and Cook counties and breeding has not been confirmed there.

EASTERN PHOEBE *Sayornis phoebe*

Minnesota status. Regular. Migrant and summer resident.
Migration. Uncommon spring and fall migrant, occasionally common at migration peaks, throughout the state. *Spring migration period:* Mid-March through very early May with the bulk of the migration during the first three weeks of April; only in exceptional years are there arrivals before late March. Earliest dates: SOUTH, March *3*, *8*, *10*, *11*, *13*, 18, 20; NORTH, March *30*, *31*, April 6, 10, 11. *Fall migration period:* Late August through early November with the bulk of the migration in September; stragglers after late October are very unusual. Latest dates: NORTH, September 28, October 1, *12*; SOUTH, November 3, 5, 9, December *23*.
Summer. Resident throughout the state, breeding in all regions.

BLACK PHOEBE *Sayornis nigricans*

Minnesota status. Hypothetical.
Records. One observation: September 13, 1952, at Madison, Lac qui Parle County (*Flicker* 25:47–48).

SAY'S PHOEBE *Sayornis saya*

Minnesota status. Hypothetical.
Records. Two observations: September 3, 1963, at St. Charles, Winona County. (*Loon* 41:10–11); September 3, 1973, Rock County (*Loon* 46:37–39).

YELLOW-BELLIED FLYCATCHER
Empidonax flaviventris

Minnesota status. Regular. Migrant and summer resident.
Migration. Uncommon spring and fall migrant, occasionally common at migration peaks, throughout the state.

Spring migration period: Early May through early June with a peak in late May and early June. Earliest dates: SOUTH, April 30, May 2, 3; NORTH, May 17, 18, 19. Latest dates: SOUTH, June 5, 6, 10; NORTH, none can be given because of breeding birds. *Fall migration period:* Late July through late September with the bulk of the migration from mid-August through early September. Earliest dates: NORTH, none can be given because of breeding birds; SOUTH, July *3*, *12*, 30, 31. Latest dates: NORTH, September 15, 19, 20, October *2*; SOUTH, September 19, 25, 28.

Summer. Resident throughout the northeastern and north central regions (see map 45). Reported as far west as Moose River, Marshall County (family group), and as far south as Bruno, Pine County (singing males); the only breeding records are from northern Lake County.

45. Yellow-bellied Flycatcher

ACADIAN FLYCATCHER *Empidonax virescens*

Minnesota status. Regular. Summer resident in Houston County.
Migration. All observations are of birds on breeding territory in June and July.
Summer. In 1967 a nesting pair was discovered in Beaver Creek Valley State Park, Houston County (*Loon* 40:4–6). A pair was present in the same spot from 1968 through 1973, and nests were found in 1968 and 1970. The only other report is of singing birds in 1940 on the Root River, Houston County, 2½ miles east of Rushford.

WILLOW FLYCATCHER *Empidonax traillii;*
ALDER FLYCATCHER *Empidonax alnorum*

Taxonomic note. Traill's Flycatcher is divided into two species (*Auk* 90:415–416): "*Empidonax traillii* (Audubon), the generally more southern and western bird, of more open country, whose vocalization has been interpreted as 'fitz-bew', and *Empidonax alnorum* Brewster, the generally more northern bird, of the boreal forest region, whose vocalization has been interpreted as 'fee-bee-o'. . . . [W]here circumstances do not permit specific identification, 'Traill's Flycatcher' remains available for the complex." Both species occur in Minnesota, and they are considered together because little information based on song type is available for the two species.
Minnesota status. Regular. Migrant and summer resident.
Migration. Uncommon migrant, occasionally common at migration peaks, throughout the state in both seasons. *Spring migration period:* Early May through early June with the bulk of the migration in the second part of May. Earliest dates: SOUTH, April *26*, May 1, 3, 4; NORTH, May

10, 11, 12. *Fall migration period:* Early August through late September with a peak in late August and early September. Latest dates: NORTH, September 20, 22, 25; SOUTH, September 17, 21, 24.

Summer. Both species occur as residents, the Willow Flycatcher in the southern and western regions and the Alder Flycatcher in the northern regions. Since few ornithologists have undertaken to report field data by song type, a great deal of fieldwork must be done before the respective ranges and any areas of overlap can be mapped.

LEAST FLYCATCHER *Empidonax minimus*

Minnesota status. Regular. Migrant and summer resident.
Migration. Common spring and fall migrant throughout the state. *Spring migration period:* Late April through late May with the bulk of the migration in mid- and late May. Earliest dates: SOUTH, April *22*, 26, 27, 28; NORTH, April *24*, *28*, *29*, May 4, 6. *Fall migration period:* Early August through early October with the bulk of the migration from late August through mid-September. Latest dates: NORTH, September 24, 25, 26, *30*; SOUTH, October 7, 8, 10.
Summer. Resident throughout the state. The species frequents groves on the prairie.

EASTERN WOOD PEWEE *Contopus virens*

Minnesota status. Regular. Migrant and summer resident.
Migration. Uncommon spring and fall migrant, occasionally common at migration peaks, throughout the state. *Spring migration period:* Very late April through early June with the bulk of the migration in the second half of May. Earliest dates: SOUTH, April *22*, *24*, 27, 29, May 1; NORTH, April *25*, May *4*, 14, 15, 16. *Fall migration period:* Early August through very early October. Latest dates: NORTH, September 26, 27, 28; SOUTH, October 1, 5, 6.
Summer. Resident throughout the state. The species frequents groves on the prairie.

WESTERN WOOD PEWEE
Contopus sordidulus

Minnesota status. Hypothetical.
Records. One bird was seen and heard on September 26, 1971, in Cottonwood, Lyon County (*Loon* 44:115–116).

OLIVE-SIDED FLYCATCHER
Nuttallornis borealis

Minnesota status. Regular. Migrant and summer resident.
Migration. Uncommon spring and fall migrant throughout the state. *Spring migration period:* Early May through

mid-June with stragglers even later. Earliest dates: SOUTH, April *30*, May 5, 6, 7; NORTH, May 6, 8, 13. Latest dates: SOUTH, June 9, 11, 14, *18*, *26*, July *4*; NORTH, none can be given because of breeding birds. *Fall migration period:* Early August through late September with the bulk of the migration in late August and early September. Earliest dates: NORTH, none can be given because of breeding birds; SOUTH, August 3, 11, 13. Latest dates: NORTH, September 17, 19, 21; SOUTH, September 20, 24, 26 October *1*, *2*.

Summer. Resident in the northeastern and north central regions as far west as Kittson County and Many Point Lake, Becker County (see map 46). Breeding evidence has been obtained from areas as far south as Sturgeon Lake, Pine County. The Isanti County record (June 12, 1927) mentioned by Roberts (1932) and in the fifth edition of the AOU *Check-List* could have been a migrant bird.

46. Olive-sided Flycatcher

Family ALAUDIDAE: Larks

HORNED LARK *Eremophila alpestris*

Minnesota status. Regular. Migrant and summer resident; regular in winter.

Migration. Common to abundant spring and fall migrant throughout the state. *Spring migration period:* Mid-January through mid-April with the bulk of the migration from mid-February through late March. Earliest dates: SOUTH, none can be given because of wintering birds; NORTH, February 10, 11, 12. *Fall migration period:* Late September through late November with the bulk of the migration in October. Latest dates: NORTH, November 13, 18, 21, December *20*; SOUTH, none can be given because of wintering birds.

Summer. Resident throughout the state; very scarce in the north central and northeastern regions where little suitable habitat is available in heavily forested areas.

Winter. Uncommon to common in winter in the southern part of the state north to Aitkin and Otter Tail counties. Most numerous in the southwestern region. It is not known whether the birds present in winter are local summer residents or visitors from farther north.

Family HIRUNDINIDAE: Swallows

VIOLET-GREEN SWALLOW
Tachycineta thalassina

Minnesota status. Hypothetical.
Records. A pair was seen on October 25–26, 1942, at Rochester, Olmsted County (*Auk* 60:455).

TREE SWALLOW *Iridoprocne bicolor*

Minnesota status. Regular. Migrant and summer resident.
Migration. Abundant spring and fall migrant throughout
the state. *Spring migration period:* Late March through
mid-May with a peak in late April and early May. Earliest
dates: SOUTH, March *18*, 22, 23, 26; NORTH, March *22*,
April 7, 8, 9. *Fall migration period:* Mid-July through early
November with the bulk of the migration from early August
through early October. Latest dates: NORTH, September 27,
October 3, *25*, *26*, November *6*; SOUTH, November 2, 3, *8*,
9.
Summer. Resident throughout the state; numerous in all
regions.

BANK SWALLOW *Riparia riparia*

Minnesota status. Regular. Migrant and summer resident.
Migration. Common spring and fall migrant throughout
most of the state; usually uncommon in the north central and
northeastern regions. *Spring migration period:* Early April
through mid-May with a peak in late April and early May.
Earliest dates: SOUTH, April 7, 8, 11; NORTH, April 16, 19,
20. *Fall migration period:* Late July through late September
with the bulk of the migration in August. Latest dates:
NORTH, September 3, 5, 13; SOUTH, September 19, 23, 28,
October *5*, *8*.
Summer. Resident throughout the state wherever suitable
habitat is available. Least numerous in heavily forested
areas where stream banks are scarce or absent.

ROUGH-WINGED SWALLOW
Stelgidopteryx ruficollis

Minnesota status. Regular. Migrant and summer resident.
Migration. Common spring and fall migrant in the south-
ern, central, and northwestern regions; uncommon to rare in
the spring and very rare in the fall in the north central and
northeastern regions. *Spring migration period:* Mid-April
through late May with a peak in late April and early May.
Earliest dates: SOUTH, March *19*, April 9, 10, 13; NORTH,
April *19*, 26, 29, 30. *Fall migration period:* Mid-July
through early October with a peak in early September.
Latest dates: NORTH, July 25, September 10 (only dates);
SOUTH, October 5, 10, 13.
Summer. Resident throughout the state. Numerous
in the southern and central regions and less numerous
in the northern regions; very scarce in the northeastern
region.

BARN SWALLOW *Hirundo rustica*

Minnesota status. Regular. Migrant and summer resident.
Migration. Common spring and fall migrant throughout the state; occasionally abundant, especially in the western prairie areas. *Spring migration period:* Early April through late May with a peak in late April and early May. Earliest dates: SOUTH, April 1, 5, 9; NORTH, April 14, 19, 27. *Fall migration period:* Late July through late October with the bulk of the migration in September. Latest dates: NORTH, October 9, 19, 25; SOUTH, October 28, 29, November 1.
Summer. Resident throughout the state. Most numerous on the prairie; least numerous in heavily wooded areas. The Barn Swallow is the most common species of swallow on the prairie.

CLIFF SWALLOW *Petrochelidon pyrrhonota*

Minnesota status. Regular. Migrant and summer resident.
Migration. Common to abundant spring and fall migrant throughout the state. Most numerous in the northwestern region; least numerous in the southwestern and south central regions. *Spring migration period:* Early April through late May with a peak in early May. Earliest dates: SOUTH, April 6, *13*, 23, 25, 26; NORTH, April *14*, *20*, 26, 28, 29. *Fall migration period:* Late July through mid-October with a peak in early September. Latest dates: NORTH, September 12, 15, *27*; SOUTH, October 8, 10, 14.
Summer. Resident throughout the state. Least numerous in the southwestern region; most numerous in the northwestern and northeastern regions, especially in St. Louis and Marshall counties.

PURPLE MARTIN *Progne subis*

Minnesota status. Regular. Migrant and summer resident.
Migration. Abundant spring and fall migrant throughout the state. The largest concentrations (two thousand to three thousand birds) occur in the fall. *Spring migration period:* Late March through late May with the bulk of the migration from mid-April through early May. Earliest dates: SOUTH, February *14*, March *13*, 24, 27, 28; NORTH, April 10, 11, 12. *Fall migration period:* Late July through early October with a peak in the second part of August. Latest dates: NORTH, September 8, 9, 17, *26*; SOUTH, October 4, 6, 7, *19*, *21*.
Summer. Resident throughout the state. Most numerous along the Mississippi River and in the central and western parts of the state in and about towns and cities.

Family CORVIDAE:
Jays, Magpies, and Crows

GRAY JAY *Perisoreus canadensis*

47. Gray Jay

Minnesota status. Regular. Primarily permanent resident; also erratic fall migrant and winter visitant.

Distribution. Permanent resident throughout the northeastern and north central regions. Family groups have been reported as far west as eastern Marshall County and Itasca State Park and as far south as Mille Lacs Lake, Aitkin County (see map 47).

Migration. Irregular fall eruptions are most noticeable along the shore of Lake Superior in St. Louis County; the movements begin in mid-September, peak in October, and end in late November. During eruptions the species is common in the north central and northeastern regions and occasionally uncommon in the central and east central regions. No spring movements noted. Usually very rare in fall and winter beyond normal range as far south as the Twin Cities in the eastern part of the state, Stearns County in the central part, and Clay County in the western part; not recorded farther south and west. Earliest dates (beyond normal range): October 5, 15, 19, 23. Latest dates (beyond normal range): February 9, 11, April (no date).

BLUE JAY *Cyanocitta cristata*

Minnesota status. Regular. Primarily permanent resident; regular migrant in the north.

Distribution. Permanent resident throughout the state, breeding in all regions.

Migration. Common to abundant spring and fall migrant in the northern regions, especially along the shore of Lake Superior. *Spring migration period:* Late April through early June with the bulk of the migration in May. *Fall migration period:* Late August through mid-October with the bulk of the migration in September.

Winter. Present throughout the state; least numerous in the northern regions. It is not known whether the winter population in any area of the state is the same as the summer population.

BLACK-BILLED MAGPIE *Pica pica*

Minnesota status. Regular. Migrant and winter visitant; casual summer resident.

Migration. Common fall migrant in the northwestern region and in the adjacent counties of the north central region (regular range); rare migrant throughout the rest of the north-

ern region; accidental elsewhere. In the spring uncommon in
the regular range; rare in the rest of the northern regions; casual elsewhere. *Fall migration period:* Early September
through mid-November with a peak during the first three
weeks of October. Earliest dates: REGULAR RANGE,
August *29*, September 2, 5, 7; BEYOND REGULAR
RANGE, September *24*, 28, 30, October 2. *Spring migration period:* Mid-February through early April with
stragglers into May. Latest dates: REGULAR RANGE,
March 27, 29, April 4, *25*, May 6; BEYOND REGULAR
RANGE, May 4, 12, 15, *26*.
Winter. Uncommon visitant in the northwestern region and
in the adjacent counties of the north central region; very rare
in the rest of the northern regions; accidental elsewhere.
Most numerous in invasion years (about once a decade).
Invasions during the 1920s and 1930s came into the state
from the southwest; since the 1940s migration and invasions
have come from the northwest. The major invasion during
1972–1973 occurred principally in the north and west, but
some birds reached the southeastern region (*Loon* 45:14).
Summer. Breeding records have been obtained from several counties: Beltrami (1951; *Flicker* 23:90); Marshall
(1971; *Loon* 43:78–79); Clay (1972; *Loon* 45:120–121); and
Roseau (1973; M. M. Carr). The species seems to be casual
in these counties and in Clearwater and Polk counties. Accidental in summer elsewhere.

COMMON RAVEN *Corvus corax*

Minnesota status. Regular. Migrant, winter visitant, and
summer resident.
Migration. Uncommon fall migrant in the northern regions
(common along the shore of Lake Superior); casual in the
central regions (regular but rare in Pine County); accidental
in the southern regions. Uncommon to rare spring migrant in
the northern regions and in Pine and Mille Lacs counties; unknown elsewhere. *Fall migration period:* Early September
through early November with a peak from late September
through mid-October. Earliest dates: NORTH, none can be
given because of breeding birds; SOUTH, September 25,
October 3, 7. *Spring migration period:* Probably late February through late April; most nonbreeding birds leave by
the end of March. Latest dates: SOUTH, no records after
December; NORTH, none can be given because of breeding
birds.
Winter. Uncommon to common winter visitant (with
concentrations at dumps and at locations where animals
have been killed along roadways) in the northern regions

48. Common Raven

and in adjacent Pine and Mille Lacs counties. Most numerous along the North Shore of Lake Superior. Accidental elsewhere. During the nineteenth century the species was common in the northern regions, but it was quite rare from about 1900 until the 1940s; since the 1950s, however, its numbers have again been increasing.

Summer. Resident in the north central and northeastern regions and in the adjacent parts of Pine and Mille Lacs counties (see map 48). Most numerous in the Superior National Forest. Not known at Itasca State Park until the late 1960s. Probably always regular in some localities in Pine County as far south as Hinckley.

COMMON CROW *Corvus brachyrhynchos*

Minnesota status. Regular. Migrant and summer resident; regular in winter.

Migration. Common spring and fall migrant, becoming abundant on peak days, throughout the state. *Spring migration period:* Early February through mid-April with the bulk of the migration from very late February through early April. Earliest dates: None can be given because of wintering birds. *Fall migration period:* Early September through late November with stragglers still present into early winter; the bulk of the migration is from mid-September through late October. Latest dates: None can be given because of wintering birds.

Summer. Resident throughout the state; numerous in all regions.

Winter. Common as far north as Chisago and Stevens counties; uncommon from there northward to Duluth and Clay County; rare or casual farther north. It is not known whether wintering flocks are local summer residents.

CLARK'S NUTCRACKER
Nucifraga columbiana

Minnesota status. Casual. Fall migrant.

Records. All but one of the records are from September (earliest dates: September 8, 9, 12) through December (latest dates: December 6, 8–18), occurring at intervals of several years. Major incursions resulting in four or five records took place in 1894 (in the southwestern region), 1969 (in the northeastern region), and 1972 (Cook, Itasca, Stearns, Hennepin, and Lyon counties). One overwintering bird was reported at Christmas Lake, Hennepin County, from November 20, 1972, to April 8, 1973 (*Loon* 45:20–21). Three specimens are available (MMNH #2795, #3417, and #8689).

Family PARIDAE:
Titmice, Verdins, and Bushtits

BLACK-CAPPED CHICKADEE
Parus atricapillus

Minnesota status. Regular. Primarily permanent resident; also erratic migrant.

Distribution. Permanent resident, breeding throughout the state.

Migration. At irregular intervals fall migration is detected along the shore of Lake Superior; at this time hundreds of birds can be counted on peak days. The movement is from early September through late November with a peak from mid-September through mid-October. Recent documented invasions occurred in 1959 and 1968. A much smaller spring migration in early and mid-May is sometimes detected along Minnesota Point, Duluth.

BOREAL CHICKADEE *Parus hudsonicus*

Minnesota status. Regular. Permanent resident; casual winter visitant outside the regular range.

Distribution. Permanent resident throughout the northeastern and north central regions (see map 49). Breeding has been reported as far south as Big Sandy Lake, Aitkin County.

Migration and winter. During eruptions, which occur at irregular intervals, this species becomes a casual migrant and winter visitant in the central regions (accidental in the southern regions). Increased numbers are found at these times within the usual breeding range of the species. *Fall migration period:* Late September (north) through late October. Earliest dates (beyond normal range): July 7–August 8 (Lyon County), October *3*, *5*, 23, 24, 29. *Spring migration period:* None recognized. Latest dates (beyond normal range): March 22, 26, April 7, *30*, May *29*.

49. Boreal Chickadee

TUFTED TITMOUSE *Parus bicolor*

Minnesota status. Regular. Permanent resident; casual winter visitant outside the regular range.

Distribution. Permanent resident in the southeastern region and locally northward along the St. Croix, Minnesota, and Mississippi rivers (see map 50). Numbers vary markedly from year to year, and breeding populations are localized, especially in the northern part of the range. The species appears to have increased in abundance and possibly to have extended its breeding range since the 1940s. It is known to nest regularly as far north as Washington and Hennepin

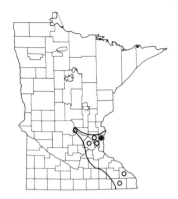

50. Tufted Titmouse

counties, and on one occasion a family group was observed at a feeder at St. Cloud, Stearns County.

Winter. Outside the breeding season individuals and small groups (two to six birds) have been found casually through- out the state as far north as Duluth and Leech Lake and accidentally as far north as Cook and Polk counties. These records involve birds seen only in fall or spring and over- wintering birds. Earliest dates (beyond breeding range): September 24, 28, October 18. Latest dates (beyond breed- ing range): March 28, 31, April 2, *12*.

Family SITTIDAE: Nuthatches

WHITE-BREASTED NUTHATCH
Sitta carolinensis

Minnesota status. Regular. Primarily permanent resident; also regular winter visitant in the northeastern region.

Distribution. Permanent resident throughout the state; very scarce and local during the breeding season in the northeast- ern region (no breeding records on file). Common in all seasons throughout the rest of the state.

Winter. Since there are only casual summer records for Duluth and for southern St. Louis and Lake counties, and since the species becomes uncommon in these areas in winter, it would seem that this nuthatch is a visitant. The species usually arrives in mid-September and departs by the end of April.

RED-BREASTED NUTHATCH *Sitta canadensis*

Minnesota status. Regular. Permanent resident; also mi- grant and winter visitant.

Distribution. Regular permanent resident; widely distrib- uted in the northeastern and north central regions (see map 51). The number present in the state varies markedly from year to year, especially in winter; for example, in some winters the species is common, but in others it is uncommon to rare. The summer population does not seem to fluctuate so drastically. Casual resident in the east central region, breeding as far south as the Twin Cities area (nests or family groups have been reported in Hennepin, Ramsey, and Washington counties); much more numerous and regular in this region in winter (varying from rare to common) than in summer (rare or absent); breeding is reported about every ten years.

Migration. Uncommon spring and fall migrant throughout the state; occasionally common in the eastern regions. In the northeastern and north central regions where the species is a permanent resident, it becomes most numerous in spring

51. Red-breasted Nuthatch

and fall. *Fall migration period:* Mid-August probably through early November with the bulk of the migration in late August and September. Earliest dates (beyond regular range): August 11, 12, 16. *Spring migration period:* Probably early April through late May. Latest dates (beyond regular range): May 19, 21, 22, 29, June 3.

Winter. Visitant throughout the state; numbers vary irregularly from rare to common in different years. Most numerous in the north central and northeastern regions.

Family CERTHIIDAE: Creepers

BROWN CREEPER *Certhia familiaris*

Minnesota status. Regular. Migrant, summer resident, and winter visitant.

Migration. Common spring and fall migrant throughout the state. *Spring migration period:* Mid-March through late May with the bulk of the migration in April. Earliest dates: SOUTH, none can be given because of wintering birds; NORTH, March 22, 27, 29, 30. *Fall migration period:* Early September (north) and mid-September (south) through mid-November (north) and probably late November (south). Latest dates: None can be given because of stragglers and overwintering birds.

Winter. Visitant from mid-St. Louis, Clay, and Beltrami counties southward throughout the state. Rare in the northern regions; uncommon in the central and southern regions.

Summer. Resident in the north central and northeastern regions primarily; probably also resident throughout much of the wooded portion of the state (see map 52). Nests have been found as far south as Hennepin County and Frontenac, Goodhue County.

52. Brown Creeper

Family CINCLIDAE: Dippers

DIPPER *Cinclus mexicanus*

Records. One bird was observed in four different streams along the North Shore of Lake Superior in Cook County from January 29 to April 4, 1970 (*Loon* 42:136–137). Local residents also indicated that this bird had been present in previous years on North Shore streams.

Family TROGLODYTIDAE: Wrens

HOUSE WREN *Troglodytes aedon*

Minnesota status. Regular. Migrant and summer resident.
Migration. Common in spring and fall throughout the state; normally encountered as individuals or in pairs. *Spring mi-*

gration period: Mid-April through late May with a peak in early May. Earliest dates: SOUTH, March *30*, April *1*, *3*, *8*, 18, 19; NORTH, March *30*, April 22, 25, 26. *Fall migration period:* Mid-August through mid-October with a peak in the second half of September. Latest dates: NORTH, October 1, 3, 6; SOUTH, October 15, 20, 21, November *17*.

Summer. Resident throughout the state; widely distributed and numerous in all regions.

WINTER WREN *Troglodytes troglodytes*

Minnesota status. Regular. Migrant and summer resident; casual in winter.

Migration. Uncommon spring and fall migrant throughout the state. Most numerous in the eastern regions and least numerous in the western regions. *Spring migration period:* Late March through late May with a peak in the second half of April. Earliest dates: SOUTH, March 23, 24, 29; NORTH, April 7, 9, 10. Latest dates: SOUTH, May 18, 20, 21, *28*; NORTH, none can be given because of breeding birds. *Fall migration period:* Late August through mid-November with the bulk of the migration in late September and early October. Earliest dates: NORTH, none can be given because of breeding birds; SOUTH, September 19, 22, 24. Latest dates: NORTH, October 5, 6, 8; SOUTH, November 10, 11, 14.

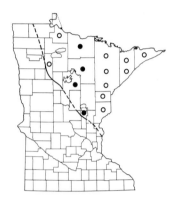

53. Winter Wren

Summer. Resident primarily in the north central and northeastern regions (see map 53); also reported occasionally in adjacent Pine and Mille Lacs counties. The species is now common in Itasca State Park. The southernmost breeding record is of a family group observed near Onamia. Two summer observations have been made as far south as Anoka and Washington counties (one in each county but in different years).

Winter. Casual winter visitant in the southeastern and east central regions as far north as Anoka County.

BEWICK'S WREN *Thryomanes bewickii*

Minnesota status. Casual. Migrant and summer resident.

Records. Although enough records are available to permit the description of migration periods and breeding areas for this species, there are long periods of time at irregular intervals when the species is not found in the state at all. There are no specimens or photographs on file.

Migration. Most records are from the spring migration in the southeastern and east central regions as far north as Anoka County and in adjacent Sibley, Rice, and Steele counties. There are also single April records for Aitkin and Lac qui Parle counties. *Spring migration period:* April. Earliest dates: March 30, April 1, 9. *Fall migration period:*

Very few records; all records are from the southeastern area of the state described above with the exception of one September record from Duluth. Latest dates: October 7, 31.

Summer. Seven records of family groups or nests from Fillmore, Hennepin, and Anoka counties and summer observations from Houston and Washington counties and from Sand Dunes State Forest in Sherburne County.

CAROLINA WREN *Thryothorus ludovicianus*

Minnesota status. Casual. Migrant, summer resident, and winter visitant.

Records. Although enough records are available to permit the description of migration periods and breeding and wintering areas, there are long periods of time at irregular intervals when the species is not found in the state at all. One published photograph (*Loon* 44:23–24); no specimens.

Migration. Almost all records during the migration seasons are from the Twin Cities area and the southeastern region; the exceptions are single records from Martin and Rice counties. `Spring migration period:* Mid-April through mid-May. Earliest dates: April 12, 19, 20. *Fall migration period:* Probably October and early November; very few dates. Latest dates: October 14, November 9, 12.

Summer. Five records of family groups or nests from Houston, Fillmore, Ramsey, and Washington counties and summer observations from Stearns and Hennepin counties.

Winter. Eight records of single birds attempting to winter in Martin, Pope, Hennepin, Ramsey, Dodge, Washington, Itasca, and Cass counties. Most of these birds remained in one area from late November into January and then disappeared, but one bird was observed through early February and another into March.

LONG-BILLED MARSH WREN
Telmatodytes palustris

Minnesota status. Regular. Migrant and summer resident; accidental in winter.

Migration. Common in spring and fall throughout most of the state; uncommon in the north central region; rare in the northeastern region. The species is usually encountered in its breeding habitat. *Spring migration period:* Late April through late May with a peak in mid-May. Earliest dates: SOUTH, March 22, 26, April 1, 14, 26, 30; NORTH, April 29, May 15, 16, 17. *Fall migration period:* Mid-August through mid-October. Latest dates: NORTH, October 5, 14, 17, November 10; SOUTH, October 15, 17, 21, November 2, 26.

Summer. Resident throughout the state; scarce in the

northeastern region and in the adjacent parts of the north central region where suitable cattail marshes are scarce.

Winter. One record on January 27, 1953, in Hennepin County.

SHORT-BILLED MARSH WREN
Cistothorus platensis

Minnesota status. Regular. Migrant and summer resident.

Migration. Common in spring and fall throughout most of the state; uncommon in the northeastern region. Most numerous in the western regions. The species is not usually encountered outside its breeding habitat during migration. *Spring migration period:* Late April through late May with the bulk of the migration in early and mid-May. Earliest dates: SOUTH, April *14*, *16*, 25, 27; NORTH, May 2, 5, 9. *Fall migration period:* Early August through mid-October with the bulk of the migration in the second half of September. Latest dates: NORTH, September 11, 17, 24; SOUTH, October 10, 11, 15, *26*.

Summer. Resident throughout the state. Least numerous in the northeastern region; most numerous in the western regions where prime habitat of grassy marshes and wet grassy uplands is abundant.

ROCK WREN *Salpinctes obsoletus*

Minnesota status. Accidental. Two spring records and two fall records.

Records. April.18, 1948, Salt Lake, Lac qui Parle County (*Flicker* 20:111); May 13, 1922, Pipestone County (MMNH #6269); October 28, 1962, near Dalton, Otter Tail County (*Flicker* 34:130); October 29, 1966, Grand Marais, Cook County (*Loon* 39:135).

Family MIMIDAE:
Mockingbirds and Thrashers

MOCKINGBIRD *Mimus polyglottos*

Minnesota status. Regular. Migrant, summer resident, and winter visitant.

Migration. Rare spring migrant and very rare fall migrant throughout the state. *Spring migration period:* Mid-April through late May with the bulk of the migration throughout May. Earliest dates: SOUTH, April *6*, 14, 19; NORTH, April *20*, 30, May 2, 4. *Fall migration period:* Late August through late November with most records between October 30 and November 25. Latest dates: None can be given because of wintering birds.

Summer. The first state record is from June 1, 1883, in

Otter Tail County, but the species occurred casually in summer as well as during migration and winter until about 1950. Since then it has become regular but rare with summer observations from sixteen counties in all regions except the southwest. The first nesting record was at Royalton, Morrison County, in 1968 (*Loon* 41:128), and birds have continued to nest there; this site remains the only confirmed breeding location, although local residents report that the species nests at Lutsen and Tofte in Cook County.

Winter. Very rare winter visitant in the eastern and central regions as far north as Cook County; casual in the western regions. Most overwintering attempts are unsuccessful; the birds die or disappear in January. One bird survived until mid-February in St. Louis County, and four birds survived until spring in the Twin Cities area.

GRAY CATBIRD (Catbird) *Dumetella carolinensis*

Minnesota status. Regular. Migrant and summer resident; accidental in winter.

Migration. Common spring and fall migrant throughout most of the state; rare in the heavily forested areas south of the Canadian border. During migration it is difficult to distinguish the resident birds from the migrants, and no concentrations have been reported. *Spring migration period:* Late April through late May with the bulk of the migration during the last three weeks of May. Earliest dates: SOUTH, April 24, 25, 26; NORTH, April 29, May 2, 3. *Fall migration period:* Probably from early August through late October with the bulk of the migration in September. Latest dates: NORTH, September 28, 29, 30, October *8, 13, 26, 27*, November *5*; SOUTH, October 20, 22, 24, November *9* (five records from November 17 to November 30 probably represent wintering birds).

Summer. Resident throughout the state. Widespread and numerous except in the heavy coniferous forests where the species occurs only in brushy openings.

Winter. There are ten late November and December records for the southern half of the state and two winter records for the northern half. One bird appeared during November, 1971, and remained at a feeder in Bloomington, Hennepin County, until March 2, 1972 (*Loon* 44:93–94). There are only two January records, and stragglers are generally not successful in overwintering in the area.

BROWN THRASHER *Toxostoma rufum*

Minnesota status. Regular. Migrant and summer resident; casual in winter.

Migration. Common spring and fall migrant in areas where. the species is resident; no concentrations reported. Less numerous in fall than in spring. *Spring migration period:* Early April through mid-May; most birds do not arrive until late April. Earliest dates: SOUTH, April 3, 6, 8; NORTH, April *7*, *11*, 22, 25, 26. *Fall migration period:* August through October; only stragglers are seen after early October. Latest dates: NORTH, October 22, 29, 31, November *10*; SOUTH, October 25, 27, 28, November *10* (later November dates are probably for wintering birds).

Summer. Resident throughout the state; absent from large areas of dense forest (mixed conifers). The species seems to occur in logged openings in the forest but not in natural ones.

Winter. There are forty-two records for the three winter months. Most records represent birds trying to overwinter at feeding stations from Cook County southward. The majority of these birds are not successful, but some have survived, including two as far north as Duluth. The overwintering birds usually arrive in very late October or during the first half of November and leave in late March or early April.

Family TURDIDAE:
Thrushes, Solitaires, and Bluebirds

AMERICAN ROBIN (Robin) *Turdus migratorius*

Minnesota status. Regular. Migrant, summer resident, and winter visitant.

Migration. Abundant spring and fall migrant throughout the state. *Spring migration period:* Early March through early May with the bulk of the migration from late March through late April. Earliest dates: SOUTH, early March to mid-March; NORTH, mid-March to late March; no exact dates can be given because of wintering birds. *Fall migration period:* Late August through late November with the bulk of the migration from late September through late October. Latest dates: None can be given because of wintering birds.

Summer. Resident throughout the state from the prairie to the dense northern forests, nesting in heavily wooded areas as well as around human habitations.

Winter. Rare to uncommon winter visitant throughout most of the state; occasionally common in the Twin Cities area and in the southeastern region; frequently abundant along the North Shore of Lake Superior. In the Lake Superior area abundance is dependent on the berry crop of the mountain ash (*Sorbus americana*).

VARIED THRUSH *Ixoreus naevius*

Minnesota status. Regular. Migrant and winter visitant.

Migration and winter. Very rare winter visitant. Although the species may occur anywhere in the state, most reports are from the eastern regions, reflecting human population centers. Most observations are of birds wintering at feeders; many of these birds do not survive, but some have successfully overwintered as far north as Lake County. There are a few reports of birds away from feeders in spring, fall, and midwinter, especially on the North Shore of Lake Superior. Before 1960 this bird occurred only casually in the state and was first reported at Duluth between February and April in 1941. There are two specimens in the Bell Museum of Natural History and one specimen in the Science Museum of Minnesota (St. Paul Arts and Science Center). Because little information is available, no migration periods can be defined. Earliest dates: NORTH, October *16*, *22*, November 22, 25, 26; SOUTH, October *30*, November 13, 20. Latest dates: SOUTH, February 30, April 6, May *24*; NORTH, April 4, 7, 14, May *7*.

WOOD THRUSH *Hylocichla mustelina*

Minnesota status. Regular. Migrant and summer resident.

Migration. Uncommon in the southeast quarter of the state and rare elsewhere in the spring; almost all birds seen are on breeding territories. The species is less numerous in the fall when the local birds gradually leave the nesting areas. There is no population north of the state. *Spring migration period:* Late April through late May. Earliest dates: SOUTH, April *9*, 23, 24, 27; NORTH, May 8, 14, 15. *Fall migration period:* Mid-August through early October; almost all birds leave by mid-September. Latest dates: NORTH, September 9 (only date); SOUTH, October 12, 14, 15.

Summer. Resident throughout the state except in the heavy coniferous forests adjacent to the Canadian border. Nests have been found as far north as Maple Lake, Polk County, and Deer River, Itasca County, and singing males have been heard in the northern hardwood forests near Lake Superior in Cook County. The species has never been reported from northern Lake County, northern and central St. Louis County, Koochiching County, Beltrami County, or Lake of the Woods County. It is most numerous in the southeastern part of the state from Hennepin County southward and eastward; to the north and west of this area the species is scarce. On the prairie, for instance, suitable habitat is lacking. Furthermore, the species does not seem to occur in the forested central region, despite the existence of suitable woodland habitat, and in the northern half of the state it does not regularly occupy all areas of the maple-basswood forest which seems to be its preferred habitat. Roberts (1932) did not believe it could occur in the coniferous half of the state, and he discounted many northern records; as a result, the recent records from that area are possibly an expansion of our knowledge rather than an expansion of the range.

HERMIT THRUSH *Catharus guttatus*

Minnesota status. Regular. Migrant and summer resident.
Migration. Common spring migrant throughout the state, becoming abundant when adverse weather halts migration. Common to uncommon fall migrant throughout the state. *Spring migration period:* Late March through late May with the bulk of the migration from mid-April through early May. Earliest dates: SOUTH, March *17*, 24, 26, 28; NORTH, March *23*, April 6, 7, 8. Latest dates: SOUTH, May 17, 22, 23; NORTH, none can be given because of breeding birds. *Fall migration period:* Early September through very early November with the bulk of the migration from late September through mid-October. Earliest dates: NORTH, none can be given because of breeding birds; SOUTH, September 3 (only date). Latest dates: NORTH, October 26, 27, 28, November *11*; SOUTH, October 29, November 3, 4, *10*, *20*, December *9*, *11*.
Summer. Resident throughout the northeastern and north central regions and adjacent Roseau, Mille Lacs, and Pine counties (see map 54). There are breeding records as far west as Warroad, Roseau County, and Itasca State Park, Clearwater County, and as far south as Onamia, Mille Lacs County, and Sturgeon Lake, Pine County. Although old single records exist for Otter Tail, Isanti, and Washington counties, the status of the species there as a breeding bird has never been established; no modern records are available from these counties.
Winter. One record: One bird at a feeder in Duluth from December 17, 1973, to at least February 24, 1974 (J. C. Green et al.).

54. Hermit Thrush

SWAINSON'S THRUSH *Catharus ustulatus*

Minnesota status. Regular. Migrant and summer resident.
Migration. Common spring and fall migrant throughout the state. *Spring migration period:* Late April through early June with most of the migration taking place between May 5 and May 25. Earliest dates: SOUTH, April 22, 23, 25; NORTH, April *22*, *27*, May 3, 4, 5. Latest dates: SOUTH, June 1, 2, *8*; NORTH, none can be given because of breeding birds. *Fall migration period:* Late July through late October

with the bulk of the migration from late August through late September. Earliest dates: NORTH, none can be given because of breeding birds; SOUTH, July 24, 27, August 8. Latest dates: NORTH, October 20, 22, 25, *29*, November *11*; SOUTH, October 16, 18, 20, *29*, November *13*, *24*.

Summer. Resident throughout the northeastern and north central regions and the adjacent counties in the northwestern region (see map 55). In the northwestern region the only modern records are from eastern Marshall County, although there is a nineteenth-century nesting record from St. Vincent, Kittson County. A number of old summer observations are available from Pine County, but the present status of the species is unknown.

Winter. One bird attempted to winter at a feeder in St. Paul during 1973; it was first seen on November 23 and was found dead on December 30 (*Loon* 46:42).

55. Swainson's Thrush

GRAY-CHEEKED THRUSH *Catharus minimus*

Minnesota status. Regular. Migrant.
Migration. Uncommon spring and fall migrant throughout the state. More numerous in spring than in fall. *Spring migration period:* Mid-April through early June; most of the birds pass through the state in May. Earliest dates: SOUTH, April 18, 19, 20; NORTH, April 26, 27, May 1. Latest dates: SOUTH, June 1, 3, 4; NORTH, June 1, 5, 9. *Fall migration period:* Mid-August through mid-October with the bulk of the migration from early September through early October. Earliest dates: NORTH, August 16, 17, 26; SOUTH, August 22, September 2, 6. Lates dates: NORTH, October 9, 10, 14, *28*, *29*–November *5*; SOUTH, October 8, 9, 14.

VEERY *Catharus fuscescens*

Minnesota status. Regular. Migrant and summer resident.
Migration. Common spring migrant and uncommon fall migrant throughout the state. *Spring migration period:* Very late April through late May; most birds do not arrive until the second week of May. Earliest dates: SOUTH, April *18*, 28, 29; NORTH, April *30*, May 3, 5, 6. *Fall migration period:* Late July through late September; only stragglers remain after early September. Latest dates: NORTH, September 19, 20, *27*, *28*; SOUTH, September 21, 23, 25, *29*, October *22*.

Summer. Resident throughout the state; very scarce and local south and west of a line between Washington, Stearns, and Otter Tail counties. There are breeding records as far south as the Des Moines River, Jackson County (1902). The modern status of the species in the southwestern quarter of the state is poorly known. Only summer observations (no breeding records) are available from Pope and Lyon counties. In the southeastern region and in wooded portions of the adjacent counties the species is largely restricted to a few areas like Nerstrand Woods in Rice County, Forestville Woods in Fillmore County, and the Whitewater area in Wabasha and Winona counties. The Veery has never been very numerous in the southern regions and is probably even less numerous there now, owing to the destruction of wooded habitat.

EASTERN BLUEBIRD *Sialia sialis*

Minnesota status. Regular. Migrant and summer resident; casual in winter.

Migration. Common spring migrant throughout most of the state; usually uncommon in the northeastern and north central regions. Common to locally abundant fall migrant throughout the state. Numbers fluctuate yearly. The species may have been more abundant in the past. *Spring migration period:* Early March through mid-May with the bulk of the migration in April. Earliest dates: SOUTH, before 1940, February 22, 23, 27; since 1940, March 7, 8, 10; NORTH, March *15*, *23*, April 7, 8, 10. *Fall migration period:* Early September through late November with stragglers through December; the peak of the migration is from late September through late October. Latest dates: NORTH, November 20, 23; SOUTH, none can be given because stragglers linger into early winter.

Summer. Resident throughout the state wherever suitable habitat and nesting sites are available. Not found in the dense northern forests and quite scarce on the open prairie.

Winter. Very rare in early winter in the southeastern quarter of the state (from St. Cloud southward and eastward); casual along the North Shore of Lake Superior; accidental elsewhere. In late winter, after early January, casual in the lower Mississippi River valley and along the North Shore of Lake Superior; unknown elsewhere. There are only three records of birds wintering into February.

MOUNTAIN BLUEBIRD *Sialia currucoides*

Minnesota status. Casual. Migrant; two winter records.

Records. There are eight spring records between March 15 and April 7 in Sherburne, Lac qui Parle, Beltrami, Mower, Clay, Aitkin, Lyon, and Wadena counties; six records are of single birds, the other two are of pairs. Two fall records: one bird in Becker County (September, no date); a pair in Hennepin County (October 14). Two winter records, both from the North Shore of Lake Superior: three birds at Duluth, November 22, 1942, to March 16, 1943; one bird in Cook County, January 20–24, 1971. Two specimens (a pair) at St. Cloud State College; one specimen at the Bell Museum of Natural History (MMNH #25706).

TOWNSEND'S SOLITAIRE *Myadestes townsendi*

Minnesota status. Casual. Migrant and winter visitant.
Records. The twenty-five records of this bird indicate that it is a casual fall migrant and winter visitant, mostly in the southern half of the state. The only records for the northern half of the state are four records (none from midwinter) from the northeastern region. Six of the records are of individual birds, each of which stayed at the same location for several weeks; three of the birds are known to have over-wintered, departing in the second half of April. One specimen at St. John's College, Collegeville; one specimen in the Bell Museum of Natural History (MMNH #5771). Earliest dates: October 11, 26, November 7. Latest dates: April 20, 26, 27, May 4.

Family SYLVIIDAE: Gnatcatchers and Kinglets

BLUE-GRAY GNATCATCHER *Polioptila caerulea*

Minnesota status. Regular. Migrant and summer resident.
Migration. Almost all birds seen during the migration seasons are on breeding territories; abundance varies from rare to common. *Spring migration period:* Late April through May. Earliest dates: April *18, 23, 25, 27. Fall migration period:* Birds gradually depart from the state in late July and August. Latest dates: August 29, September 1, 5.
Summer. Resident in the southeastern part of the state (see map 56). Breeding birds have been recorded as far north as Grand Lake, Stearns County, and Copas, Washington County. Recent observations during spring migration have also been made in Chisago County; Royalton, Morrison County; Collegeville, Stearns County; and Lake Shetek, Murray County (1900). These observations may indicate possible breeding locations. There are summer records along the Minnesota River to St. Peter and also a single summer observation from Fairmont, Martin County (1942).

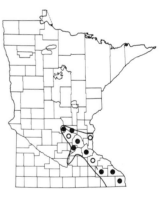

56. Blue-gray Gnatcatcher

GOLDEN-CROWNED KINGLET *Regulus satrapa*

Minnesota status. Regular. Migrant, summer resident, and winter visitant.
Migration. Common spring and fall migrant throughout the state. *Spring migration period:* Mid-March through mid-May with the bulk of the migration from late March through late April. Earliest dates: SOUTH, none can be given because

57. Golden-crowned Kinglet

of wintering birds; NORTH, March 14, 16, 19. Latest dates: SOUTH, May 9, 10–14, 16; NORTH, none can be given because of breeding birds. *Fall migration period:* Early September through early December with most of the migration from late September through early November. Earliest dates: NORTH, none can be given because of breeding birds; SOUTH, September 19, 21, 22. Latest dates: NORTH, November 21, 22, 25–28; SOUTH, none can be given because of wintering birds.

Summer. Resident primarily in the northern regions but also sparingly in the eastern part of the central regions (see map 57). There are summer observations in the north as far west as Agassiz National Wildlife Refuge and Tamarac National Wildlife Refuge and breeding records as far south as Onamia, Mille Lacs County, and Lake Vadnais, Ramsey County.

Winter. Uncommon winter visitant in the southern half of the state; rare to casual in the northern half.

RUBY-CROWNED KINGLET *Regulus calendula*

Minnesota status. Regular. Migrant and summer resident; accidental in winter.

Migration. Common spring and fall migrant throughout the state. *Spring migration period:* Late March through late May with the bulk of the migration from mid-April through early May. Earliest dates: SOUTH, March *3*, *12*, 21, 22, 23; NORTH, March *11*, *19*, April 1, 3, 9. Latest dates: SOUTH, May 20, 22, 23, *29*, June *3*; NORTH, none can be given because of breeding birds. *Fall migration period:* Late August through mid-November with the bulk of the migration from mid-September through mid-October. Earliest dates: NORTH, none can be given because of breeding birds; SOUTH, August 20, 24, 31. Latest dates: NORTH, October 28, 29, November 5, *15*, *22*; SOUTH, November 15, 16, 18, *24*, December *4*, *9–17*.

58. Ruby-crowned Kinglet

Summer. Regular resident in the northeastern and north central regions. The species has been observed as far west as Itasca State Park and eastern Marshall County (see map 58); it is more numerous in the former region than in the latter. A nesting record from St. Cloud, Stearns County, indicates that the species occasionally breeds outside this area, and single summer observations have been recorded in Anoka and Dakota counties. It is strange that this species with its distinctive song was completely overlooked as a summer resident in Minnesota until the 1940s.

Winter. The species has been reported six times during the Audubon Christmas Count, and stragglers may occasionally linger until very early January, especially in the southern half of the state.

Family MOTACILLIDAE: Pipits

WATER PIPIT *Anthus spinoletta*

Minnesota status. Regular. Migrant.

Migration. Uncommon to occasionally common spring migrant and common to occasionally abundant fall migrant throughout the state. *Spring migration period:* Very late March through late May with the bulk of the migration from late April through mid-May. Earliest dates: SOUTH, March 23, 30, April 1, 4; NORTH, April *19*, May 4, 6, 7. Latest dates: SOUTH, May 22, 25, 28; NORTH, May 24, 27, 31. *Fall migration period:* Mid-September through early November with the bulk of the migration from late September through late October. Earliest dates: NORTH, September *7*, *8*, 13, 14, 16; SOUTH, September *12*, 16, 19, 20. Latest dates: NORTH, November 2, 5; SOUTH, November 1, 5, *14*, *16*, *29*.

SPRAGUE'S PIPIT *Anthus spragueii*

Minnesota status. Regular. Migrant and summer resident.

Migration. Very rare migrant throughout the western prairie regions; accidental elsewhere. *Spring migration period:* Mid-April through early May (possibly later). Earliest dates: April 11, 25, 27. Latest dates (beyond breeding areas): May 1 (only date). *Fall migration period:* September. Earliest dates (beyond breeding areas): September 7 (only date). Latest dates: September 23, 28, October *15*.

Summer. Resident on the prairie in the northwestern region. The species has been reported in summer as far south as Foxhome, Wilkin County. There are nesting records from Kittson County (1929), Pennington County (1933), Marshall County (1937), and Clay County (1962). Since all recent investigations have been from a specific locality in Clay County, the abundance of the species as a breeding bird on the prairie is not known; but it is probably much less common than it was before intensive cultivation developed in the Red River Valley.

Family BOMBYCILLIDAE: Waxwings

BOHEMIAN WAXWING *Bombycilla garrulus*

Minnesota status. Regular. Migrant and winter visitant; accidental in summer.

Migration. Erratic in abundance and distribution. The species may occur anywhere in the state, but it is present most regularly in the northern regions. In numbers the species varies from rare to abundant. *Fall migration period:* No regular period of influx; small flocks are usually seen in northern Minnesota in early November. Earliest dates:

NORTH, October *21*, *25*, 29, 30, 31; SOUTH, October *9*, 24, November 10, 11. *Spring migration period:* No regular period of departure; most flocks leave by mid-April, but stragglers may remain into May. Latest dates: SOUTH, May 8, 12, 16; NORTH, May 10, 16.

Winter. Regular winter visitant; numbers vary yearly from rare to abundant. The species may occur anywhere in the state, but it is most regular and numerous in the northeast and least so in the southwest. Peak numbers can be found any time from December through March.

Summer. Two records: July 14, 1945, at Many Point Lake in Becker County; June 20, 1972, on State Highway 6 in Cass County.

CEDAR WAXWING *Bombycilla cedrorum*

Minnesota status. Regular. Migrant, summer resident, and winter visitant.

Migration. Common to abundant spring and fall migrant throughout the state. Spring flocks usually contain fewer than a hundred birds, but fall and winter flocks may be much larger. *Spring migration period:* Little regularity has been noted in the movements of the species; arrivals and peak numbers vary from year to year, and it is difficult to distinguish migrants from winter visitants. Following winters in which the species has been absent from an area, however, it has been noted that the migrant flocks usually arrive between mid-May and mid-June. No dates can be given. *Fall migration period:* From sometime in August throughout the fall. No dates can be given because of wintering birds.

Summer. Resident throughout the wooded portions of the state. The status of the species on the prairie is uncertain. Flocks are found in prairie towns during the summer, but these seem to be nonbreeding birds. There are only two breeding records for the west central, southwestern, and south central regions: Jackson County (1898); Lac qui Parle County (1948).

Winter. Common to occasionally abundant visitant anywhere in the state, but its presence in any area is irregular and its numbers vary sharply.

Family LANIIDAE: Shrikes

NORTHERN SHRIKE *Lanius excubitor*

Minnesota status. Regular. Migrant and winter visitant.

Migration. Uncommon spring and fall migrant anywhere in the state. *Fall migration period:* Early October into winter with most arrivals in late October and early

November. Earliest dates: NORTH, September *14*, October 5, 8; SOUTH, October 6, 8, 9. *Spring migration period:* Probably late winter through mid-April; most birds depart in late March or during the first week in April. Latest dates: SOUTH, April 15, 19; NORTH, April 19, 21, *30*.

Winter. Uncommon winter visitant throughout the state. Most numerous in the northern regions. Numbers vary from year to year.

LOGGERHEAD SHRIKE *Lanius ludovicianus*

Minnesota status. Regular. Migrant and summer resident; accidental in winter.

Migration. Uncommon during the migration seasons throughout most of the state; rare in the north central and northeastern regions. Most birds seen are on their breeding territories. *Spring migration period:* Mid-March through April; most arrivals occur in late March and April. Earliest dates: SOUTH, March *7*, *9*, *11*, 15, 17; NORTH, March *18*, 24, 27, April 3. *Fall migration period:* Probably from sometime in August through late October; almost all birds leave by late September. Latest dates: NORTH, October 7, 13; SOUTH, October 22, 29, November *24*, *25*.

Summer. Resident throughout the state but very scarce in the northeastern region and in adjacent counties in the north central region. The species has nested as far north as Chisholm, St. Louis County.

Winter. Two records: December 10, 1967, Nobles County; December 30, 1967, Hennepin County.

Family STURNIDAE: Starlings

STARLING *Sturnus vulgaris*

Minnesota status. Regular; introduced. Primarily permanent resident; also regular migrant.

Distribution. Permanent resident throughout the state. This European species, which was introduced in the state of New York in 1890, made its first appearance in Minnesota in 1929 in Fillmore County. By the end of the 1930s it was widely distributed throughout the state, but it did not become abundant until the 1940s. Now it is found as a breeding species everywhere in the state, including wilderness areas like the Boundary Waters Canoe Area, but it reaches its greatest abundance in farming areas.

Migration. Some birds remain in the state all year around. During migration large flocks are seen, especially in late fall, but unfortunately people do not pay much attention to this pest species and as a result there is not enough data to describe the migration movements.

Family VIREONIDAE: Vireos

WHITE-EYED VIREO *Vireo griseus*

Minnesota status. Hypothetical.

Records. Two observations, both of single birds: May 23–24, 1965, Wacouta, Goodhue County (*Loon* 37:149); July 31, 1941, St. Cloud, Stearns County (*Loon* 37:52).

BELL'S VIREO *Vireo bellii*

59. Bell's Vireo

Minnesota status. Regular. Migrant and summer resident.

Migration. Rare spring and fall migrant in the breeding range in the southeastern quarter of the state; most birds seen are on nesting territories. The few spring migration records from outside the known summer range may represent undiscovered breeding locations: Frog Lake, Stevens County; Albert Lea, Freeborn County; Victoria, Carver County; Christmas Lake, Hennepin County. *Spring migration period:* Throughout May. Earliest dates: May 5, 7, 13. *Fall migration period:* Birds gradually leave the nesting grounds in July and August. Latest dates: August 15, 21.

Summer. Resident primarily along the Mississippi River in the southeastern quarter of the state (see map 59). In June, 1972, a singing male was collected in Rock County (MMNH #26035). Very scarce except in Winona and Houston counties; one May record and one June record from St. Cloud. The northernmost nesting location on record is Fort Snelling, Hennepin County.

YELLOW-THROATED VIREO *Vireo flavifrons*

60. Yellow-throated Vireo

Minnesota status. Regular. Migrant and summer resident.

Migration. Uncommon spring and fall migrant throughout most of the state; casual in the northeastern region and in the adjacent counties of the north central region. *Spring migration period:* Late April through early June; the bulk of the migration is in early and mid-May. Earliest dates: SOUTH, April 27, 29, 30; NORTH, May 9, 14, 17. *Fall migration period:* Probably late July through early October; the bulk of the migration is from late August through mid-September. Latest dates: NORTH, September 6, 13, 15; SOUTH, October 3, 4, 5, *19, 26*.

Summer. Resident throughout most of the state except the northeastern region and the adjacent counties in the north central region (see map 60). In the western part of the state breeding evidence has been found as far north as Pennington County (one nest), and there have been summer observations as far north as the Canadian border (Roseau, Kittson, and Lake of the Woods counties). In the northeastern quarter of the state breeding evidence has been found only as far north as St. Croix State Park, Pine County, and Bay Lake, Crow Wing County, with a few summer observations as far to the northeast as Duluth.

SOLITARY VIREO *Vireo solitarius*

Minnesota status. Regular. Migrant and summer resident.
Migration. Uncommon to occasionally common spring and fall migrant throughout the state. *Spring migration period:* Late April through early June; the bulk of the migration is from early to mid-May. Earliest dates: SOUTH, April 21, 25, 29; NORTH, April *26*, May 3, 4, 6. Latest dates: SOUTH, June 2, 4; NORTH, none can be given because of breeding birds. *Fall migration period:* Probably early August through mid-October; the bulk of the migration is from late August through early October. Earliest dates: NORTH, none can be given because of breeding birds; SOUTH, August 22, 23, 24. Latest dates: NORTH, October 3, 6, *11*, *17*, *21*; SOUTH, October 14, 15, 17, *23*, *27*.

61. Solitary Vireo

Summer. Resident throughout most of the northeastern and north central regions (see map 61). There are summer observations as far south as Cromwell, Carlton County, and Emily, Crow Wing County. The western boundary of the range is poorly known. A nineteenth-century breeding record exists for Detroit Township, Becker County, but the present range boundary seems to be Itasca State Park, Clearwater County.

RED-EYED VIREO *Vireo olivaceus*

Minnesota status. Regular. Migrant and summer resident.
Migration. Common spring and fall migrant throughout the state. *Spring migration period:* Early May through early June; the bulk of the migration is in the second half of May. Earliest dates: SOUTH, May 1, 3, 4; NORTH, May 7, 13, 14. *Fall migration period:* Probably from late July and early August through mid-October. The bulk of the migration is in the first half of September; it is very unusual to see an individual of this species after the first week in October. Latest dates: NORTH, September 27, 28, October 3, *8*, *13*; SOUTH, October 13, 14, 18, *26*, November *6*.
Summer. Resident throughout the state. The Red-eyed Vireo is the most widespread and numerous vireo species.

PHILADELPHIA VIREO *Vireo philadelphicus*

Minnesota status. Regular. Migrant and summer resident.
Migration. Uncommon spring and fall migrant throughout the state. *Spring migration period:* Early May through early June; the bulk of the migration is in the second half of May. Earliest dates: SOUTH, May 5, 6; NORTH, May 12, 14, 15.

62. Philadelphia Vireo

Latest dates: SOUTH, June 2, 3, 4; NORTH, none can be given because of breeding birds. *Fall migration period:* Mid-August through early October; the bulk of the migration is in early and mid-September. Earliest dates: NORTH, none can be given because of breeding birds; SOUTH, July *30*, August *11*, 18, 19, 20. Latest dates: NORTH, October 9, 11, 12; SOUTH, October 5, 6, 9, *29*.

Summer. Resident primarily in the northeastern region as far south as Duluth (see map 62). Only two records outside this region: fledglings being fed by parents at Many Point Lake, Becker County, in 1961; one bird banded near Little Falls, Morrison County, on June 16, 1966. The species is also scarce in the northeast, and it may be overlooked when present because its song is similar to that of the Red-eyed Vireo.

WARBLING VIREO *Vireo gilvus*

Minnesota status. Regular. Migrant and summer resident.
Migration. In the spring common throughout most of the state; uncommon to rare in the northeastern region and in the adjacent counties of the north central region (most birds seen at this season are on breeding territories). Uncommon to rare in the fall with a gradual exodus from the nesting grounds. *Spring migration period:* Throughout May; the bulk of the migration takes place in the middle of May. Earliest dates: SOUTH, April 29, 30, May 1; NORTH, May 8, 11, 12. *Fall migration period:* Probably from late July through late September; most birds leave by early September. Latest dates: NORTH, September 20, 21, 22, *27*; SOUTH, September 26, 27, October *2*.

Summer. Resident throughout the state; quite scarce north of Duluth and in the adjacent counties in the north central region. Summer records are available from almost all counties, but there are no breeding records from northeast of a line between Duluth and Cass and Polk counties.

Family PARULIDAE: Wood Warblers

BLACK-AND-WHITE WARBLER *Mniotilta varia*

Minnesota status. Regular. Migrant and summer resident.
Migration. Common spring and fall migrant throughout the state. *Spring migration period:* Late April through early June with a peak during the first two weeks of May. Earliest dates: SOUTH, April *15*, *17*, 25, 26; NORTH, April *26*, 30, 31, May 2. Latest dates: SOUTH, June 3 (only date); NORTH, none can be given because of breeding birds. *Fall migration period:* Early August through mid-October with the bulk of the migration from late August through late September.

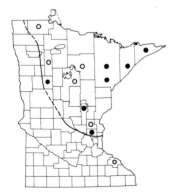

63. Black-and-white Warbler (1910)

Earliest dates: NORTH, none can be given because of breeding birds; SOUTH, August 9, 12, 17. Latest dates: NORTH, October 8, 9, 11, *19*, November *10*; SOUTH, October 10, 11, 12, *23*, *29*.

Summer. Resident primarily in the northeastern and north central regions (see map 63). In the central regions the species occurs east of the Mississippi River but is quite scarce south and west of Mille Lacs Lake. It formerly occurred in the southeastern region and in the Red River Valley in the northwestern region, but there have been no summer reports from these areas in over fifty years.

PROTHONOTARY WARBLER *Protonotaria citrea*

Minnesota status. Regular. Migrant and summer resident.
Migration. Rare in spring with most observations on or near breeding grounds. Spring vagrants have been reported from Duluth, Agassiz National Wildlife Refuge, and Swift County. Very rare in fall; all observations have been made within the breeding range. *Spring migration period:* Early to late May. Earliest dates: April *11*, May 2, 3. *Fall migration period:* Mid-July through mid-August. Latest dates: August 15, 17, 21, September *3*.
Summer. Resident in the southeastern region and along the Mississippi, Rum, and St. Croix rivers in the central regions (see map 64). Although the species has been reported as far north as Collegeville and Milaca in the spring, no breeding evidence has yet been obtained for Stearns or Mille Lacs counties.

64. Prothonotary Warbler

WORM-EATING WARBLER *Helmitheros vermivorus*

Minnesota status. Casual. Spring migrant; one fall record.
Records. Casual spring migrant in the southern part of the state. There are eight records from the Twin Cities area and one record from Lac qui Parle County. The records range from April 28 through May 22; most of the dates are during the first two weeks of May. One specimen was collected on April 30, 1962, in Hennepin County (MMNH #17835). The fall record was a bird seen near Garrison, Crow Wing County, on November 18, 1973 (*Loon* 46:35–36).

GOLDEN-WINGED WARBLER *Vermivora chrysoptera*

Minnesota status. Regular. Migrant and summer resident.
Migration. Uncommon spring migrant in the forested part of the state as far north as Pine and Hubbard counties; rare to casual north and east of Pine and Hubbard counties; also rare in the unforested areas of the state. Rare fall migrant

anywhere in the state. *Spring migration period:* Early May through early June with a peak on about May 10. Earliest dates: SOUTH, April 30, May 1, 3; NORTH, May 5, 9. *Fall migration period:* Probably from late July through late September. Latest dates: NORTH, September 12, 24, 28; SOUTH, September 25, 30, October 2.

Summer. Resident primarily in the central part of the state (see map 65). There is some indication that the range of this species has changed in historical times. Because of the interest in the species and its congener, the Blue-winged Warbler, with which it is known to hybridize, the available information about the breeding range of the Golden-winged Warbler will be discussed in full. (Since all the easily observable hybrids come from within the range of the Blue-winged Warbler, the records of hybrids will be noted in the discussion of that species.)

It is difficult to document any change in the range of the Golden-winged Warbler because ornithological exploration has been uneven, with the result that small local colonies may have been overlooked. Roberts, from his experience with the Golden-winged Warbler in Stearns and Hennepin counties, regarded it as a bird of the deciduous forests. He found nests in Hennepin County, but the species apparently had disappeared from that area before the turn of the century. In *The Birds of Minnesota* (1932) he implied that the species occurred during the breeding season throughout the southeastern part of the state, but his information seems to be based only on the notes of J. C. Hvoslef from Lanesboro, Fillmore County. (Hvoslef's notes, written in Norwegian, are filed in the University of Minnesota Archives.) No one else at the time reported the presence of the species in areas south of Hennepin County during the breeding season. The translation of Hvoslef's notes will be quoted in full to indicate the slimness of the evidence: "Shot one, male, June 15, 1888. This is the fourth observed at Lanesboro." "May 14, '89 (2). This is a rare bird here, still I have seen it several times both in Apr. and fall." It is strange that in 1889 Hvoslef did not mention the bird he shot during the previous summer; perhaps the June date is in error.

The only evidence for Golden-winged Warblers in summer in southeastern Minnesota became available after *The Birds of Minnesota* was published and does not include any description of the birds. A male and a female were seen together, and later a male was seen carrying food near Lamoille, Winona County, in 1934. The only additional evidence is a note in a letter dated August 24, 1954, from

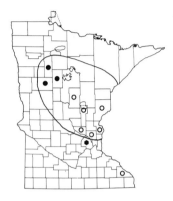

65. Golden-winged Warbler

F. R. Keating: "Golden Wings nesting in the immediate vicinity of Rochester [Olmsted County]."

Some evidence suggests that the Golden-winged Warbler may have expanded its range to the north during this century. Until the 1940s there were only three records from Itasca Park, all of them reported verbally to Roberts; the first record was in 1919. The species is now found regularly in Itasca State Park. In Pine County, where the species is also quite numerous now, Surber did not report it at all during the summers of 1918 and 1919. All the summer specimens in the Bell Museum of Natural History are from the north central region of the state and, with one exception, were collected in the last twenty years.

BLUE-WINGED WARBLER *Vermivora pinus*

Minnesota status. Regular. Migrant and summer resident.
Migration. Birds seen within the breeding range are usually on breeding territory (see map 66). Rare spring migrant and casual fall migrant outside the breeding range. These birds may be migrants that have overshot their summer range, or they may be representatives of undiscovered colonies. Various locations where the species has been reported outside the known breeding range are listed here in the hope that observers will be alert for evidence of further range expansion: Hennepin County (Christmas Lake, Minneapolis); Anoka County (Carlos Avery Wildlife Refuge); Wright County (Cokato); Sherburne County (near St. Cloud); Stearns County (St. Cloud); Blue Earth County (near Cambia); Rice County (Northfield); Lyon County (fall record). One unsubstantiated record from Duluth has been published (*Jack-Pine Warbler* 36:56). *Spring migration period:* Late April through early June. Earliest dates: April 27, 30. *Fall migration period:* Probably late July through early September. Latest dates: September 6, 7, 10.

66. Blue-winged Warbler

Summer. Resident in the southeastern region and in Dakota and Washington counties (see map 66). This represents an expansion from the breeding range in Fillmore County and probably Houston County at the turn of the century. During the 1920s migrants were reported in Goodhue and Winona counties, but the first evidence of breeding did not come until around 1940 for Winona and Washington counties. Apparently the major expansion took place in the late 1940s, but because of the increase in the amount of ornithological exploration at that time it is difficult to be certain of this. Since a number of migrants have been reported recently (during the 1960s) from the Twin Cities to St. Cloud, evidence of breeding should be looked for in that area.

Since the expansion of the Blue-winged Warbler population in Minnesota, hybrids between the Blue-winged Warbler and the Golden-winged Warbler have been observed in the state. All but one of the breeding specimens of the two species are from the 1940s and 1950s; according to L. L. Short (personal communication), the specimens are not phenotypically pure, although the amount of hybridization is not great. Observations of the obvious hybrids — the Lawrence's Warbler and the Brewster's Warbler — have been reported regularly since the mid-1960s, mostly from Hennepin, Goodhue, and Winona counties.

TENNESSEE WARBLER *Vermivora peregrina*

67. Tennessee Warbler

Minnesota status. Regular. Migrant and summer resident.
Migration. Abundant spring and fall migrant throughout the state. *Spring migration period:* Late April through mid-June with a peak in the south between May 8 and May 25 and in the north between May 15 and May 30. Earliest dates: SOUTH, April 28, 29; NORTH, May 7, 8. Latest dates: SOUTH, June 4, 6; NORTH (urban Duluth), June 16, 17. *Fall migration period:* Mid-July through mid-October with a peak in late August and early September. Earliest dates: NORTH (urban Duluth; Morrison County), July 16, 17, 18; SOUTH, July 21, 23, 31. Latest dates: NORTH, October 10, 12, 13, *19*; SOUTH, October 24, 26, 29.
Summer. Resident in the northeastern and north central regions as far south as Duluth and Itasca State Park (see map 67). The species is scarce throughout most of this area except along the Canadian border in Cook County, northern Lake County, and northern St. Louis County.

ORANGE-CROWNED WARBLER
Vermivora celata

Minnesota status. Regular. Migrant; accidental summer visitant.
Migration. Common spring and fall migrant throughout the state. Banding data seem to indicate that the species is more numerous in the western regions than in the eastern regions. *Spring migration period:* Mid-April through late May with a peak in late April and early May. Earliest dates: SOUTH, April *11*, 16, 18, 19; NORTH, April *17*, 21, 22, 24. Latest dates: SOUTH, May 26, 27; NORTH, May 29, 31. *Fall migration period:* Mid-August through late October with a peak in September. Earliest dates: NORTH, August *3*, 16, 22, 26; SOUTH, August *15*, 22, 25. Latest dates: NORTH, October 10, 12, *23*; SOUTH, October 24, 28, November *3*, *5*, December *4–13*.

Summer. Although there is no evidence of breeding, several summer records are available: Isanti County (singing male, June 11, 1915); Clearwater County (singing male, June 10, 1935); St. Louis County, near Hibbing (one banded bird on May 16, June 15, and June 23, 1965, and another banded bird on June 15, 1965).

NASHVILLE WARBLER *Vermivora ruficapilla*

Minnesota status. Regular. Migrant and summer resident.
Migration. Abundant spring and fall migrant throughout the state. *Spring migration period:* Late April through early June. Earliest dates: SOUTH, April 25, 29, 30; NORTH, May 3, 4. Latest dates: SOUTH, June 1, 3; NORTH, none can be given because of breeding birds. *Fall migration period:* Late July through late October with the bulk of the migration from late August through early October. Earliest dates: NORTH, none can be given because of breeding birds; SOUTH (Minneapolis, Winona), July 19, 21. Latest dates: NORTH, October 19, 20, 22; SOUTH, October 26, 28, 29, November *20–29*.
Summer. Resident primarily in the northeastern and north central regions; also resident in parts of the adjacent regions to the south and west (see map 68). The species is less numerous in the latter regions (except in northern Pine County), where it inhabits tamarack bogs.

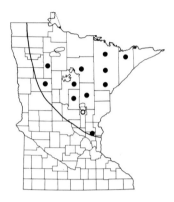

68. Nashville Warbler

NORTHERN PARULA (Parula Warbler)
Parula americana

Minnesota status. Regular. Migrant and summer resident.
Migration. Rare spring and fall migrant throughout most of the state; occasionally uncommon in the eastern regions at the peak of the spring migration. *Spring migration period:* Mid-April through early June with the bulk of the migration from early to late May. Earliest dates: SOUTH, April *12*, *13*, *15*, *17*, 22, 29; NORTH, April *30*, May 7, 9, 11. Latest dates: SOUTH, June 2, 5; NORTH, none can be given because of breeding birds. *Fall migration period:* Late August through early October. Earliest dates: NORTH, none can be given because of breeding birds; SOUTH, August 23, 31 (only dates). Latest dates: NORTH, September 20, 23, 24; SOUTH, October 2, 6, *22*, November *9*.
Summer. Resident primarily in the northeastern and north central regions (see map 69); very scarce in the northern part of the east central region. In the northwestern region the species has been observed as far west as central Polk County. Breeding has not been confirmed for the east central or northwestern regions.

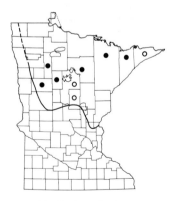

69. Northern Parula

YELLOW WARBLER *Dendroica petechia*

Minnesota status. Regular. Migrant and summer resident.
Migration. Common throughout the state during the spring; many of the birds seen are probably on their nesting territories. Uncommon in the fall with a gradual exodus from the state. *Spring migration period:* Very late April through late May; the bulk of the migration takes place between May 5 and May 20. Earliest dates: SOUTH, April 28 (several years); NORTH, May 4, 5. *Fall migration period:* Probably late July through late September; the migration is usually over by September 10. Latest dates: NORTH, September 19, 21, 23; SOUTH, September 25, 28, 30.
Summer. Resident throughout the state, breeding in all regions. Numerous almost everywhere except in the heavily forested areas of the northern regions where suitable habitat (brushy bogs and stream edges) is limited.

MAGNOLIA WARBLER
Dendroica magnolia

70. Magnolia Warbler

Minnesota status. Regular. Migrant and summer resident.
Migration. Common spring and fall migrant throughout the state. *Spring migration period:* Early May through early June with a peak in mid-May. Earliest dates: SOUTH, May 1 (several years); NORTH, May 6, 7, 9. Latest dates: SOUTH, June 3, 4, 7, *26* (Minneapolis); NORTH, none can be given because of breeding birds. *Fall migration period:* Early August through early October; the bulk of the migration is from late August through late September. Earliest dates: NORTH, none can be given because of breeding birds; SOUTH, August 12, 18, 19. Latest dates: NORTH, October 3, 5, 7; SOUTH, October 9, 10, 14, November *1*.
Summer. Resident primarily in the northeastern and north central regions (see map 70). The species is most numerous in the eastern part of this range.

CAPE MAY WARBLER *Dendroica tigrina*

71. Cape May Warbler

Minnesota status. Regular. Migrant and summer resident.
Migration. Generally uncommon in the eastern one-third of the state and rare elsewhere at both seasons; occasionally common or even abundant in the east during the spring. *Spring migration period:* Early to late May. Earliest dates: SOUTH, May 3, 4; NORTH, May 2, 5, 7. Latest dates: SOUTH, May 31; NORTH, none can be given because of breeding birds. *Fall migration period:* Early August through early October. Earliest dates: NORTH (nonbreeding areas), July 29, August 7; SOUTH, August 18, 24. Latest dates: SOUTH, September 28, 29, October 2, November *28*–December *4*; NORTH, September 29, October 4, 7, *26*.

Summer. Resident primarily in the northern part of the northeastern region (see map 71). The species apparently increased in numbers in the 1960s. Observations have been made as far south as southern St. Louis County and Itasca State Park. The only other summer locality in which the species has been observed is Clover Township, Pine County, reported in 1919.

BLACK-THROATED BLUE WARBLER
Dendroica caerulescens

Minnesota status. Regular. Migrant and summer resident.
Migration. Rare spring and fall migrant throughout the state. The majority of the reports are from the eastern one-third of the state, but this may reflect the concentration of bird-watchers there. On the basis of these reports the species is most abundant in Duluth in the spring and in the Twin Cities in the fall. *Spring migration period:* Early to late May. Earliest dates: SOUTH, May 3, 4, 7; NORTH, May 16, 20, 21. Latest dates: SOUTH, May 23, 25, 28; NORTH, none can be given because of breeding birds. *Fall migration period:* Mid-August through early October. Earliest dates: NORTH, none can be given because of breeding birds; SOUTH, August 14, 28, 29. Latest dates: NORTH, September 16, 17, *26*; SOUTH, October 10, 12, *31*–November *1*.

72. Black-throated Blue Warbler

Summer. Resident primarily in the northeastern and north central regions (see map 72). The species is scarce throughout most of this range except in Cook County. The most southerly records are observations from Mille Lacs Lake and northern Pine County and a specimen collected at Waconia, Carver County (July 16, 1898); if the date for the specimen is correct, the bird may have been a vagrant.

YELLOW-RUMPED WARBLER (Myrtle Warbler) *Dendroica coronata*

Minnesota status. Regular. Migrant and summer resident; accidental in winter.
Migration. Abundant spring and fall migrant throughout the state. *Spring migration period:* Very late March through very early June with the bulk of the migration from mid-April through mid-May. The species is not usually seen before April 10 in the south and April 15 in the north. Earliest dates: SOUTH, March 30, 31, April 2; NORTH, April 6, 9. Latest dates: SOUTH, May 28, 31, June 2; NORTH, none can be given because of breeding birds. *Fall migration period:* Although some birds begin to wander away from the breeding areas in mid-July, migration usually starts in the north in early August and in the south in late August, continuing through early November with stragglers remaining until early winter; the bulk of the migration takes place

73. Yellow-rumped Warbler

from mid-September through late October. Earliest dates: NORTH, none can be given because of breeding birds; SOUTH, August 13, 15, 26. Latest dates: NORTH, November 1, 2, *25*; SOUTH, November 8, 9, *16*, *28*.

Summer. Resident primarily in the northeastern and north central regions (see map 73). The species is most numerous in the northern part of these regions.

Winter. Four individuals are known to have attempted to overwinter at feeding stations — three in the southern half of the state (Ramsey, Hennepin, and Goodhue counties) and one in the northern half (Cass County). One of these birds survived the winter and disappeared in early March.

Taxonomic note. The Audubon's Warbler, *D. c. auduboni*, has been observed three times during the spring migration in the Twin Cities area.

BLACK-THROATED GRAY WARBLER
Dendroica nigrescens

Minnesota status. Accidental. Two spring records.
Records. One observation on April 24, 1938, in Minneapolis (L. M. Aler; description in MMNH files); one specimen (MMNH #12245) collected on May 14, 1956, at Madison, Lac qui Parle County.

BLACK-THROATED GREEN WARBLER
Dendroica virens

Minnesota status. Regular. Migrant and summer resident.
Migration. Uncommon to locally common spring migrant from the Twin Cities and Stearns County northward and eastward; rare in the south and west. Less numerous in the fall (abundance in the eastern part of the state can still be classified as uncommon). *Spring migration period:* Late April through early June with the bulk of the migration in May. Earliest dates: SOUTH, April 25, 28; NORTH, May 1, 3, 4. Latest dates: SOUTH, May 26, 30, June 2, *8*; NORTH, none can be given because of breeding birds. *Fall migration period:* Mid-August through early October. Earliest dates: NORTH, none can be given because of breeding birds; SOUTH, August 17, 18, 29. Latest dates: NORTH, September 27, 28, October 1, *8*; SOUTH, September 29, October 1, 2, *13*, *22*, November *2*, *3*.

Summer. Resident primarily in the northeastern and north central regions (see map 74). The species formerly bred in the Big Woods of Hennepin and Wright counties; the most recent record for that area was reported from Lake Minnetonka, Hennepin County, in about 1930.

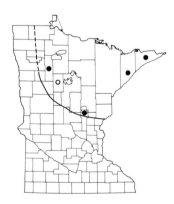

74. Black-throated Green Warbler

HERMIT WARBLER *Dendroica occidentalis*

Minnesota status. Accidental. One spring record.

Records. The only record is a specimen (MMNH #7735) collected near Cambridge, Isanti County, on May 3, 1931 (*Auk* 48:435).

CERULEAN WARBLER *Dendroica cerulea*

Minnesota status. Regular. Migrant and summer resident.
Migration. Rare spring and fall migrant; all reports have been from within the breeding range or south of it. *Spring migration period:* Early to late May. Earliest dates: SOUTH, May 3, 4; NORTH, May 14, 26. Latest dates: SOUTH (Cottonwood County), May 28. *Fall migration period:* A gradual exodus from the breeding range takes place with no distinct migration movements noted. Latest dates: SOUTH, August 21, 23; NORTH, no data.
Summer. Resident within a wide belt on both sides of the Mississippi River (see map 75) as far north as Mahnomen County (*Loon* 39:108–109). The species has been reported in summer as far west as Lake Carlos State Park, Douglas County, near St. Peter, Nicollet County, and as far northeast as Mille Lacs Lake.

75. Cerulean Warbler

BLACKBURNIAN WARBLER *Dendroica fusca*

Minnesota status. Regular. Migrant and summer resident.
Migration. Common spring migrant in the forested part of the state and uncommon on the prairie; uncommon fall migrant throughout the state. *Spring migration period:* Early May through early June; only occasionally seen before May 8. Earliest dates: SOUTH, April 30, May 1, 3; NORTH, May 1, 4, 5. Latest dates: SOUTH, June 1, 2; NORTH, none can be given because of breeding birds. *Fall migration period:* Mid-August through late September. Earliest dates: NORTH, none can be given because of breeding birds; SOUTH, July 31, August 17, 18. Latest dates: NORTH, September 17, 19, October 17, 22; SOUTH, September 23, 28, October 2.
Summer. Resident primarily in the northeastern and north central regions (see map 76). The species is also found sparingly along the eastern margin of the northwestern region and in the northern counties of the central and east central regions. South of these counties it has been observed a few times (but not since the early 1930s) in the cedar and tamarack bogs of Isanti and Sherburne counties.

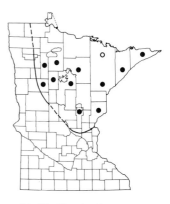

76. Blackburnian Warbler

CHESTNUT-SIDED WARBLER
Dendroica pensylvanica

Minnesota status. Regular. Migrant and summer resident.
Migration. Common spring and fall migrant throughout most of the state; probably uncommon on the western margin of the prairie. *Spring migration period:* Early May through very early June with the bulk of the migration dur-

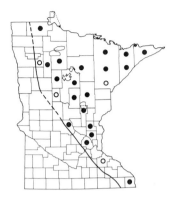

77. Chestnut-sided Warbler

78. Bay-breasted Warbler

ing the last half of May. Earliest dates: SOUTH, May 1, 2, 3; NORTH, April *25*, May 5, 6, 7. Latest dates: SOUTH (Cottonwood County), June 3. *Fall migration period:* Mid-August through mid-September. Earliest dates: SOUTH (Lac qui Parle County), August 13. Latest dates: NORTH, September 27, 29; SOUTH, October 1, 3, 4.

Summer. Resident primarily in the northeastern and north central regions and in the adjacent counties in the northwestern, central, and east central regions (see map 77). In the early twentieth century the species was fairly well represented in the southeastern region and in the area around the Twin Cities, but as the forests were cut and as urbanization progressed, it began to disappear. Roberts (1932) found nests as far south as Houston County, but no nests have been reported for thirty-five years from the Twin Cities area southward. Nevertheless, recent isolated summer observations from Winona, Rice, and Dakota counties suggest that the species may still occur there as a resident. In 1932 Roberts also stated that the species nested infrequently in the prairie groves, but no data (early or recent) are available to confirm this.

BAY-BREASTED WARBLER *Dendroica castanea*

Minnesota status. Regular. Migrant and summer resident.
Migration. Generally uncommon spring migrant throughout most of the state; occasionally common at the peak of migration. Usually common fall migrant, especially in the eastern part of the state. *Spring migration period:* Early May through early June; the species is rarely seen before May 15. Earliest dates: SOUTH, May 4, 5; NORTH, May 14, 15. Latest dates: SOUTH, June 1, 4, *14*; NORTH (Duluth, Two Harbors), June 6, 9. *Fall migration period:* Mid-July (north) and mid-August (south) through mid-October; rarely seen after the end of September. Earliest dates: NORTH (Duluth), July 17, 26; SOUTH, August 13, 23, 27. Latest dates: NORTH, September 28, October 1; SOUTH, October 19, 20.

Summer. Resident primarily in Cook, Lake, and northern St. Louis counties (see map 78). The species has been reported as far south and west as Itasca State Park, but it is quite scarce away from the northeastern tip of the state. Several birds were reported in a tamarack bog in Sherburne County, July 9–20, 1925; three males and one female in breeding condition were collected, but no young were observed.

BLACKPOLL WARBLER *Dendroica striata*

Minnesota status. Regular. Migrant.
Migration. Common spring and fall migrant throughout the

state (including the western prairie). *Spring migration period:* Very late April through early June with the bulk of the migration during the second half of May. Earliest dates: SOUTH, April *26*, 30, May 1, 2; NORTH, May 4, 7. Latest dates: SOUTH, June 3, 4, 6; NORTH, June 8, 9, 10, *14*. *Fall migration period:* Early August through early October. Earliest dates: NORTH, August 8, 16; SOUTH, August 16, 22. Latest dates: NORTH, September 27, 28, October *8*, *9*; SOUTH, October 1, 2, *25*.

PINE WARBLER *Dendroica pinus*

Minnesota status. Regular. Migrant and summer resident.
Migration. Rare to occasionally uncommon spring and fall migrant throughout the state. *Spring migration period:* Mid-April through late May with the bulk of the migration taking place in late April and early May. Earliest dates: SOUTH, April 15, 17, 20; NORTH, April *17*, 23, 26. Latest dates: SOUTH (beyond breeding areas), May 25, 26, June *8*; NORTH, none can be given because of breeding birds. *Fall migration period:* Mid-August through mid-October. Earliest dates: NORTH, none can be given because of breeding birds; SOUTH (beyond breeding areas), August *3*, 14, 19, 22. Latest dates: NORTH, October 7, 8, *25*; SOUTH, October 12, 13, 15.

79. Pine Warbler

Summer. Resident in the northeastern and north central regions and in the adjacent counties to the west and south (see map 79). The species is most numerous in the pine country between Mille Lacs Lake and Red Lake. There are two records (probably of vagrant birds) from the prairie: Herman, Grant County (June 20, 1879); Buffalo River State Park, Clay County (June 10, 1969).

KIRTLAND'S WARBLER *Dendroica kirtlandii*

Minnesota status. Accidental. One spring record.
Records. The only acceptable record of this rare species is a specimen that was collected on May 13, 1892, in Hennepin County (MMNH #5724).

PRAIRIE WARBLER *Dendroica discolor*

Minnesota status. Accidental. Two spring records.
Records. Both records are observations from Hennepin County: May 12, 1961 (*Flicker* 33:92); May 30, 1968 (*Loon* 40:59–60).

PALM WARBLER *Dendroica palmarum*

Minnesota status. Regular. Migrant and summer resident.
Migration. Abundant spring and fall migrant in the eastern two-thirds of the state, particularly along the shore of Lake

80. Palm Warbler

Superior in the fall; uncommon to rare migrant in the western prairie areas. *Spring migration period:* Mid-April through late May with the bulk of the migration from late April through mid-May. Earliest dates: SOUTH, April *10, 11*, 17, 23; NORTH, April *15, 23*, 29. Latest dates: SOUTH, May 25, 27, 31, June *4*; NORTH, none can be given because of breeding birds. *Fall migration period:* Mid-August through early November with the bulk of the migration from mid-September through mid-October. Earliest dates: NORTH, none can be given because of breeding birds; SOUTH, August 25, 30. Latest dates: NORTH, October 16, 17, *19, 26*, November *19*; SOUTH, November 2, 3, *10*.

Summer. Resident in the northeastern and north central regions and in adjacent Marshall and Roseau counties (see map 80). Scarce throughout most of the range except where extensive areas of open or parklike tamarack–black spruce bogs, the preferred habitat of the species, are present.

OVENBIRD *Seiurus aurocapillus*

Minnesota status. Regular. Migrant and summer resident.
Migration. Common spring and fall migrant throughout the state. *Spring migration period:* Late April through early June with a peak in mid-May. Earliest dates: SOUTH, April 27, 28; NORTH, May 3, 4. *Fall migration period:* Probably from early August through mid-October with the bulk of the migration in September. Latest dates: NORTH, September 24, 28, October *7, 16*; SOUTH, October 15, 16, November *3, 15, 21*–December *2*.

Summer. Resident throughout the wooded portions of the state. With the clearing of woodland habitats the species has become less numerous from the Twin Cities southward than it was formerly. Its status as a breeding bird in groves and river bottoms on the prairie is uncertain; no information is available from the period before intensive farming began. Recently there have been summer observations from as far west as Norman County in the northern part of the state, Pope County in the central part, and Rice and Olmsted counties in the southern part.

NORTHERN WATERTHRUSH
Seiurus noveboracensis

Minnesota status. Regular. Migrant and summer resident.
Migration. Uncommon spring and fall migrant throughout the state. *Spring migration period:* Mid-April through early June with the bulk of the migration from late April through mid-May. Earliest dates: SOUTH, April *8*, 16, 18, 22; NORTH, May 2, 3. Latest dates: SOUTH, May 30, June 1; NORTH, none can be given because of breeding birds. *Fall migration period:* Probably late July through mid-October

81. Northern Waterthrush

with the bulk of the migration from mid-August through
early October. Earliest dates: NORTH, none can be given
because of breeding birds; SOUTH, August 4, 9. Latest
dates: NORTH, October 1, 2, 3, *25*; SOUTH, October 15, 19,
21.

Summer. Resident primarily in the northeastern and north
central regions (see map 81). The species is scarce south
and west of a line between Duluth and Leech Lake, although it has been reported as far south as the St. Croix
River bottoms, Pine County, and Mille Lacs Lake and as far
west as Clearwater County. There is one early July record
from Stearns County, but the status of the species in that
area is not known.

LOUISIANA WATERTHRUSH *Seiurus motacilla*

Minnesota status. Regular. Migrant and summer resident.
Migration. Rare spring migrant in the breeding range in the
southeastern quarter of the state; most birds seen there are
probably on or near their nesting locations. Very rarely seen
in the fall. *Spring migration period:* Mid-April probably
through mid-May. Earliest dates: April *1*, 17, 18. *Fall migration period:* Gradual exodus during August. Latest dates:
September 4, 14, 20.

Summer. Resident primarily in the southeastern region;
also present along the St. Croix and Mississippi rivers into
the central regions (see map 82). Roberts (1932) assigned to
this species the waterthrushes that Surber found in the upper
reaches of the St. Croix River in Pine County in 1918 and
1919; Surber believed that the birds were Northern Waterthrushes (discussed in the preceding account).

82. Louisiana Waterthrush

KENTUCKY WARBLER *Oporornis formosus*

Minnesota status. Casual. Migrant and summer visitant.
Migration. Casual spring vagrant from the Twin Cities
southeastward; the records from May 12 through May 29
include only one specimen (MMNH #17324). Only two fall
records: western Lake Superior (found on board a ship),
July 24, 1964; Anoka County, August 19, 1963.

Summer. Singing males sometimes have been observed for
several weeks, indicating that occasionally the species attempts to nest in Minnesota, but no females or broods have
been found. The records are from Winona County (Winona,
1952 and 1965; Whitewater State Park, 1958) and Anoka
County (at the same location near Coon Rapids in 1964 and
1965).

CONNECTICUT WARBLER *Oporornis agilis*

Minnesota status. Regular. Migrant and summer resident.
Migration. Usually rare spring and fall migrant through-

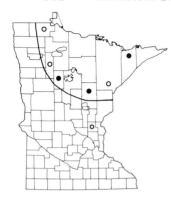

83. Connecticut Warbler (1920)

84. Mourning Warbler

out the state; very occasionally uncommon in the eastern part of the state at the migration peak. *Spring migration period:* Early May through early June; the bulk of the migration is in late May. Earliest dates: SOUTH, May 9, 10; NORTH, May 6, 7. Latest dates: SOUTH, June 5, 9, *19*; NORTH, none can be given because of breeding birds. *Fall migration period:* Mid-August through late September. Earliest dates: NORTH, none can be given because of breeding birds; SOUTH, August 17, 19. Latest dates: NORTH, September 19, 24; SOUTH, September 25, 28.

Summer. Resident in the northeastern and north central regions (see map 83). Scarce throughout most of the area but plentiful in the northwestern corner (from Koochiching County northwestward) in tamarack–black spruce bogs and in forests of upland jack pine and aspen. From 1914 through 1917 this warbler was found regularly in tamarack bogs near Cambridge, Isanti County, but it did not seem to be present in the area in 1927; there have been no subsequent reports.

MOURNING WARBLER *Oporornis philadelphia*

Minnesota status. Regular. Migrant and summer resident.
Migration. Common spring and fall migrant throughout the state. Possibly more numerous in the western part of the state than in the eastern part. *Spring migration period:* Early May through early June with the bulk of the migration during the last half of May. Earliest dates: SOUTH, May 2, 5; NORTH, May 10, 11, 12. Latest dates: SOUTH (southern and west central regions only), June 3, 4, 5, *10*; NORTH, none can be given because of breeding birds. *Fall migration period:* Probably late July through early October. Earliest dates: None can be given because of breeding birds. Latest dates: NORTH, September 20, 21; SOUTH, October 1, 5, 7, *14*.

Summer. Resident throughout much of the wooded portion of the state from the Twin Cities northward (see map 84). Successful nestings have been reported only as far south as Cambridge in Isanti County, but there are a number of records of singing males in Hennepin, Anoka, and Washington counties.

COMMON YELLOWTHROAT (Yellowthroat) *Geothlypis trichas*

Minnesota status. Regular. Migrant and summer resident.
Migration. Common spring and fall migrant throughout the state. *Spring migration period:* Very late April through at least the end of May. Earliest dates: SOUTH, April *19*, *23*, 30, May 1; NORTH, April *22*, May 1, 3. *Fall migration period:* At least mid-August through late October; rarely

seen after October 10. Latest dates: NORTH, October 1, 2, 4, 9; SOUTH, October 25, 26, December *15*, *25*.

Summer. Resident throughout the state. Most widespread and numerous warbler species in the state.

YELLOW-BREASTED CHAT *Icteria virens*

Minnesota status. Casual. Migrant and summer resident.
Migration. Very rare to casual spring migrant in the southeastern and southwestern parts of the state. The number of birds fluctuates sharply from year to year, and in many years no birds are reported. Spring records outside the known breeding range include a number from the Twin Cities area and one each from Stearns and Polk counties. Casual in the fall. Most of the fall records are from the western margin of the state, including one from Clay County (north of the known breeding range). *Spring migration period:* Probably throughout May. Earliest dates: May 2, 5, 6. *Fall migration period:* Probably throughout August and into September. Latest dates: August 27, 29, September 4, October *15*.

85. Yellow-breasted Chat

Summer. Casual resident in the southeastern and southwestern corners of the state (see map 85), with nesting records as far north as Ortonville, Big Stone County. In some years this bird cannot be found in the state at all, but in other years it is more numerous and breeds in the state. Several periods of unusual abundance have been documented: along the lower Mississippi River (Winona and Houston counties) in 1948 and 1953–1955; along the Cannon River (Goodhue County) in 1950–1952; along the Minnesota River (Lac qui Parle and Big Stone counties) in 1939–1944. There are specimens from Jackson, Lac qui Parle, and Houston counties.

HOODED WARBLER *Wilsonia citrina*

Minnesota status. Accidental. Five spring records and one fall record.
Records. One bird seen on April 30, 1972, Minneapolis (*Loon* 44:58–59); one bird seen on May 17, 1942, Minneapolis (*Flicker* 14:41–43); one bird seen from May 22 to May 25, 1973, Minneapolis (*Loon* 45:133–134); one bird banded and photographed, June 2, 1962, Washington County (*Flicker* 34:130; cover); one bird banded, June 2, 1973, Isle, Mille Lacs County (*Loon* 45:65); one bird seen on September 10, 1969, Ramsey County (*Loon* 42:36).

WILSON'S WARBLER *Wilsonia pusilla*

Minnesota status. Regular. Migrant; accidental summer visitor.

Migration. Common spring and fall migrant throughout the state. *Spring migration period:* Very late April through early June with the bulk of the migration during the last three weeks of May. Earliest dates: SOUTH, April *21–22*, 30, May 2; NORTH, May 8. Latest dates: SOUTH, June 3, 4, 7, *11*, *15*; NORTH, June 6, 8. *Fall migration period:* Early August through mid-October with the bulk of the migration from late August through mid-September. Earliest dates: NORTH, August 4, 6, 8; SOUTH, August 12, 15, 20. Latest dates: NORTH, September 27, 29; SOUTH, October 5, 10, 11, *18*, *20*, November *4*.

Summer. The only evidence that this warbler is a summer resident in Minnesota is found in the reports by Roberts and Dart of three observations of single birds and one observation of a pair (seen several times) in Marshall County in 1900 and 1901 (Roberts, 1932). The AOU *Check-List* (1957) gives Duluth as a breeding locality, but there is no information, published or in the Minnesota files, about this record.

CANADA WARBLER *Wilsonia canadensis*

Minnesota status. Regular. Migrant and summer resident.
Migration. Uncommon to occasionally common spring migrant and uncommon fall migrant throughout the state. *Spring migration period:* Early May through early June with the bulk of the migration during the last half of May. Earliest dates: SOUTH, May 1, 4, 6; NORTH, May *5*, 9, 12, 13. Latest dates: SOUTH, June 3, 6; NORTH, none can be given because of breeding birds. *Fall migration period:* Mid-August through late September with very few birds seen after mid-September. Earliest dates: NORTH, none can be given because of breeding birds; SOUTH, August *9*, 13, 14, 15. Latest dates: NORTH, September 15, 18, 20; SOUTH, September 29, 30.

86. Canada Warbler

Summer. Resident primarily in the northeastern and north central regions (see map 86). More numerous in the northeastern region than in the north central region. Nesting activity has been reported as far west as Itasca State Park and as far south as Onamia, Mille Lacs County.

AMERICAN REDSTART *Setophaga ruticilla*

Minnesota status. Regular. Migrant and summer resident.
Migration. Common spring and fall migrant throughout the state. *Spring migration period:* Throughout the month of May with a peak usually between May 14 and May 24 in the south and between May 20 and May 30 in the north. Earliest dates: SOUTH, April 30, May 1, 2; NORTH, April *30*, May 6, 7. *Fall migration period:* Late July through mid-October

with the bulk of the migration from late August through mid-September; most birds leave by late September in the north and by early October in the south. Latest dates: NORTH, October 12, *19, 21, 22, 24, 26*; SOUTH, October 14, 15, *22, 29*.

Summer. Resident throughout the state; very scarce south of the Minnesota River from Blue Earth and Faribault counties westward.

Family PLOCEIDAE: Weaver Finches

HOUSE SPARROW *Passer domesticus*

Minnesota status. Regular; introduced. Permanent resident.

Distribution. Permanent resident throughout the state wherever there are settlements or farms; does not occur in heavily wooded areas. This Old World species was introduced in the Twin Cities area in 1875 and became established as a breeding bird two years later. Roberts (1932) described its acclimatization in Minnesota as follows: "From this time [1877] it spread steadily throughout the state, following the lines of railroads and establishing itself first in cities and towns. It took some years to develop a breed hardy enough to endure the long cold winters, and for a time many perished when conditions were especially severe. It reached Lanesboro, Fillmore County, in the southeastern part of the state in the fall of 1886; Duluth in 1887; Tower, on the Iron Range in St. Louis County, in 1892; and about the same time the Red River Valley in the northwestern corner of the state."

Migration. Although this species is not thought to migrate, flocks which perhaps were migrants have been reported in the fall along the North Shore of Lake Superior. Since most people ignore this bird, the information available on it is not sufficient to permit a description of its migration movements.

Family ICTERIDAE: Meadowlarks, Blackbirds, and Orioles

BOBOLINK *Dolichonyx oryzivorus*

Minnesota status. Regular. Migrant and summer resident.

Migration. Common spring and fall migrant throughout most of the state; uncommon and of only local occurrence in the northeastern and north central regions. *Spring migration period:* Late April through late May with a peak in mid-May. Earliest dates: SOUTH, April 23, 25, 26; NORTH, April *19, 29*, May *4, 6*. *Fall migration period:* Probably late July through mid-September with stragglers into October and November; the peak occurs in late August. Latest dates: NORTH, September 1, 9, *29*, November *3*, *10*; SOUTH, September 21, 30, October 4, *12*, *15*.

Summer. Resident throughout the state wherever a suitable habitat of grassy lowlands is present. Most numerous on the prairies in the west central and northwestern regions of the state; least numerous in the heavily wooded north central and northeastern regions.

EASTERN MEADOWLARK *Sturnella magna*

Minnesota status. Regular. Migrant and summer resident; regular in winter.

Migration. Common spring and fall migrant in the eastern half of the state; rare in the western regions. *Spring migration period:* Early March through early May with a peak in early April. Earliest dates: SOUTH, none can be given because of wintering birds; NORTH, March *9*, 17, 18, 20. *Fall migration period:* September through mid-November with a peak in early and mid-October. Latest dates: NORTH, November 9, 13, *23*, *28*; SOUTH, none can be given because of wintering birds.

Summer. Resident eastward from Lake of the Woods, Clearwater and Otter Tail counties in the north and southward through the middle of the central region to Blue Earth and Faribault counties in the south.

Winter. Because this species is difficult to distinguish from the Western Meadowlark except by song, the winter records for the two species may be unreliable. Meadowlarks occur uncommonly throughout the winter in the southern half of the state. No doubt some of these birds, especially in the east central and southeastern regions, are Eastern Meadowlarks, but there is not enough reliable evidence available to permit accurate mapping of the winter range and abundance of this species.

WESTERN MEADOWLARK *Sturnella neglecta*

Minnesota status. Regular. Migrant and summer resident; regular in winter.

Migration. Common to abundant spring and fall migrant throughout most of the state; uncommon to rare in the north central and northeastern regions. *Spring migration period:* Early March through early May with a peak in late March and early April. Earliest dates: SOUTH, none can be given because of wintering birds; NORTH, March *2*, 29, April 1, 5. *Fall migration period:* September through mid-November with a peak in mid-October. Latest dates: NORTH, October 25, 26, 30, November *29*, December *22*, *23* (the extreme dates are from the northwestern region); SOUTH, none can be given because of wintering birds.

Summer. Resident throughout the state with the possible exception of Lake and Cook counties. Locally numerous in the north central and northeastern regions; widespread and numerous elsewhere. The species has been reported as far north and east as St. Louis County (Lake Vermillon, Duluth).

Winter. Since it is difficult to distinguish this species in winter from the Eastern Meadowlark, the winter range and abundance of the Western Meadowlark are poorly known; both species occur in winter in the southern half of the state. The Western Meadowlark is probably a regular but uncommon winter visitant at least in the southwestern region of the state.

YELLOW-HEADED BLACKBIRD
Xanthocephalus xanthocephalus

Minnesota status. Regular. Migrant and summer resident; accidental in winter.

Migration. Common to abundant spring and fall migrant throughout the breeding range in the state; rare in the northeastern region and in the adjacent counties in the north central region and not known to nest there. *Spring migration period:* Early April through late May with a peak in late April. Earliest dates: SOUTH, March 25, 29, 31; NORTH, April 8, 11, 12. *Fall migration period:* Late August through mid-November with a peak in September; unusual after early October. Latest dates: NORTH, October 24, 25, December 5; SOUTH, November 2, 8, 9, *15, 29.*

Summer. Resident throughout the state with the exception of the northeastern region, adjacent Itasca and Koochiching counties, and much of Pine and Aitkin counties. The northeastern margin of the breeding range includes the mouth of the Rainy River, Lake of the Woods County; Cass Lake; Aitkin, Aitkin County; and Duluth.

Winter. Three of the winter records are of single birds attempting to overwinter: Dakota County (December, 1934, to January 5, 1935); Hennepin County (winter of 1938–1939); Carver County (December 26, 1960, to January 1, 1961). The other record is of a flock of twenty-five birds on February 26, 1943, in Cottonwood County; these birds may have been exceptionally early spring migrants.

RED-WINGED BLACKBIRD *Agelaius phoeniceus*

Minnesota status. Regular. Migrant and summer resident; regular in winter.

Migration. Abundant spring and fall migrant throughout the state. One of the two or three most numerous birds in the state. *Spring migration period:* Late February through early May with the bulk of the migration from mid-March through mid-April. Earliest dates: SOUTH, late February to early March; NORTH, mid-March to late March; no dates can be given because of wintering birds. *Fall migration period:* Early August through early December with the bulk of the migration from early October through mid-November. Latest dates: None can be given because of wintering birds, but most migrants leave by late November.

Summer. Resident throughout the state.

Winter. Regular in the southern half of the state, occurring in small groups of a few birds or in flocks of ten to a hundred birds, especially in the east central and southeastern regions. In the northern half of the state the species is rare or casual and is most frequently reported in December and early January.

ORCHARD ORIOLE *Icterus spurius*

Minnesota status. Regular. Migrant and summer resident.
Migration. Rare spring migrant in the southern half of the state west of the Mississippi River and north along the Red River to Clay County; very rare after the gradual exodus from the state in the fall. Accidental spring migrant northeast of the breeding range; no fall records. *Spring migration period:* Throughout May. Earliest dates: SOUTH, May 2, 4, 7; NORTH, May 11, 15, 17. *Fall migration period:* Probably late July through very early September. Latest dates: NORTH, no data; SOUTH, August 24, 28, September 3.

Summer. Resident throughout the southern half of the state in the area lying west of the Mississippi River and northward along the western margin of the state (see map 87). At the turn of the century the species was found as a summer resident in the Red River Valley as far north as the Canadian border, but there have been no records north of Clay County in the last forty years. At present, the species is scarce north of the Twin Cities in the east and north of the headwaters of the Minnesota River in the west; it is also very scarce in the south central region. Breeding has been reported in the northern part of the range as far east as Wadena in Wadena County and St. Cloud in Stearns County.

87. Orchard Oriole

NORTHERN ORIOLE (Baltimore Oriole)
Icterus galbula

Minnesota status. Regular. Migrant and summer resident; accidental in winter.

Migration. Common spring migrant throughout most of the state; rare in Lake and Cook counties. Uncommon fall migrant throughout most of the state; casual in the northeastern tip of the state. *Spring migration period:* Late April through early June with a peak between May 5 and May 20. Earliest dates: SOUTH, April 27, 28; NORTH, May 2, 5, 7. *Fall migration period:* August through late September; almost all birds leave by mid-September. Latest dates: NORTH, September 7, 8, 10; SOUTH, September 24, 27, October 1, *8*.

Summer. Resident throughout the state; very scarce in Lake and Cook counties.

Winter. In the metropolitan areas of Duluth and the Twin Cities a number of birds have attempted to overwinter at feeding stations; these birds usually appear in November and disappear in mid-December. Latest dates: NORTH, December 22; SOUTH, December 25, January 5.

Taxonomic note. The Bullock's Oriole, *I. g. bullockii*, has been identified once in Minnesota; an immature male was banded and photographed at a feeding station in Duluth, mid-October to December 13, 1968 (*Loon* 41:41–42).

RUSTY BLACKBIRD *Euphagus carolinus*

Minnesota status. Regular. Migrant and winter visitant.

Migration. Common spring migrant and abundant fall migrant throughout the state. *Spring migration period:* Mid-March through mid-May with the bulk of the migration during the month of April. Earliest dates: SOUTH, none can be given because of wintering birds; NORTH, March *16*, *21*, 28, April 1, 2. Latest dates: SOUTH, May 12, 17, 18; NORTH, May 17, 18, 20, *24*, *25*. *Fall migration period:* Early September through early December with the bulk of the migration from late September through early November. Earliest dates: NORTH, August *20*, September 2, 4; SOUTH, September 8, 12, 13. Latest dates: NORTH, November 14, 19, *26*, *29*; SOUTH, none can be given because of wintering birds.

Summer. Not known to breed in Minnesota; summer observations of single birds apparently of this species reported from different localities in Cook County (June, 1968; July, 1972).

Winter. Uncommon to locally common visitant in the southern half of the state; rare visitant in the northern half.

BREWER'S BLACKBIRD
Euphagus cyanocephalus

Minnesota status. Regular. Migrant and summer resident; casual in winter.

Migration. Common spring and fall migrant throughout

most of the state; uncommon in the most heavily wooded portions of the northern regions. *Spring migration period:* Mid-March through early May with a peak in April. Earliest dates: SOUTH, March 14, 15, 16; NORTH, March *25*, April 2, 7, 11. *Fall migration period:* Mid-August through late November with the bulk of the migration from mid-September through mid-October. Latest dates: NORTH, November 8, 11, 13; SOUTH, none can be given because of wintering birds.

Summer. Resident throughout the state with the exception of the heavily wooded portions of the northern regions, especially along the Canadian border from Lake of the Woods to the Pigeon River. Breeding evidence has been reported as far north as Kittson County; Hibbing, St. Louis County; and Tofte, Cook County. The species is scarce south of the Minnesota River, especially in the west; in that area breeding has been reported only from Lac qui Parle, Cottonwood, Freeborn, and Winona counties. The species expanded its range in Minnesota from the Red River Valley (where it was always found) to east central Minnesota between 1914 and 1918 and to northeastern Minnesota in 1928 (Roberts, 1932).

Winter. Stragglers occasionally linger into early winter in the southern half of the state, but most of them disappear by February. There are four winter records for the northern half of the state; one of the birds remained in the state until early February.

COMMON GRACKLE *Quiscalus quiscula*

Minnesota status. Regular. Migrant and summer resident; regular in winter.

Migration. Abundant spring and fall migrant throughout the state. *Spring migration period:* Mid-March through early May with a peak in late March and early April. Earliest dates: SOUTH, none can be given because of wintering birds; NORTH, March *14*, *15*, 21, 24, 26. *Fall migration period:* Flocking begins in late July; migration from late August through late November with a peak from mid-October through early November; stragglers frequently remain until early winter. Latest dates: None can be given because of wintering birds; most birds leave by mid-November in the north and early December in the south.

Summer. Resident throughout the state. Least numerous in the heavily wooded parts of the northern regions. The species is known to breed along the brushy edges of lakes and flowages away from settled areas.

Winter. Individuals or small flocks can be found anywhere at this season, especially around feeders or dumps; rare in the north and uncommon in the south. Most reports are from early winter, but some birds remain in the state throughout the season.

BROWN-HEADED COWBIRD *Molothrus ater*

Minnesota status. Regular. Migrant and summer resident; casual in winter.
Migration. Abundant spring migrant and uncommon fall migrant throughout the state. *Spring migration period:* Mid-March through mid-May with a peak during the second half of April and early May. Earliest dates: SOUTH, March *12*, *13*, 18, 19, 21; NORTH, April 4, 6, 10. *Fall migration period:* Very poorly defined. Flocking begins in late June, and the local adults in the north disappear in July; some migration is noted throughout the fall. Latest dates: NORTH, October 31, November 1, 4; SOUTH, November 17, 24, 25.
Summer. Resident throughout the state.
Winter. Casual in early winter in the south; accidental in late winter in the south and at any time in the north.

Family THRAUPIDAE: Tanagers

WESTERN TANAGER *Piranga ludoviciana*

Minnesota status. Casual. Spring migrant.
Records. Nine of the ten records, obviously associated with the height of the spring migration, occurred between May 8 and May 30 in Hennepin County (photographed; *Loon* 38:106), St. Louis County (photographed; *Loon* 40:23), Cook County, Becker County, Mille Lacs County, and Stevens County. The tenth record is of a male seen at Agassiz National Wildlife Refuge, Marshall County, on June 28, 1971. In addition, one specimen of a Western Tanager–Scarlet Tanager hybrid was collected on August 17, 1950, in Anoka County (MMNH #9481).

SCARLET TANAGER *Piranga olivacea*

Minnesota status. Regular. Migrant and summer resident.
Migration. Uncommon spring and fall migrant in the eastern and central regions; rare in the western regions. *Spring migration period:* Early May through early June. Earliest dates: SOUTH, April 29, May 1; NORTH, May *1*, 9, 10. *Fall migration period:* Mid-August through mid-October with the bulk of the migration in the second part of September. Latest dates: NORTH, September 25, 29, October 1, November *14*, *26*; SOUTH, October 13, 14, *26*.
Summer. Resident throughout most of the state (as far north as Norman, Beltrami, and Cook counties). Most numerous in the central wooded portion of the state and least numerous on the southern and western prairies.

SUMMER TANAGER *Piranga rubra*

Minnesota status. Casual. Spring migrant.

Records. Nine records between May 3 and June 14 from the following counties: Goodhue, Winona, Hennepin (female, 1973; *Loon* 45:63–64), St. Louis (male, 1964, and female, 1965, in the same yard, both photographed; *Loon* 36:63, 37:113), Becker, Lac qui Parle, and Pipestone (MMNH #1037).

Family FRINGILLIDAE: Grosbeaks, Finches, Sparrows, and Buntings

CARDINAL *Cardinalis cardinalis*

Minnesota status. Regular. Permanent resident; visitant outside regular range.

Distribution. Permanent resident primarily in the central and southern regions (see map 88). The species has extended its range significantly in the last one hundred years. In the nineteenth century it was a visitant, entering the state from the southeast along the Mississippi River; by the mid-1930s it was established as a resident from the Twin Cities southward and eastward, and by the 1960s it had expanded its range northward to Morrison County and westward to Lac qui Parle County. In the last ten years there have been three breeding records north of Mille Lacs Lake (Aitkin, Crow Wing, and Cass counties) and a number of summer sight records as far northwest as Red Lake and as far northeast as Duluth. The species is not yet known as a breeding bird in the southwestern tip of the state.

Winter. North of the breeding range outlined above and in the southwestern tip of the state the species occurs as a rare visitant in fall, winter, and spring. It has been reported as far north as Cook and Beltrami counties. Earliest dates: September *13*, October 17, 18, 21. Latest dates: May 24, 25, 28.

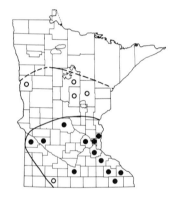

88. Cardinal

ROSE-BREASTED GROSBEAK
Pheucticus ludovicianus

Minnesota status. Regular. Migrant and summer resident.

Migration. Common spring and fall migrant throughout most of the state; uncommon in the fall northeast of Duluth and in the prairie regions. *Spring migration period:* Late April through early June with a peak in mid-May. Earliest dates: SOUTH, April 23, 24, 25; NORTH, May 2, 4, 8. *Fall migration period:* Mid-August through late October with a peak during the first half of September; almost all birds leave by early September in the north and by early October in the south. Latest dates: NORTH, October 29, 30, November 3, *8*, *11*, *20*; SOUTH, October 26, 27, November 1.

Summer. Resident throughout the state. Most numerous in the deciduous forests of the central and southern regions.

Winter. One immature bird attempted to winter at Winona, Winona County; it was last seen on January 4, 1973 (*Loon* 45:26).

BLACK-HEADED GROSBEAK
Pheucticus melanocephalus

Minnesota status. Accidental. Two spring records and one summer record.

Records. The earliest spring date is for a second-year male at a feeder two miles from Mendota Heights in St. Paul, Ramsey County, between April 19 and April 26, 1972 (*Loon* 44:121–122). The other spring bird was a male recorded on June 6, 1940, at Minnesota Point, Duluth (Mrs. W. C. Olin). The summer record is of a male reported in Mendota Heights, Dakota County, from mid-July through August 9, 1967; this bird was seen feeding a juvenile at the feeder on August 6 (*Loon* 39:130).

BLUE GROSBEAK *Guiraca caerulea*

Minnesota status. Regular. Spring migrant, summer visitant, and possible resident.

Migration. Rare; found only in the southwestern tip of the state (Rock, Murray, and Nobles counties). Earliest dates: May 20, 23. Latest date: September 4.

Summer. The species occurs only in a small area in the southwestern corner of the state: from the Iowa border as far north as Beaver Creek, Rock County; southwest of Chandler, Murray County; and east to Kinbrae and Worthington, Nobles County. First found in the state in 1961 along the border between South Dakota and Minnesota in Rock County. In the last ten years the species has gradually expanded its range eastward into Murray and Nobles counties. The only breeding evidence is an observation of two adults and three immatures near Beaver Creek, Rock County, on September 4, 1972.

INDIGO BUNTING *Passerina cyanea*

Minnesota status. Regular. Migrant and summer resident.

Migration. Common spring and fall migrant throughout most of the state; rare in the heavily forested parts of the northern regions; uncommon along the western prairie margin. *Spring migration period:* Early May through early June with a peak in mid-May. Earliest dates: SOUTH, April *28*,

May 2, 4; NORTH, May 9, 15, 18. *Fall migration period:* Late July through mid-October with the bulk of the migration in September. Latest dates: NORTH, September 7, 18, 26, October *28*; SOUTH, October 11, 13, 15.

Summer. Resident throughout the state with records north to Cook, northern Lake, northern St. Louis, Lake of the Woods, and Roseau counties. Most numerous in the southeastern, south central, east central, and central regions.

LAZULI BUNTING *Passerina amoena*

Minnesota status. Accidental. Four spring records.

Records. Four observations of birds identified or described as males of this species: May 8–10, 1930, Jackson County (Roberts, 1932); May 18–19, 1964, Clay County (*Loon* 36:105); May 25, 1956, Lac qui Parle County (bird banded); June 4, 1935, Lac qui Parle County. In addition, there are four records of specimens or birds described as hybrids. Three of these were males that appeared to be closer to the Lazuli Bunting than to the Indigo Bunting in appearance: May 16, 1964, Rock County (MMNH #19922); June 24, 1943, Sherburne County (*Loon* 37:53); June 26, 1929, Marshall County (MMNH #7493). One specimen (MMNH #19921) from Rock County on July 4, 1964, had only 25 percent of the plumage characteristics of the Lazuli Bunting (*Loon* 37:47).

PAINTED BUNTING *Passerina ciris*

Minnesota status. Accidental. Three spring records.

Records. May 2, 1893, Lac qui Parle County (MMNH #4724); May 12–16, 1965, Cook County (photographed; *Loon* 37:150); May 27–28, 1969, Cottonwood County (MMNH #25661).

DICKCISSEL *Spiza americana*

Minnesota status. Regular. Migrant and summer resident.

Migration. Usually a common spring migrant and an uncommon fall migrant in the southern half of the state; populations fluctuate yearly from abundant to uncommon. In the northern half of the state the species is uncommon to rare in the northwest and rare to casual in the northeast. *Spring migration period:* Early May through early June with a peak in late May. Earliest dates: SOUTH, April *24*, May 1, 4, 5; NORTH, May 2, 4, 10. *Fall migration period:* Gradual exodus from the state in August and September. Latest dates: NORTH, no data; SOUTH, September 29, October 3, 4.

Summer. Resident usually in the southern half of the state north to Chisago, Stearns, Stevens, and Traverse counties. In years of peak abundance the species extends its range northward, usually into the western part of the state; there are summer observations from Roseau, Lake of the Woods, Norman, Clay, Mahnomen, Becker, and Hubbard counties and a nesting record from Fosston, Polk County. In the northeastern quarter of the state the range usually extends only to southern Pine and Morrison counties, although there are old summer observations, mostly in the 1930s, from Lake County (Two Harbors), St. Louis County (Virginia), Itasca County (Lake Pokegama), and Crow Wing County (Brainerd).

EVENING GROSBEAK *Hesperiphona vespertina*

Minnesota status. Regular. Migrant, winter visitant, and summer resident.

Migration. Common but erratic throughout the wooded portions of the state in spring and fall; uncommon on the northern prairie and rare on the central and southern prairies. *Fall migration period:* Late July (north) through early December with the bulk of the migration in October and November. Earliest dates: NORTH, none can be given because of nesting birds; SOUTH, September *4*, *6*, *15*, October *5*, 17, 18, 22. *Spring migration period:* March through early June (north) with the bulk of the migration from mid-April through mid-May. Latest dates: SOUTH, May 13, 16, 19, *23*, *24*; NORTH, none can be given because of nesting birds.

Winter. Visitant throughout the state, usually in flocks at feeding stations in settlements but occasionally in the coniferous forests when there is a good cone crop. Erratic in distribution and variable in numbers from year to year, but usually common in the north and uncommon in the south.

Summer. Resident in the northeastern and north central regions (see map 89). Formerly present only sparingly in the coniferous forests; more numerous during the last twenty years with some evidence that the species has expanded its breeding range to the south and west into Crow Wing, Cass, Clearwater, and Beltrami counties.

89. Evening Grosbeak

PURPLE FINCH *Carpodacus purpureus*

Minnesota status. Regular. Migrant, winter visitant, and summer resident.

Migration. Common spring and fall migrant throughout most of the state; uncommon along the prairie margins. Locally abundant, especially in the spring in the eastern part of the state. *Fall migration period:* Mid-July (north) through late November; usually leaves the north by early November. Earliest dates: NORTH, none can be given because of breeding birds; SOUTH, September 3, 4, 10. *Spring*

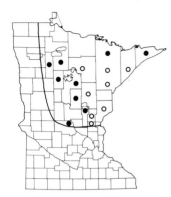

90. Purple Finch

migration period: Late February through late May with a peak in the south from late February through early April and in the north from late April through mid-May. Latest dates: SOUTH, May 20, 21, 25; NORTH, none can be given because of breeding birds.

Winter. Visitant throughout the state. Usually rare or absent in the northern regions; uncommon in the west central, southwestern, and south central regions; common in the central, east central, and southeastern regions. Numbers vary; invasions occur erratically in both the north and the south, usually in late winter or early spring.

Summer. Resident throughout the northeastern and north central regions and the adjacent counties in the central part of the state (see map 90) with breeding records from as far south as Collegeville, Stearns County, and Isanti County. There are a few summer observations from the Twin Cities but no nesting evidence.

HOUSE FINCH *Carpodacus méxicanus*

Minnesota status. Hypothetical.

Records. A specimen was taken in the spring of 1876, but the skin has since disappeared; this bird was thought to be an escaped cage bird. There were two observations in 1971 and 1972 from Hennepin County (*Loon* 43:127; 44:53–54), but the details of the descriptions do not preclude the possibility of confusion of this species with the Purple Finch. Because the species is expanding its range throughout the eastern United States, it should be looked for in Minnesota.

PINE GROSBEAK *Pinicola enucleator*

Minnesota status. Regular. Migrant and winter visitant.

Migration. Common fall migrant in the northeastern and north central regions; uncommon to rare in adjacent western and central regions. The species usually does not reach the southeastern region until winter and is accidental in the south central and southwestern regions. Less numerous in spring except in invasion years. *Fall migration period:* Mid-October through late November and probably into December, depending on the availability of food. Earliest dates: NORTH, August *20*, September *15*, *29*, October *6*, 18, 23, 25; SOUTH, September *22*, October *15*, *25*, November 1, 7, 11. *Spring migration period:* Gradual exodus with most birds departing from the south by late February or early March and from the north by late March or early April. Latest dates: SOUTH, March 3, 13, 19, April *1*, *12*; NORTH, April 9, 10, *22*, *30*, May *5*, *6*.

Winter. Usually a common winter visitant in the northeastern and north central regions; numbers vary from uncommon to abundant (invasion years). In the northwestern, west central, central, east central, and southeastern regions the species is usually a rare to uncommon winter visitant, occasionally becoming locally common in invasion years. In the south central and southwestern regions it is accidental. The erratic distribution and varying numbers reflect the availability of winter food such as cones and berries.

GRAY-CROWNED ROSY FINCH
Leucosticte tephrocotis

Minnesota status. Accidental. One fall record and three winter records.

Records. On October 28, 1972, one bird visited a feeder at Grand Rapids, Itasca County (*Loon* 45:20). On January 3, 1889 a male was shot from a flock of Snow Buntings near Minneapolis (MMNH #216). The species was not recorded again in winter until 1967, when two birds visited a feeder at Bagley, Clearwater County, from late December until March, 1968 (*Loon* 40:99). From January 25 to February 16, 1972, one bird visited a feeder at Little Marais, Lake County; the bird was seen and photographed by many people (*Loon* 44:117–118).

EUROPEAN GOLDFINCH *Carduelis carduelis*

Minnesota status. Hypothetical.

Records. The only record is of one bird, possibly an escaped cage bird, seen at a feeder in St. Paul, April 23–30, 1967 (*Loon* 39:105).

HOARY REDPOLL *Acanthis hornemanni*

Minnesota status. Regular. Migrant and winter visitant.

Migration. In the fall rare in the northern regions, rare to casual in the central regions, and accidental in the southern regions. In the spring rare to uncommon in the northern regions, rare in the central regions, and accidental in the southern regions. *Fall migration period:* Late October into December. Earliest dates: NORTH, October 27, 28, 30; SOUTH, October 21, November 3 (only dates). *Spring migration period:* Probably February through April. Latest dates: SOUTH, March 28, 31, April 6; NORTH, April 20, 22, 23.

Winter. Rare winter visitant, occasionally uncommon during invasion years, in the northern half of the state; rare winter visitant in the rest of the central regions and accidental in the southern regions. The species is often present in flocks of Common Redpolls. Numbers vary from year to year.

COMMON REDPOLL *Acanthis flammea*

Minnesota status. Regular. Migrant and winter visitant.

Migration. Common migrant, abundant during invasion years, in fall and spring throughout the state. *Fall migration period:* Mid-October through late November. Earliest dates: NORTH, October *4*, *5*, 12, 16; SOUTH, October *14*, 19, 21, 22. *Spring migration period:* Early February through early May with the bulk of the migration from mid-March through mid-April. Latest dates: SOUTH, April 16, 17, 18, May *1*; NORTH, May 13, 14, *20*, *26*.

Winter. Usually a common winter visitant throughout the state, but the numbers vary from uncommon to abundant. In invasion years flocks of one thousand to five thousand birds can be seen.

PINE SISKIN *Spinus pinus*

Minnesota status. Regular. Migrant, winter visitant, and summer resident.

91. Pine Siskin

Migration. Usually common fall and spring migrant (abundant during invasion years) in the eastern and central regions of the state; usually uncommon to rare in the western regions in both seasons. The species becomes locally common in the fall in the Red River Valley and in other western prairie areas where recently farmers have begun to grow crops of sunflowers. *Fall migration period:* Mid-September through late November. Earliest dates: None can be given because of breeding birds, but early arrivals in the south are usually in late September and early October. *Spring migration period:* Early March through late May with the bulk of the migration in April and early May. Latest dates: None can be given because of breeding birds, but late departures in the south are usually in mid-May.

Winter. Erratic winter visitant throughout the state. Distribution and numbers vary more sharply than for other winter finches. In the northern half of the state the species may be common in invasion years and absent in other years. In the southern half of the state it is more regular in occurrence but usually is uncommon.

Summer. Resident primarily in the northeastern and north central regions (see map 91). There is nesting evidence from Hennepin County (*Flicker* 33:55–56; *Loon* 38:108–109), and the species probably bred in Lac qui Parle County (one adult and two young birds seen on June 24, 1955), Winona County (one female with brood, patch-banded on July 28, 1969), and Rice County (two adults and two young birds seen on June 22, 1970). The most southerly nestings seem to occur after large winter invasions.

AMERICAN GOLDFINCH *Spinus tristis*

Minnesota status. Regular. Migrant and summer resident; regular in winter.

Migration. Common to abundant spring and fall migrant throughout the state; most numerous in the southern half of the state. *Spring migration period:* Mid-April (south) through early June (north) with the bulk of the migration from late April through late May. Earliest dates: SOUTH, none can be given because of wintering birds; NORTH, April 21, May 5, 6. *Fall migration period:* Early September through late November with the bulk of the migration in September and October. Latest dates: NORTH, none can be given because of winter stragglers, but most late departures are in early November; SOUTH, none can be given because of wintering birds.

Summer. Resident throughout the state; most numerous in the southern half of the state but present throughout the north in large numbers except in heavily wooded areas.

Winter. Regular and common in winter in the southern half of the state. It is not known whether the winter flocks are visitants from farther north or local summer residents. In the northern half of the state the species is usually absent or rare, but in some winters it has been present in invasion numbers locally.

RED CROSSBILL *Loxia curvirostra*

Minnesota status. Regular. Migrant and winter visitant; erratic summer resident and visitant.

Migration. Erratic migrant throughout the state in both seasons. When present, the species is usually uncommon, but it may be locally common in the north. Unpredictable in distribution and numbers from season to season and from year to year. *Fall migration period:* Erratic movements with no regular migration period; flocks may invade anywhere in the state from mid-June through August; winter invasions usually occur in mid- to late fall and are usually restricted to the north. Earliest dates: None can be given. *Spring Migration period:* No regular migration period; winter invasion flocks usually leave by mid-April; birds remaining later may breed locally anywhere in the northern half of the state and sometimes farther south. Latest dates: SOUTH, birds reported at feeders in May probably are breeding locally; NORTH, none can be given.

Winter. Erratic winter visitant throughout the state. Completely absent in some years, uncommon to locally common in other years. Numbers and movements depend on the cone crop in Minnesota and Canada.

92. Red Crossbill

Summer. Irregular resident primarily in the northern regions (see map 92), although breeding has occurred as far south as Stillwater, Washington County. The presence of nesting birds (usually in spring) depends on the availability of cones for food. The species nests in coniferous forests and in towns with plantings of conifers. Nesting is irregular, and the boundary on the map is only an approximate one.

WHITE-WINGED CROSSBILL *Loxia leucoptera*

Minnesota status. Regular. Migrant and winter visitant; erratic summer resident and visitant.

Migration. Usually an uncommon fall migrant in the northern regions, varying from rare to abundant (in invasion years); usually rare in the central and southern regions, varying from uncommon to locally common (in invasion years). *Fall migration period:* August through December. An invasion peak may occur at any season, most commonly in late fall or early winter. Earliest dates: NORTH, none can be given because of breeding birds; SOUTH, September 22, October 3, 5. *Spring migration period:* Gradual exodus of winter flocks through the end of April. Latest dates: SOUTH, May 11, 14, 17; NORTH, none can be given because of breeding birds.

Winter. Uncommon to common winter visitant in the northern regions (in invasion years abundant in the northeast); rare to uncommon in the central regions; rare in the southern regions. The numbers vary considerably from year to year, and the abundance terms represent only approximate population densities. Invasions usually peak in early winter.

Summer. The species is probably a very scarce resident in the northern coniferous forests; no nests have been found there, but fully fledged juvenile birds being fed by adults have been observed in Cook County, St. Louis County (Duluth), and Clearwater County (Itasca State Park). The species also occurs as a summer visitant in the northern forested regions, and flocks of juveniles and adults periodically invade these areas from late June through August.

GREEN-TAILED TOWHEE *Chlorura chlorura*

Minnesota status. Accidental. One winter record.
Records. One bird remained at a feeder in Duluth, St. Louis County, from early December, 1966, to mid-January, 1967. It was seen by many people (*Loon* 39:135) and photographed (National Photoduplicate File #592.1-1T).

RUFOUS-SIDED TOWHEE
Pipilo erythrophthalmus

Minnesota status. Regular. Migrant and summer resident; casual in winter.

Migration. Uncommon migrant throughout most of the state; rare or casual along the eastern Canadian border and the western prairie margin. *Spring migration period:* Mid-April through late May with a peak in late April. Earliest dates: SOUTH, March *23*, April 10, 13, 17; NORTH, April *5*, 26, 27, 30. *Fall migration period:* Early September through early November; most birds leave by mid-October. Latest dates: NORTH, October 9, 20, November 4, *15*, *21–25*, December *2*; SOUTH, October 12, 21, 28, November *15*, *21*.

Summer. Resident primarily in the southeastern, east central, and north central regions (see map 93). Absent on the prairie and in the northeastern coniferous forests (north of Duluth).

Winter. There are nine records of birds that have attempted to overwinter; three of these birds are known to have survived until February. Eight of the records are from the Twin Cities area, and one is from Lac qui Parle County.

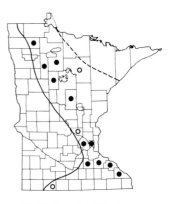

93. Rufous-sided Towhee

LARK BUNTING *Calamospiza melanocorys*

Minnesota status. Regular. Migrant; casual summer resident.

Migration. Rare to occasionally common spring migrant along the western margin of the state from Jackson County north to Mahnomen County and the Red River Valley; less numerous in the fall in this area. Casual elsewhere with spring and fall records from Cook, Lake, St. Louis, Cass, Mille Lacs, Sherburne, Ramsey, Kandiyohi, Rice, and Fillmore counties. *Spring migration period:* Mid-May through possibly mid-June with a peak in late May. Earliest dates: SOUTH, April *22*, May 11, 12, 15; NORTH, May *9*, *11*, 23 24. *Fall migration period:* Gradual exodus from breeding grounds in August and September; vagrants occur elsewhere into November. Latest dates: NORTH, September 12, 18, October *29*, November *9*; SOUTH, September 1, 5, October *20*.

Summer. Casual resident primarily in the southwestern region (see map 94). The species is not present in the state every year, and breeding has been recorded in only a few years (1895, 1897, 1900, 1901, 1927, 1929, 1936, 1964). Anderson and Getman speculate that the suitability of the remaining prairie in southern Minnesota as a nesting habitat for the Lark Bunting is influenced by the amount of precipitation, especially at nesting time (*Loon* 37:63–69).

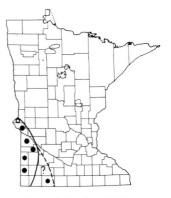

94. Lark Bunting (1940)

SAVANNAH SPARROW
Passerculus sandwichensis

Minnesota status. Regular. Migrant and summer resident.
Migration. Common spring and fall migrant throughout the state; most numerous on the western prairie in both seasons and least numerous in the northeastern region in the fall. *Spring migration period:* Early April through late May with the bulk of the migration during the first half of May. Earliest dates: SOUTH, March *21*, *24*, April 5, 9, 10; NORTH, March *30*, April *5*, 12, 21, 22. *Fall migration period:* Mid-August through late October with the bulk of the migration from mid-September through early October. Latest dates: NORTH, October 26, 29, 30; SOUTH, October 28, 31, November 1, *11*, *17–22*.
Summer. Resident throughout the state; numerous wherever there are low-lying grassy fields.

GRASSHOPPER SPARROW
Ammodramus savannarum

Minnesota status. Regular. Migrant and summer resident.
Migration. Uncommon to locally common spring migrant throughout most of the state; rare to casual in the north central and northeastern regions. Less numerous everywhere in the fall. *Spring migration period:* Late April through late May with a peak in early May. Earliest dates: SOUTH, April *14*, 18, 23, 24; NORTH, April 25, 26, 29. *Fall migration period:* Gradual departure from breeding areas in August and September; since few birds breed north of Minnesota, migration concentrations are not seen in the state. Latest dates: NORTH, September 17, October *10* (only dates); SOUTH, September 30, October 1, 3.
Summer. Resident throughout the state. The species is generally scarce in the north central and northeastern regions, and no nests have been reported from these two regions. Summer observations have been made as far north as Cook, northern St. Louis, Lake of the Woods, and Roseau counties.

BAIRD'S SPARROW *Ammodramus bairdii*

Minnesota status. Casual. Summer resident only in Clay County since about 1960; formerly more widespread.
Migration. Birds seen during the migration seasons are on breeding territories; there are no recent reliable records of transients. Earliest dates: May 5, 10, 17. Latest dates: July 21, 22, August 4.
Summer. Resident on the virgin prairie of the Glacial Lake Agassiz beach ridge east of Felton and Averill, Clay County; not present every year. The species was formerly a

resident throughout the Red River Valley from northern Traverse County to Kittson County. The disappearance of its habitat as a result of farming is probably the main reason for its current scarcity. The only nesting records are from western Pennington County (1930) and near Euclid, Polk County (1937).

HENSLOW'S SPARROW *Ammodramus henslowii*

Minnesota status. Regular. Migrant and summer resident.
Migration. Rare during the migration seasons in the southern half of the state and along the western margin north to Mahnomen County; most birds seen are on breeding territories. Accidental elsewhere. *Spring migration period:* Late April through late May. Earliest dates: April 19, 24, 25. *Fall migration period:* Gradual exodus from breeding areas in August and September. Latest dates: September 27, October 2, 3, *13*, *19*.
Summer. Resident in the southern half of the state and along the western margin to Mahnomen and Norman counties (see map 95). Most numerous south and east of St. Cloud. There are nineteenth-century summer observations from as far north as Kittson County, but modern records extend only to Clay County (Felton), Norman County (Syre), and Mahnomen County (Waubun).

95. Henslow's Sparrow

LE CONTE'S SPARROW *Ammospiza leconteii*

Minnesota status. Regular. Migrant and summer resident.
Migration. Uncommon to locally common spring and fall migrant in the western regions; uncommon to rare migrant in the central and eastern regions. *Spring migration period:* Late April through late May with the bulk of the migration during the first half of May. Earliest dates: SOUTH, April *6*, *8*, 21, 24; NORTH, April 29, May 4, 6. *Fall migration period:* Probably from sometime in August through mid-October. Latest dates: NORTH, October 3, 6, November *8*; SOUTH, October 11, 12, 17, *26*, November *1*, *2*, *9*.
Summer. Resident primarily in the northwestern region. The species also occurs sparingly in areas of wet and grassy habitat in the other northern regions and in the central part of the state, generally east of the Mississippi River (see map 96). Although large juveniles were recorded in Jackson County in 1928, no modern breeding evidence from the southern regions is available.

96. Le Conte's Sparrow (1930)

SHARP-TAILED SPARROW *Ammospiza caudacuta*

Minnesota status. Regular. Migrant and summer resident.
Migration. Rare to occasionally uncommon spring and fall migrant throughout most of the state; casual in the north

97. Sharp-tailed Sparrow

central and northeastern regions. *Spring migration period:* Throughout May with a peak in late May. Earliest dates: SOUTH, May 4, 7, 15; NORTH, no data. *Fall migration period:* Late August through mid-October with a peak around the end of September. Latest dates: NORTH, October 1, 5; SOUTH, October 11, 12, *18*.

Summer. Resident only in the northwestern region (see map 97). There are July records from the 1920s in Renville and Hennepin counties, but no evidence of breeding was reported.

VESPER SPARROW *Pooecetes gramineus*

Minnesota status. Regular. Migrant and summer resident; accidental in winter.

Migration. Common spring and fall migrant throughout most of the state; in the northeastern region the species is uncommon in the spring and rare in the fall. *Spring migration period:* Late March through late May with a peak in the south in mid-April and in the north in late April and early May. Earliest dates: SOUTH, March 23, 24, 28; NORTH, April *4*, *5*, 12, 16, 17. *Fall migration period:* August (north) through late October with a peak in mid- and late September. Latest dates: NORTH, October 24, 25, 27, November *8–12*, *20*, *21*; SOUTH, October 26, 27, 28. November *15*.

Summer. Resident throughout the state. Least numerous in the northeastern region; no breeding evidence from Lake and Cook counties.

Winter. Four winter records: December 5, 1966, Duluth; December 22, 1935, Fillmore County; December 25, 1957, four birds, Martin County; January 11, 1923, Anoka County.

LARK SPARROW *Chondestes grammacus*

Minnesota status. Regular. Migrant and summer resident.

Migration. Uncommon spring migrant in the southeastern, east central, and northwestern regions; casual in the north central and northeastern regions; rare elsewhere in the state. In the fall less numerous everywhere and absent in the north central and northeastern regions. *Spring migration period:* Early April through mid-May with a peak in early May. Earliest dates: SOUTH, April 4, 6, 8; NORTH, April *5*, *16*, 29, May 3, 6. *Fall migration period:* August and September. Latest dates: NORTH, September 3 (only date); SOUTH, September 17, 18, 20, October *4*.

Summer. Resident in the southeastern, east central, central, and northwestern regions; also probably resident south of the Minnesota River in the western and central areas (see

98. Lark Sparrow

map 98). The main breeding distribution of this species in Minnesota appears to be in two separate areas — one in the northwest and the other in the southeast.

DARK-EYED JUNCO (Slate-colored Junco)
Junco hyemalis

Minnesota status. Regular. Migrant, summer resident, and winter visitant.

Migration. Abundant spring and fall migrant throughout the state. *Spring migration period:* Early March through very early June with the bulk of the migration from late March through late April. Earliest dates: None can be given because of wintering birds. Latest dates: SOUTH, May 8, 10, 22, 24, 27; NORTH, none can be given because of breeding birds. *Fall migration period:* Late August through early December with the bulk of the migration in October. Earliest dates: NORTH, none can be given because of breeding birds; SOUTH, August 18, 25, September 15, 17, 20. Latest dates: None can be given because of wintering birds.

99. Dark-eyed Junco

Summer. Resident primarily in the northeastern and north central regions (see map 99) but very scarce along the western and southern margins of the two regions. Two records for the east central region; Pine County (young birds seen being fed), 1918; Chisago County (two young birds seen), 1950.

Winter. Visitant throughout the state. Common in the southern and central regions; rare in the northern regions.

Taxonomic note. The Oregon Junco, *J. h. oreganus*, occurs as a spring and fall migrant and as a winter visitant.

GRAY-HEADED JUNCO *Junco caniceps*

Minnesota status. Accidental. Two fall records and two winter records.

Records. One bird was seen and photographed at a feeder in Tofte, Cook County, October 27–29, 1968 (*Loon* 41:10); another bird was seen and photographed at a feeder in Duluth, November 24–29, 1969, and February 28, 1970 (*Loon* 42:116); the third bird was seen at a feeder in Boyd, Lac qui Parle County, from January 1 to February 24, 1973 (*Loon* 45:26).

TREE SPARROW *Spizella arborea*

Minnesota status. Regular. Migrant and winter visitant.

Migration. Abundant fall and spring migrant throughout the state. *Fall migration period:* Mid-September through late November with the bulk of the migration in October. Earliest dates: NORTH, September 10, 18, 20, 22; SOUTH, September 16, 21, 27, 28, October 2. *Spring migration* *period:* Early March through late May with the bulk of the migration from early April through early May. Latest dates: SOUTH, April 27, 30, May 4; NORTH, May 22, 23, 27.

Winter. Common to locally abundant winter visitant in the southern half of the state; rare winter visitant elsewhere in the state.

CHIPPING SPARROW *Spizella passerina*

Minnesota status. Regular. Migrant and summer resident.
Migration. Common migrant throughout the state in spring and fall; occasionally abundant on the North Shore of Lake Superior in the spring. *Spring migration period:* Late March through late May with the bulk of the migration from mid-April through mid-May. Earliest dates: SOUTH, March *15*, 24, 25; NORTH, April *1*, *7*, *9*, 16, 17. *Fall migration period:* From early August (in the northeast) through late October with the bulk of the migration in September. Latest dates: NORTH, October 12, 16, *26*, *29*; SOUTH, October 27, 30, November 2, *22–27*.
Summer. Resident throughout the state; most numerous in the eastern and central regions.

CLAY-COLORED SPARROW *Spizella pallida*

Minnesota status. Regular. Migrant and summer resident.
Migration. Uncommon to locally common spring and fall migrant throughout most of the state; rare in the southern regions. *Spring migration period:* Late April through late May with a peak in mid-May. The species formerly arrived regularly in mid-April in the southernmost counties, but it is now very scarce there as a breeding bird. Earliest dates: SOUTH, April *4*, *6*, *8*, 20, 22, 23; NORTH, April 25, 26, 27. *Fall migration period:* Mid-August through mid-October with a peak in mid- and late September. Latest dates: NORTH, October 6, 9, 12; SOUTH, October 15, 19, 20.
Summer. Resident throughout the state; very scarce in the southern regions. Old nesting records from Fillmore (1888), Mower (1903), and Goodhue (1921) counties; no recent observations south of Dakota and Lyon counties.

FIELD SPARROW *Spizella pusilla*

Minnesota status. Regular. Migrant and summer resident; accidental in winter.
Migration. In the southeastern and east central regions the species is common in spring and fall; in the south central, southwestern, central, and west central regions it is uncommon in both seasons; in the northern regions it is very rare during migration. *Spring migration period:* Late March through early May with a peak in mid-April. Earliest dates:

SOUTH, March 9, 23, 29; NORTH, April 12, 23 (only dates). *Fall migration period:* September and October. Latest dates: NORTH, September 27, October 2, *16*; SOUTH, October 27, 29, November *11*, *16*, *29*.

Summer. Resident in the southern half of the state (see map 100); most numerous in the southeastern and east central regions. There are a few summer observations from farther north (Otter Tail, Hubbard, Wadena, Crow Wing, Itasca, Aitkin, and southern St. Louis counties), but no nesting evidence is available from these areas.

Winter. One record of a bird at a feeder in Winona, Winona County, from October 1, 1969, to February 26, 1970.

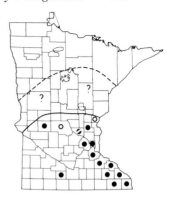

100. Field Sparrow

HARRIS' SPARROW *Zonotrichia querula*

Minnesota status. Regular. Migrant and winter visitant.

Migration. Common to locally abundant migrant in the western half of the state; uncommon to locally common migrant in the eastern half. *Spring migration period:* Very late March through very early June with a peak in mid-May. Earliest dates: SOUTH, March *19*, *20*, 26, 27, 31; NORTH, April 22, 24, 28. Latest dates: SOUTH, May 23, 26, June *19*; NORTH, May 30, 31, June 2, *7*. *Fall migration period:* Mid-September through late November with the bulk of the migration from late September through late October. Earliest dates: NORTH, September *3*, 10, 13, 14; SOUTH, August *30*, September 17, 19. Latest dates: NORTH, October 29, November 1, *13*, December *13*, *20*; SOUTH, November 20, 21.

Winter. Regular but rare winter visitant in the southwestern region; casual elsewhere. This species was not known to winter in the state until the mid-1950s, but during the 1960s it began to appear regularly in the southwest. Although its numbers dwindle in late winter, there are February records of the species in ten counties throughout the southwestern quarter of the state (from Watonwan County to Pope County). Most reports are of individual birds seen at feeders, but a few small groups have been seen in Rock and Jackson counties. Elsewhere in the state a few individual birds have attempted to overwinter at feeders as far north as Moorhead and Duluth. Most disappear by midwinter, but there are February records for Carlton County (as late as February 10 in 1965) and Hennepin County (as late as February 7 in 1969).

WHITE-CROWNED SPARROW
Zonotrichia leucophrys

Minnesota status. Regular. Migrant; casual in winter.

Migration. Uncommon to locally common spring and fall

migrant throughout the state. *Spring migration period:* Mid-April through late May with a peak in mid-May. Earliest dates: SOUTH, March *30*, April *9*, 14, 16; NORTH, April *14*, 19, 20, 23. Latest dates: SOUTH, May 21, 22, 26, *30*; NORTH, May 30, 31, June 3, *6–9, 7–13*. *Fall migration period:* Early September through early November with stragglers into December; the bulk of the migration occurs from late September through mid-October. Earliest dates: NORTH, September 3, 5, 7; SOUTH, September *12*, 19, 20, 25. Latest dates: NORTH, October 22, 27, November *13*, *29*, December *5*; SOUTH, October 29, November 7, *25*, December *1–8*.

Winter. There are a few records, most of them recent, of birds attempting to overwinter in the state: December 22, 1970, Redwood County; December 26, 1935, Dakota County; January 1, 1964, Olmsted County; January 1, 1964, Scott County; January 31, 1970, Cook County; February 11, 1964, Anoka County; March 7, 1964, Hennepin County (two birds).

WHITE-THROATED SPARROW
Zonotrichia albicollis

Minnesota status. Regular. Migrant, summer resident, and winter visitant.

Migration. Abundant spring and fall migrant throughout the state. *Spring migration period:* Late March through late May with the bulk of the migration from late April through mid-May. Earliest dates: SOUTH, March 20, 22; NORTH, April *5*, 11, 12, 21. Latest dates: SOUTH (beyond breeding areas), May 19, 20, 25, June *1*, *4*. *Fall migration period:* Mid-August (north) through November with stragglers into early winter; the bulk of the migration is from mid-September through early October. Earliest dates: SOUTH (beyond breeding areas), August *27*, September 3, 7, 12. Latest dates: NORTH, November 25, 27, 29; SOUTH, November 30, December 2, 6.

Summer. Resident primarily in the northeastern and north central regions and in the adjacent counties in the central and east central regions (see map 101); scarce along the western and southern margins of these areas. Breeding evidence has been obtained from locations as far south as Cedar Creek Forest, Anoka County, and as far west as eastern Marshall County.

Winter. Very rare visitant. Most frequent reports are of individual birds overwintering at feeders in the eastern part of the state, but there are records from all parts of the state except the western regions.

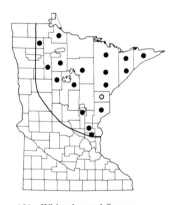

101. White-throated Sparrow

FOX SPARROW *Passerella iliaca*

Minnesota status. Regular. Migrant; casual in winter.
Migration. Uncommon migrant in spring and fall throughout the state, becoming locally common in spring in the
eastern regions. *Spring migration period:* Mid-March
through mid-May with a peak in early April (south) to late
April (north). Earliest dates: SOUTH, March 11, 12, 14;
NORTH, March 31, April 1, 2. Latest dates: SOUTH, May 11,
17, 19; NORTH, May 19, 20, 21. *Fall migration period:*
Mid-September through mid-November with stragglers into
early winter; the bulk of the migration is from early October through mid-October. Earliest dates: NORTH, August
26, September 8, 9, 12; SOUTH, September *4*, 12, 14, 15.
Latest dates: NORTH, November 19, 20, 21, *30*, December
19, *23*; SOUTH, November 28, 30, December 6, *12*, *16*.
Winter. There are at least fifteen records of single birds at
feeding stations in late December, January, or February,
reported from a total of ten counties. Two-thirds of the
records are from the southern half of the state; the northern
records are from St. Louis and Cook counties.

LINCOLN'S SPARROW *Melospiza lincolnii*

Minnesota status. Regular. Migrant and summer resident.
Migration. Uncommon migrant in spring and fall throughout the state, becoming locally common in spring in the
eastern regions. *Spring migration period:* Mid-April
through late May with the bulk of the migration from late
April through mid-May. Earliest dates: SOUTH, March *30*,
April 7, 10, 13; NORTH, March *31*, April *12*, 21, 26, 27.
Latest dates: SOUTH, May 21, 22, June *5*, *26*; NORTH
(beyond breeding areas), May 31. *Fall migration period:*
Late July (north) through early November with the bulk of
the migration from mid-September through early October.
Earliest dates: NORTH (beyond breeding areas), July 28,
29; SOUTH, July *12*, August 12, 14, 17. Latest dates:
NORTH, October 16, 20, 26, November *2*; SOUTH, October
31, November 1, 2, *6*, 7.
Summer. Resident primarily in the northeastern region (see
map 102). The species is very scarce even in its main range
in Cook and Lake counties and in the northern two-thirds of
St. Louis County; nests have been found as far south as
Kelsey, St. Louis County. Outside this area the range is
very poorly known, and only single reports are available
from Itasca County, Crow Wing County (Whitefish Lake),
Cass County (Leech Lake), and Beltrami County (Waskish).

102. Lincoln's Sparrow

SWAMP SPARROW *Melospiza georgiana*

Minnesota status. Regular. Migrant and summer resident; casual in winter.

Migration. Common spring and fall migrant throughout most of the state; uncommon fall migrant in the northern regions. *Spring migration period:* Late March through late May with the bulk of the migration from mid-April through mid-May. Earliest dates: SOUTH, March 12, 24, 25; NORTH, April 16, 17, 18. *Fall migration period:* Early August through late November with the bulk of the migration from mid-September through mid-October. Latest dates: NORTH, October 20, 24, 26, November *4*; SOUTH, November 18, 23, 25.

Summer. Resident throughout the state wherever there is suitable habitat.

Winter. There are over a dozen records of wintering birds; all but two of them are from the Twin Cities area and southeastward, where the species has been seen in all winter months at feeders and in swampy locations (up to four birds in a group). Other records: December 20, 1966, Lyon County; January 22–April 14, 1970, Duluth.

SONG SPARROW *Melospiza melodia*

Minnesota status. Regular. Migrant and summer resident; regular in winter.

Migration. Common spring and fall migrant throughout the state; least numerous in the northern regions in the fall. *Spring migration period:* Early March through early May with the bulk of the migration from late March through late April. Earliest dates: SOUTH, none can be given because of wintering birds; NORTH, March *18*, 25, 26, 30. *Fall migration period:* Late August (north) through late November (south) with the bulk of the migration from late September through late October. Latest dates: NORTH, October 31, November 2, 11, *25*; SOUTH, none can be given because of wintering birds.

Summer. Resident throughout the state. One of the most numerous and evenly distributed breeding species in the state.

Winter. Very rare winter visitant. The species is most often seen in early winter at feeders and near open water in the southeastern quarter of the state. It is only casual in the northern half of the state, and birds attempting to overwinter at feeders disappear by January or early February.

McCOWN'S LONGSPUR *Calcarius mccownii*

Minnesota status. Accidental. One fall record since 1900. The species formerly occurred as a migrant and as a summer resident.

Records. On October 20, 1935, at least two birds of this species were seen in a flock of Chestnut-collared Longspurs near Hassman, Aitkin County (*Auk* 53:342).

Former status. In the nineteenth century the species bred on the high prairie along the extreme western margin of the state from Pipestone County north to Big Stone County and more sparingly northward into the Red River Valley until it disappeared from the state in about 1900. Roberts (1932) mentioned records of breeding in Pipestone, Lincoln, and Lac qui Parle counties and a spring arrival date of May 8. There are four specimens from the nineteenth century.

LAPLAND LONGSPUR *Calcarius lapponicus*

Minnesota status. Regular. Migrant and winter visitant.

Migration. Common to locally abundant spring and fall migrant throughout the state except in heavily wooded areas. The species is most numerous in the western regions, and flocks totaling tens of thousands have been seen. The numbers present in the state vary considerably; in addition, the species may be absent from a given area in one year and abundant there the next. *Fall migration period:* Early September through mid-November with a peak period from late September through early October in the north and from late October through early November in the south. Earliest dates: NORTH, September 8, 9, 11; SOUTH, September *10*, *13*, October 2, 3, 4. Latest dates: NORTH, November 4, 5, *19*; SOUTH, none can be given because of wintering birds. *Spring migration period:* Late February through late May with a peak from late March through early April in the south and during May in the north. Earliest dates: SOUTH, none can be given because of wintering birds; NORTH, March 1, 2. Latest dates: SOUTH, May 5, 6, 8, *30*; NORTH, May 27, 28, 29.

Winter. Common winter visitant in the southern half of the state; casual in the northern regions. Since all but one of the eight northern records were observed between December 14 and January 8, the records may represent fall stragglers. The eighth record was one bird seen on January 25, 1969, at Duluth.

SMITH'S LONGSPUR *Calcarius pictus*

Minnesota status. Regular. Migrant.

Migration. Very rare spring and fall migrant in the western regions, especially in the southern half of the state; accidental in St. Louis, Stearns, and Blue Earth counties. Normally encountered in flocks of other longspurs. *Spring migration period:* Mid-April through early May. Earliest dates: SOUTH, April 10, 18, 24; NORTH, no data. Latest dates:

SOUTH, May 8, 9, 10; NORTH, May 6 (only date). *Fall migration period:* Mid-September through mid-November. Earliest dates: NORTH, September 9, 15, 21; SOUTH, October 19, 20, 24. Latest dates: NORTH, October 10, 13; SOUTH, November 2, 11, 17.

CHESTNUT-COLLARED LONGSPUR
Calcarius ornatus

Minnesota status. Regular. Migrant and summer resident. **Migration.** Rare spring and fall migrant throughout the western margin of the state; accidental elsewhere. In the spring most birds seen are on breeding territories. The species is very rarely identified in the fall. *Spring migration period:* Mid-April probably through mid-May. Earliest dates: SOUTH, April 12, 25; NORTH, April 14, 23. *Fall migration period:* Probably mid-August through mid-October; very few dates. Latest dates: NORTH, September 20, 28; SOUTH, September 19, October 12, November *17*. **Summer.** Resident in the northwestern region, primarily on the beach ridges of Glacial Lake Agassiz that border the Red River Valley from Clay to Marshall counties (see map 103). The species formerly bred throughout the western prairie from Jackson County to the Canadian border. It disappeared in the southern part of the range in about 1900, and it was last reported in Grant County in 1937. Some undiscovered colonies may exist in the southern part of the state, however, because two singing males were seen in July, 1955, near Chandler, Murray County.

103. Chestnut-collared Longspur (1940)

SNOW BUNTING *Plectrophenax nivalis*

Minnesota status. Regular. Migrant and winter visitant. **Migration.** Common fall and spring migrant throughout the state, becoming locally abundant, especially in the northern regions. Least numerous in the southeastern region. *Fall migration period:* Occasionally mid-September, but usually early October through late November with the bulk of the migration from mid-October through mid-November. Earliest dates: NORTH, September *1*, *3*, *14*, *18*, October 3; SOUTH, September *26*, October *6*, *7*, *9*, 16, 21, 24. *Spring migration period:* Mid-February through late May with the bulk of the migration from early March through late April. Latest dates: SOUTH, April 23, 27, 29, May *5*, *12*, *14*; NORTH, May 19, 21, *26*. **Winter.** Common winter visitant throughout most of the state; uncommon in the heavily wooded areas of the northeastern and north central regions.

Appendixes

APPENDIX I. Status of Species in Minnesota

Regular Species (292)

Common Loon
Red-throated Loon
Red-necked Grebe
Horned Grebe
Eared Grebe
Western Grebe
Pied-billed Grebe
White Pelican
Double-crested Cormorant
Great Blue Heron
Green Heron
Cattle Egret (photo)
Great Egret
Black-crowned Night Heron
Yellow-crowned Night Heron
Least Bittern
American Bittern
Whistling Swan
Canada Goose
White-fronted Goose
Snow Goose
Mallard
Black Duck
Gadwall
Pintail
Green-winged Teal
Blue-winged Teal
American Wigeon
Northern Shoveler
Wood Duck
Redhead
Ring-necked Duck
Canvasback
Greater Scaup
Lesser Scaup
Common Goldeneye
Bufflehead
Oldsquaw
Harlequin Duck
White-winged Scoter
Surf Scoter
Black Scoter
Ruddy Duck

Hooded Merganser
Common Merganser
Red-breasted Merganser
Turkey Vulture
Goshawk
Sharp-shinned Hawk
Cooper's Hawk
Red-tailed Hawk
Red-shouldered Hawk
Broad-winged Hawk
Swainson's Hawk
Rough-legged Hawk
Ferruginous Hawk
Golden Eagle
Bald Eagle
Marsh Hawk
Osprey
Peregrine Falcon
Merlin
American Kestrel
Spruce Grouse
Ruffed Grouse
Greater Prairie Chicken
Sharp-tailed Grouse
Bobwhite
Ring-necked Pheasant
Chukar
Gray Partridge
Sandhill Crane
King Rail
Virginia Rail
Sora
Yellow Rail
Common Gallinule
American Coot
Semipalmated Plover
Piping Plover
Killdeer
American Golden Plover
Black-bellied Plover
Ruddy Turnstone
American Woodcock
Common Snipe

Whimbrel
Upland Sandpiper
Spotted Sandpiper
Solitary Sandpiper
Greater Yellowlegs
Lesser Yellowlegs
Willet
Red Knot
Pectoral Sandpiper
White-rumped Sandpiper
Baird's Sandpiper
Least Sandpiper
Dunlin
Semipalmated Sandpiper
Western Sandpiper
Sanderling
Short-billed Dowitcher
Long-billed Dowitcher
Stilt Sandpiper
Buff-breasted Sandpiper
Marbled Godwit
Hudsonian Godwit
American Avocet
Wilson's Phalarope
Northern Phalarope
Parasitic Jaeger
Glaucous Gull
Herring Gull
Ring-billed Gull
Franklin's Gull
Bonaparte's Gull
Forster's Tern
Common Tern
Caspian Tern
Black Tern
Rock Dove
Mourning Dove
Yellow-billed Cuckoo
Black-billed Cuckoo
Screech Owl
Great Horned Owl
Snowy Owl
Hawk Owl

195

Regular Species — *Continued*

Burrowing Owl
Barred Owl
Great Gray Owl
Long-eared Owl
Short-eared Owl
Boreal Owl
Saw-whet Owl
Whip-poor-will
Common Nighthawk
Chimney Swift
Ruby-throated Hummingbird
Belted Kingfisher
Common Flicker
Pileated Woodpecker
Red-bellied Woodpecker
Red-headed Woodpecker
Yellow-bellied Sapsucker
Hairy Woodpecker
Downy Woodpecker
Black-backed Three-toed
    Woodpecker
Northern Three-toed
    Woodpecker
Eastern Kingbird
Western Kingbird
Great Crested Flycatcher
Eastern Phoebe
Yellow-bellied Flycatcher
Acadian Flycatcher
Willow Flycatcher
Alder Flycatcher
Least Flycatcher
Eastern Wood Pewee
Olive-sided Flycatcher
Horned Lark
Tree Swallow
Bank Swallow
Rough-winged Swallow
Barn Swallow
Cliff Swallow
Purple Martin
Gray Jay
Blue Jay
Black-billed Magpie
Common Raven
Common Crow
Black-capped Chickadee
Boreal Chickadee
Tufted Titmouse
White-breasted Nuthatch
Red-breasted Nuthatch
Brown Creeper
House Wren
Winter Wren
Long-billed Marsh Wren
Short-billed Marsh Wren

Mockingbird
Gray Catbird
Brown Thrasher
American Robin
Varied Thrush
Wood Thrush
Hermit Thrush
Swainson's Thrush
Gray-cheeked Thrush
Veery
Eastern Bluebird
Blue-gray Gnatcatcher
Golden-crowned Kinglet
Ruby-crowned Kinglet
Water Pipit
Sprague's Pipit
Bohemian Waxwing
Cedar Waxwing
Northern Shrike
Loggerhead Shrike
Starling
Bell's Vireo
Yellow-throated Vireo
Solitary Vireo
Red-eyed Vireo
Philadelphia Vireo
Warbling Vireo
Black-and-white Warbler
Prothonotary Warbler
Golden-winged Warbler
Blue-winged Warbler
Tennessee Warbler
Orange-crowned Warbler
Nashville Warbler
Northern Parula
Yellow Warbler
Magnolia Warbler
Cape May Warbler
Black-throated Blue Warbler
Yellow-rumped Warbler
Black-throated Green
    Warbler
Cerulean Warbler
Blackburnian Warbler
Chestnut-sided Warbler
Bay-breasted Warbler
Blackpoll Warbler
Pine Warbler
Palm Warbler
Ovenbird
Northern Waterthrush
Louisiana Waterthrush
Connecticut Warbler
Mourning Warbler
Common Yellowthroat
Wilson's Warbler

Canada Warbler
American Redstart
House Sparrow
Bobolink
Eastern Meadowlark
Western Meadowlark
Yellow-headed Blackbird
Red-winged Blackbird
Orchard Oriole
Northern Oriole
Rusty Blackbird
Brewer's Blackbird
Common Grackle
Brown-headed Cowbird
Scarlet Tanager
Cardinal
Rose-breasted Grosbeak
Blue Grosbeak
Indigo Bunting
Dickcissel
Evening Grosbeak
Purple Finch
Pine Grosbeak
Hoary Redpoll
Common Redpoll
Pine Siskin
American Goldfinch
Red Crossbill
White-winged Crossbill
Rufous-sided Towhee
Lark Bunting
Savannah Sparrow
Grasshopper Sparrow
Henslow's Sparrow
Le Conte's Sparrow
Sharp-tailed Sparrow
Vesper Sparrow
Lark Sparrow
Dark-eyed Junco
Tree Sparrow
Chipping Sparrow
Clay-colored Sparrow
Field Sparrow
Harris' Sparrow
White-crowned Sparrow
White-throated Sparrow
Fox Sparrow
Lincoln's Sparrow
Swamp Sparrow
Song Sparrow
Lapland Longspur
Smith's Longspur
Chestnut-collared Longspur
Snow Bunting

Casual Species (23)

Little Blue Heron*
Snowy Egret*
White-faced Ibis
Cinnamon Teal
European Wigeon*
Barrow's Goldeneye†
Gyrfalcon
Long-billed Curlew

Iceland Gull
Thayer's Gull*
Barn Owl
Scissor-tailed Flycatcher
Clark's Nutcracker
Bewick's Wren†
Carolina Wren*
Mountain Bluebird

Townsend's Solitaire
Worm-eating Warbler
Kentucky Warbler
Yellow-breasted Chat
Western Tanager*
Summer Tanager
Baird's Sparrow

Accidental Species (44)

Arctic Loon†
Louisiana Heron†
Brant
Black Brant*
Ross' Goose*
Fulvous Tree Duck*
Common Eider
King Eider
Swallow-tailed Kite
Prairie Falcon
Willow Ptarmigan
Whooping Crane
Black Rail†
Purple Gallinule
Purple Sandpiper

Ruff*
Red Phalarope*
Pomarine Jaeger*
Long-tailed Jaeger
Great Black-backed Gull*
Little Gull*
Ivory Gull†
Black-legged Kittiwake*
Arctic Tern*
Least Tern†
Dovekie
Ancient Murrelet
Band-tailed Pigeon*
Groove-billed Ani

Poor-will
Dipper*
Rock Wren
Black-throated Gray Warbler
Hermit Warbler
Kirtland's Warbler
Prairie Warbler†
Hooded Warbler*
Black-headed Grosbeak*
Lazuli Bunting†
Painted Bunting
Gray-crowned Rosy Finch
Green-tailed Towhee*
Gray-headed Junco*
McCown's Longspur

Hypothetical Species (12)

Glossy Ibis†
Mississippi Kite†
Turkey†
Sabine's Gull†

Williamson's Sapsucker†
Black Phoebe†
Say's Phoebe†
Western Wood Pewee†

Violet-green Swallow†
White-eyed Vireo†
House Finch†
European Goldfinch†

Extirpated Species (2)

Trumpeter Swan†

Eskimo Curlew†

Extinct Species (1)

Passenger Pigeon

* Photograph only; no specimen
† No photograph or specimen

APPENDIX II. Distribution of Breeding Species in Minnesota

Geographic Distribution

Red-necked Grebe* †
Horned Grebe (local)
Pied-billed Grebe*
Double-crested Cormorant
  (local)
Great Blue Heron
American Bittern
Canada Goose
Mallard
Green-winged Teal (local)
Blue-winged Teal
Wood Duck
Hooded Merganser
Turkey Vulture (local)
Sharp-shinned Hawk*
Cooper's Hawk
Red-tailed Hawk
Marsh Hawk
American Kestrel
Virginia Rail*
Sora
American Coot*
Killdeer
Common Snipe
Upland Sandpiper*
Spotted Sandpiper
Black Tern*
Mourning Dove*
Black-billed Cuckoo
Great Horned Owl

Whip-poor-will
Common Nighthawk
Chimney Swift
Ruby-throated Hummingbird
Belted Kingfisher
Common Flicker
Pileated Woodpecker
Red-headed Woodpecker
Yellow-bellied Sapsucker
Hairy Woodpecker
Downy Woodpecker
Eastern Kingbird
Great Crested Flycatcher
Eastern Phoebe
Least Flycatcher
Eastern Wood Pewee
Horned Lark*
Tree Swallow
Bank Swallow
Rough-winged Swallow
Barn Swallow
Cliff Swallow
Purple Martin
Blue Jay
Common Crow
Black-capped Chickadee
White-breasted Nuthatch*
House Wren
Long-billed Marsh Wren*
Short-billed Marsh Wren
Gray Catbird

Brown Thrasher
American Robin
Veery†
Eastern Bluebird
Cedar Waxwing†
Loggerhead Shrike*
Starling
Red-eyed Vireo
Yellow Warbler
Common Yellowthroat
House Sparrow
Bobolink
Western Meadowlark*
Yellow-headed Blackbird*
Red-winged Blackbird
Northern Oriole
Brewer's Blackbird*
Common Grackle
Brown-headed Cowbird
Scarlet Tanager
Rose-breasted Grosbeak
Indigo Bunting
American Goldfinch
Savannah Sparrow
Grasshopper Sparrow*
Vesper Sparrow*
Chipping Sparrow
Clay-colored Sparrow
Swamp Sparrow
Song Sparrow

* Absent or very rare in the northeastern part of the state and along the Canadian border owing to the lack of suitable habitat
† Absent or very rare on the prairie owing to the lack of suitable habitat

BREEDING THROUGHOUT MOST OF THE STATE EXCEPT ON THE PRAIRIE

Common Loon	Long-eared Owl	Chestnut-sided Warbler
Broad-winged Hawk	Saw-whet Owl	Ovenbird
Ruffed Grouse	Brown Creeper	American Redstart
American Woodcock	Wood Thrush	Eastern Meadowlark
Barred Owl	Black-and-white Warbler	Rufous-sided Towhee

BREEDING THROUGHOUT MOST OF THE STATE EXCEPT IN THE NORTHEASTERN AND NORTH CENTRAL REGIONS

Green Heron	Ring-necked Pheasant	Screech Owl
Black-crowned Night Heron	Gray Partridge	Yellow-throated Vireo
Least Bittern	Yellow-billed Cuckoo	Warbling Vireo

Ecological Distribution

PRIMARY HABITAT IN THE NORTHERN CONIFEROUS FORESTS

Black Duck	Olive-sided Flycatcher	Yellow-rumped Warbler
American Wigeon	Gray Jay	Black-throated Green
Ring-necked Duck	Common Raven	Warbler
Common Goldeneye	Boreal Chickadee	Blackburnian Warbler
Common Merganser	Red-breasted Nuthatch	Bay-breasted Warbler
Red-breasted Merganser	Winter Wren	Pine Warbler
Goshawk	Hermit Thrush	Palm Warbler
Bald Eagle	Swainson's Thrush	Northern Waterthrush
Osprey	Golden-crowned Kinglet	Connecticut Warbler
Merlin	Ruby-crowned Kinglet	Mourning Warbler
Spruce Grouse	Solitary Vireo	Wilson's Warbler (? casual)
Solitary Sandpiper (casual)	Philadelphia Vireo	Canada Warbler
Herring Gull	Golden-winged Warbler	Rusty Blackbird (? casual)
Common Tern	Tennessee Warbler	Evening Grosbeak
Hawk Owl (casual)	Orange-crowned Warbler	Purple Finch
Great Gray Owl (casual)	(? casual)	Pine Siskin
Black-backed Three-toed	Nashville Warbler	Red Crossbill
Woodpecker	Northern Parula	White-winged Crossbill
Northern Three-toed	Magnolia Warbler	(? casual)
Woodpecker (? casual)	Cape May Warbler	Dark-eyed Junco
Yellow-bellied Flycatcher	Black-throated Blue Warbler	White-throated Sparrow
Alder Flycatcher		Lincoln's Sparrow

PRIMARY HABITAT IN THE SOUTHEASTERN DECIDUOUS FORESTS

Yellow-crowned Night Heron	Bewick's Wren (casual;	Prothonotary Warbler
Red-shouldered Hawk	withdrawing southward)	Blue-winged Warbler
(expanding northward)	Carolina Wren (casual;	Cerulean Warbler
Bobwhite	withdrawing southward)	Louisiana Waterthrush
Red-bellied Woodpecker	Mockingbird (expanding	Yellow-breasted Chat (casual;
(expanding northward)	northward)	withdrawing southward)
Acadian Flycatcher	Blue-gray Gnatcatcher	Cardinal (expanding
Tufted Titmouse	Bell's Vireo	northward)

PRIMARY HABITAT ON THE PRAIRIE

Eared Grebe
Western Grebe
White Pelican
Gadwall
Pintail
Northern Shoveler
Redhead
Canvasback
Lesser Scaup (north only)
Ruddy Duck
Swainson's Hawk

Greater Prairie Chicken (north
   only)
Upland Sandpiper
Willet (casual)
Marbled Godwit
American Avocet (casual)
Wilson's Phalarope
Franklin's Gull
Forster's Tern
Burrowing Owl (casual)
Short-eared Owl

Western Kingbird
Sprague's Pipit (north only)
Orchard Oriole
Lark Bunting (casual; south
   only)
Baird's Sparrow (casual;
   north only)
Sharp-tailed Sparrow (north
   only)
Chestnut-collared Longspur
   (north only)

APPENDIX III. Primary Seasonal Occurrence of Regular Species in Minnesota

Permanent Residents

Red-shouldered Hawk
Spruce Grouse
Ruffed Grouse
Greater Prairie Chicken
Sharp-tailed Grouse
Bobwhite
Ring-necked Pheasant
Chukar
Gray Partridge

Rock Dove
Screech Owl
Great Horned Owl
Barred Owl
Pileated Woodpecker
Red-bellied Woodpecker
Hairy Woodpecker
Downy Woodpecker
Gray Jay

Blue Jay
Black-capped Chickadee
Boreal Chickadee
Tufted Titmouse
White-breasted Nuthatch
Red-breasted Nuthatch
Starling
House Sparrow
Cardinal

Summer Residents

Common Loon
Red-necked Grebe
Horned Grebe
Eared Grebe
Western Grebe
Pied-billed Grebe
Double-crested Cormorant
Great Blue Heron
Green Heron
Cattle Egret
Great Egret
Black-crowned Night Heron
Yellow-crowned Night Heron
Least Bittern
American Bittern
Canada Goose
Mallard
Black Duck
Gadwall
Pintail
Green-winged Teal
Blue-winged Teal
American Wigeon
Northern Shoveler
Wood Duck
Redhead
Ring-necked Duck
Canvasback

Common Goldeneye
Ruddy Duck
Hooded Merganser
Common Merganser
Red-breasted Merganser
Turkey Vulture
Sharp-shinned Hawk
Cooper's Hawk
Red-tailed Hawk
Broad-winged Hawk
Swainson's Hawk
Bald Eagle
Marsh Hawk
Osprey
American Kestrel
King Rail
Virginia Rail
Sora
Yellow Rail
Common Gallinule
American Coot
Killdeer
American Woodcock
Common Snipe
Upland Sandpiper
Spotted Sandpiper
Marbled Godwit
Wilson's Phalarope

Herring Gull
Franklin's Gull
Forster's Tern
Common Tern
Black Tern
Mourning Dove
Yellow-billed Cuckoo
Black-billed Cuckoo
Long-eared Owl
Short-eared Owl
Saw-whet Owl
Whip-poor-will
Common Nighthawk
Chimney Swift
Ruby-throated Hummingbird
Belted Kingfisher
Common Flicker
Red-headed Woodpecker
Yellow-bellied Sapsucker
Eastern Kingbird
Western Kingbird
Great Crested Flycatcher
Eastern Phoebe
Yellow-bellied Flycatcher
Acadian Flycatcher
Willow Flycatcher
Alder Flycatcher
Least Flycatcher

201

Summer Residents — *Continued*

Eastern Wood Pewee
Olive-sided Flycatcher
Horned Lark
Tree Swallow
Bank Swallow
Rough-winged Swallow
Barn Swallow
Cliff Swallow
Purple Martin
Common Crow
House Wren
Winter Wren
Long-billed Marsh Wren
Short-billed Marsh Wren
Gray Catbird
Brown Thrasher
American Robin
Wood Thrush
Hermit Thrush
Swainson's Thrush
Veery
Eastern Bluebird
Blue-gray Gnatcatcher
Golden-crowned Kinglet
Ruby-crowned Kinglet
Sprague's Pipit
Cedar Waxwing
Loggerhead Shrike
Bell's Vireo
Yellow-throated Vireo
Solitary Vireo
Red-eyed Vireo

Philadelphia Vireo
Warbling Vireo
Black-and-white Warbler
Prothonotary Warbler
Golden-winged Warbler
Blue-winged Warbler
Tennessee Warbler
Nashville Warbler
Northern Parula
Yellow Warbler
Magnolia Warbler
Cape May Warbler
Black-throated Blue Warbler
Yellow-rumped Warbler
Black-throated Green Warbler
Cerulean Warbler
Blackburnian Warbler
Chestnut-sided Warbler
Bay-breasted Warbler
Pine Warbler
Palm Warbler
Ovenbird
Northern Waterthrush
Louisiana Waterthrush
Connecticut Warbler
Mourning Warbler
Common Yellowthroat
Canada Warbler
American Redstart
Bobolink
Eastern Meadowlark
Western Meadowlark

Yellow-headed Blackbird
Red-winged Blackbird
Orchard Oriole
Northern Oriole
Brewer's Blackbird
Common Grackle
Brown-headed Cowbird
Scarlet Tanager
Rose-breasted Grosbeak
Blue Grosbeak
Indigo Bunting
Dickcissel
Evening Grosbeak
Purple Finch
Pine Siskin
American Goldfinch
Rufous-sided Towhee
Savannah Sparrow
Grasshopper Sparrow
Henslow's Sparrow
Le Conte's Sparrow
Sharp-tailed Sparrow
Vesper Sparrow
Lark Sparrow
Dark-eyed Junco
Chipping Sparrow
Clay-colored Sparrow
Field Sparrow
White-throated Sparrow
Swamp Sparrow
Song Sparrow
Chestnut-collared Longspur

Migrants

Red-throated Loon
White Pelican*
Whistling Swan
White-fronted Goose
Snow Goose
Greater Scaup
Lesser Scaup*
Bufflehead
White-winged Scoter
Surf Scoter
Black Scoter
Ferruginous Hawk
Golden Eagle
Peregrine Falcon*
Merlin*
Sandhill Crane*
Semipalmated Plover
Piping Plover*
American Golden Plover
Black-bellied Plover
Ruddy Turnstone

Whimbrel
Solitary Sandpiper*
Greater Yellowlegs
Lesser Yellowlegs
Willet*
Red Knot
Pectoral Sandpiper
White-rumped Sandpiper
Baird's Sandpiper
Least Sandpiper
Dunlin
Semipalmated Sandpiper
Western Sandpiper
Sanderling
Short-billed Dowitcher
Long-billed Dowitcher
Stilt Sandpiper
Buff-breasted Sandpiper
Hudsonian Godwit
American Avocet*
Northern Phalarope

Parasitic Jaeger
Ring-billed Gull*
Bonaparte's Gull
Caspian Tern*
Burrowing Owl*
Brown Creeper*
Mockingbird*
Gray-cheeked Thrush
Water Pipit
Orange-crowned Warbler
Blackpoll Warbler
Wilson's Warbler
Rusty Blackbird
Lark Bunting*
Tree Sparrow
Harris' Sparrow
White-crowned Sparrow
Fox Sparrow
Lincoln's Sparrow*
Lapland Longspur
Smith's Longspur

*Known to have bred in the state, but most individuals are migrants or visitants

Winter Visitants

Oldsquaw
Harlequin Duck
Goshawk*
Rough-legged Hawk
Glaucous Gull
Snowy Owl
Hawk Owl*
Great Gray Owl*

Boreal Owl
Black-backed Three-toed
   Woodpecker*
Northern Three-toed
   Woodpecker
Black-billed Magpie*
Common Raven*
Varied Thrush

Bohemian Waxwing
Northern Shrike
Pine Grosbeak
Hoary Redpoll
Common Redpoll
Red Crossbill*
White-winged Crossbill
Snow Bunting

*Known to have bred in the state, but most individuals are migrants or visitants

APPENDIX IV. Species Added to Minnesota List since 1973

MUTE SWAN *Cygnus olor*

Minnesota status. Accidental.

Records. Three birds were seen and photographed on May 27, 1974, on Lake Superior, near Duluth, and three birds were seen in the harbor at Grand Marais, Cook County, on January 27, 1975 (*Loon* 47:42–43).

MOUNTAIN PLOVER *Eupoda montana*

Minnesota status. Hypothetical.

Records. Three birds were observed near Moorhead, Clay County, on May 21, 1974 (*Loon* 46:115).

RUFOUS HUMMINGBIRD *Selasphorus rufus*

Minnesota status. Hypothetical.

Records. A single bird was seen near Grand Rapids, Itasca County, on August 4, 1974 (*Loon* 46:167–168).

LEWIS' WOODPECKER *Asyndesmus lewis*

Minnesota status. Accidental.

Records. A single bird was seen during the Sherburne Christmas Count on December 28, 1974, near Santiago, Sherburne County. The bird remained in the area through March, 1975 (*Loon* 47:39–40).

SCOTT'S ORIOLE *Icterus parisorum*

Minnesota status. Hypothetical.

Records. A single immature bird was seen and banded at Duluth on May 23, 1974. This individual remained in the area through June, 1974 (*Loon* 47:22–24).

BLACK-THROATED SPARROW *Amphispiza bilineata*

Minnesota status. Accidental.

Records. A single immature bird was found at Stony Point, St. Louis County, along the North Shore of Lake Superior on September 20, 1974. The bird was seen and photographed by many observers through September 23, 1974 (*Loon* 46:100–101).

BREWER'S SPARROW *Spizella breweri*

Minnesota status. Hypothetical.

Records. An individual identified as belonging to this species was seen and heard at Blue Mounds State Park, Rock County, on September 28, 1974 (*Loon* 47:40–41).

References

Selected Bibliography

This list includes articles, books, and other publications on various aspects of birding and ornithology in Minnesota. The majority of these references have not been cited in the text of the book. With the exception of several publications by T. S. Roberts, all of the references in the list have been published since 1936.

Adams, A. M., J. Bunn, B. S. Davis, A. L. Jones, and L. W. Odne. 1973. A study of the Pig's Eye Lake heron colonies. *Loon* 45:32–45.

American Ornithologists' Union. 1957. *Check-List of North American Birds*. 5th ed. Baltimore: Lord Baltimore Press.

American Ornithologists' Union Committee on Classification and Nomenclature. 1973. Thirty-second supplement to the American Ornithologists' Union *Check-List of North American Birds*. *Auk* 90:411–419, 887.

Banko, W. E. 1960. *The Trumpeter Swan; its history, habits, and population in the United States*. U.S. Fish Wildl. Serv., North American Fauna No. 63.

Barrows, V. F. 1953. Bird observations in the Virginia area. *Flicker* 25:118–124.

———. 1954. Some observations on the density of population of certain birds. *Flicker* 26:157.

Beer, J. R. 1958. Changes in Ovenbird and Mourning Warbler abundance at Basswood Lake, Minnesota. *Flicker* 30:22–23.

Beer, J. R., and L. D. Frenzel. 1956. Additional bird records for the Quetico-Superior Wilderness Research Area. *Flicker* 28:40.

Beer, J. R., and F. Priewert. 1951. Some observations of the birds of Basswood Lake. *Flicker* 23:61–68.

Bergstedt, B. V. 1972. Breeding-bird census: Burned jack pine ridge [St. Louis County]. *Amer. Birds* 27:987–988.

Bergstedt, B. V., and G. J. Niemi. 1974. A comparison of two breeding-bird censuses following the Little Sioux forest fire. *Loon* 46:28–33.

Bettenhausen, J. 1954. A bibliography of Minnesota warblers. *Flicker* 26:136–147.

Breckenridge, W. J. 1937. Annotated list of birds observed on trip to Lake Saganaga, June 23–30, 1937. Manuscript on file in the Bell Museum of Natural History, University of Minnesota, Minneapolis.

———. 1955. Comparison of the breeding-bird populations of two neighboring but distinct forest habitats [Anoka and Isanti counties]. *Audubon Field Notes* 9:408–412.

Carlsen, J. C., and S. W. Harris. 1955. Birds of Mud Lake [Agassiz] National Wildlife Refuge. *Flicker* 27:138–147.

Cohen, R. R. 1960. A study of Harbor Island, Duluth. *Flicker* 32:73–75.

Cohen, R. R., and S. B. Cohen. 1961. Second year study, Harbor Island, Duluth. *Flicker* 33:111–113.

Commons, M. E. 1938. *The log of Tanager Hill* [Hennepin County]. Baltimore: Williams and Wilkins.

Cottrille, B. D. 1962. A search for nesting Cape May Warblers. *Flicker* 34:38–40.

———. 1964. Lake County nesting records, 1962; Lake County nesting records, 1963. *Loon* 36:22–23.

Davids, R. C. 1966. Summer birds of Clearwater County. *Loon* 38:21–24.

Dodge, A. W., H. F. Fullerton, W. J. Breckenridge, and D. W. Warner. 1957. *Birds of the*

Minneapolis–St. Paul region: Combined field check list and migration chart. Bell Museum of Natural History, University of Minnesota, Minneapolis.

Dunstan, T. C. 1973. The biology of ospreys in Minnesota [Chippewa National Forest]. *Loon* 45:108–113.

Farmes, R. E. 1956. Potholes of Mahnomen County. *Flicker* 28:24–30.

Fashingbauer, B. A., A. C. Hodson, and W. H. Marshall. 1957. The inter-relations of a forest tent caterpillar outbreak, song birds, and DDT application [Hubbard County]. *Flicker* 29:132–147.

Flaccus, E., and L. F. Ohmann. 1964. Old-growth northern hardwoods forest in northeastern Minnesota. *Ecology* 45:448–459.

Frenzel, L. D., G. Juenemann, and J. Kussman. 1973. Behavioral aspects of eagle nest surveys [Chippewa National Forest]. In *Notes on a Bald Eagle nest survey workshop*, ed. C. R. Madsen, pp. 33–36. U.S. Fish Wildl. Serv.

Gabrielson, I. N. 1936. Bird notes from the Lake Francis region of southern Minnesota. *Wilson Bull.* 48:305–309.

Gates, J. M., and J. R. Beer. 1956. A marsh bird survey — spring 1955 [Ramsey County]. *Flicker* 28:16–21.

Grant, R. A. 1962. Annotated list of birds seen in the vicinity of Lake Saganaga, Ontario. *Flicker* 34:71–75.

Green, J. C. 1971. Summer birds of the Superior National Forest, Minnesota. *Loon* 43:103–107.

Green, J. C., and R. B. Janssen. 1971. An annotated list of Minnesota birds. *Loon* 43:40–54.

Grim, L. 1972. Birds of the Fort Frances–International Falls–Rainy Lake area. Mimeographed. Rainy River State Junior College, International Falls, Minnesota.

Hale, J., and H. Hale. 1952. A bird-list from the North Shore of Lake Superior. *Flicker* 24:86–88.

Hanlon, R. W. 1956. Heron Island–General Shields Lake. *Flicker* 28:130–132.

Hayward, B. 1950. Prairie fires and nesting birds [Hennepin County]. *Flicker* 22:35–38.

Heinselman, M. 1973. Fire in the virgin forests of the Boundary Waters Canoe Area, Minnesota. *J. Quaternary Res.* 3:329–382.

Hero, C. S. 1938. Marsh bird community study: A preliminary ecological investigation of the Minnesota Point sand-fill. *Flicker* 10:1–3.

———. 1942. A study of populations in a marsh bird community. *Flicker* 14:50–51.

Hickey, J. J. 1956. Notes on the succession of avian communities at Itasca Park, Minnesota. *Flicker* 28:2–10.

Hickey, J. J., J. T. Emlen, Jr., and S. C. Kendeigh. 1965. Early-summer birdlife of Itasca State Park. *Loon* 37:27–39.

Hickey, J. J., P. B. Hofslund, and H. F. Borchert. 1955. Bird nests in the Itasca State Park area, 1954. *Flicker* 27:16–21.

Hitman, B. A. 1972. Cattle Egret, Little Blue Heron, and possible Snowy Egret nestings at the Lake Johanna rookery, Pope County, Minnesota. *Loon* 44:36–43.

Hofslund, P. B. 1953. The birds of the Nortondale tract, Duluth, Minnesota. *Flicker* 25:4–9.

———. 1956. The birds of Gooseberry Falls State Park. *Flicker* 28:62–70.

———. 1959. Additions to the Gooseberry [Falls] State Park list. *Flicker* 31:139.

Huber, R. L. 1961. Swan Lake: An excellent nesting area. *Flicker* 33:61, 83–85.

Janssen, R. B. 1970. Birdfinding in Minnesota: A seasonal guide. *Loon* 42:138–141.

Jarosz, J. A. 1952. A nesting study at Hayden's Lake, Hennepin County. *Flicker* 24:145–147.

Kellehur, K. 1967. Distribution of breeding birds in deciduous forests at the prairie–hardwood forest ecotone in northwestern Minnesota. Ph.D. dissertation, University of Minnesota, Minneapolis.

Kendeigh, S. C. 1956. A trail census of birds at Itasca State Park, Minnesota. *Flicker* 28:90–104.

Kilgore, W. 1946. Chronological bibliography of Thomas Sadler Roberts', M.D., natural history writings. *Flicker* 18:72–75.

Lakela, O. 1937. The birds of Minnesota Point. *Proc. Minn. Acad. Sci.* 5:40–42.

———. 1939. A floristic study of a developing plant community on Minnesota Point, Minnesota. *Ecology* 20:544–552.

———. 1953. A check-list of birds from northeastern Minnesota based on observations made mostly in the Duluth area. *Flicker* 25:30–35.

Le Duc, P. 1970. The nesting ecology of some hawks and owls in southeastern Minnesota. *Loon* 42:48–62.

Lee, F. B. 1948. A comparison of bird occurrence and activity in two climax forests at Itasca Park, Minnesota. M.S. thesis, University of Minnesota, Minneapolis.

Le Febvre, J. H. 1959. Preliminary ornithological survey of French Creek Bog [Itasca State Park]. *Flicker* 31:106–108.

Lewis, D. K. 1955. *Checklist, birds of Itasca State Park.* Minn. Dep. Conserv.

Lindmeier, J. P. 1960. Plover, rail, and godwit nesting on a study area in·Mahnomen County, Minnesota. *Flicker* 32:5–9.

Longley, W. H. 1958. Bird life and vegetation changes — Whitewater Refuge. *Flicker* 30:84–87.

Marshall, W. H. 1952. Waterfowl of three prairie potholes [Ramsey County]. *Flicker* 24:60–68.

———. 1958. Waterfowl brood studies, Lake Itasca, Minn. *Flicker* 30:122–126.

Mathisen, J. E. 1963. The status of the Bald Eagle [in] the Chippewa National Forest. *Flicker* 35:114–117.

———. 1965. Bald Eagle status report, 1965, Chippewa National Forest. *Loon* 37:104–105.

———. 1966a. The breeding population of waterfowl [in] the Chippewa National Forest. *Loon* 38:24–30.

———. 1966b. Bald Eagle status report, 1966, Chippewa National Forest. *Loon* 38:134–136.

———. 1967. Bald Eagle–Osprey status report. *Loon* 39:121–122.

———. 1968. Bald Eagle–Osprey status report, 1968. *Loon* 40:97–99.

———. 1969. Bald Eagle–Osprey status report, 1969. *Loon* 41:84–87.

———. 1972. The status of Ospreys [in] the Chippewa National Forest. *Loon* 44:7–9.

———. 1973. Bald Eagle–Osprey status report, 1972. *Loon* 45:15–16.

Mathisen, J. E., and J. Stewart. 1970. A band for an eagle. *Loon* 42:85–87.

Minnesota Department of Natural Resources and Minnesota State Planning Agency. 1971. *Minnesota resource potentials in state outdoor recreation.* Project 80 Staff Report No. 1.

Mitchell, M. J. 1960. A resurvey of the breeding-bird population in an upland oak forest on the Anoka Sand Plain. *Audubon Field Notes* 14:488–489.

———. 1961. Breeding-bird populations in relation to grassland succession on the Anoka Sand Plain. *Flicker* 33:102–108.

Morrison, K. D., W. J. Breckenridge, and J. D. Herz. 1955. *Where to find birds in Minnesota.* Minneapolis: University of Minnesota Press.

Moyle, J. B., ed. 1964a. *Waterfowl in Minnesota.* Minn. Dep. Conserv. Tech. Bull. No. 7.

———. 1964b. *Ducks and land use in Minnesota.* Minn. Dep. Conserv. Tech. Bull. No. 8.

Niemi, G. J. 1972. Breeding-bird census: Balsam fir–birch forest [St. Louis County]. *Amer. Birds* 26:956.

———. 1973. Breeding-bird census: Balsam fir–birch forest [St. Louis County]. *Amer. Birds* 27:974.

Oehlenschlager, R. 1963. The birds of Wadena County. *Flicker* 35:46–48.

Pratt, J. 1964. *A survey of Encampment Forest, Lake County, Minnesota.* Privately printed.

Roberts, T. S. 1930. *Some changes in the distribution of certain Minnesota birds in the last fifty years.* Occas. Pap. Minn. Mus. Natur. Hist. No. 3, pp. 9–12.

———. 1932. *The birds of Minnesota.* 2 vols. Minneapolis: University of Minnesota Press.

———. 1936. *The birds of Minnesota.* 2nd rev. ed. 2 vols. Minneapolis: University of Minnesota Press.

———. 1938. *Logbook of Minnesota bird life, 1917–1937.* Minneapolis: University of Minnesota Press.

Rosendahl, C. O. 1955. *Trees and shrubs of the Upper Midwest.* Minneapolis: University of Minnesota Press.

Rosenwinkel, A. C. 1954. Mid-summer birding along the Superior "North Shore." *Flicker* 26:119–121.

Russell, R. P., Jr. 1971. Birds of Stearns County. *Loon* 43:28–31.

Rustad, O. A. 1957. A survey of the birds of Rice County, Minnesota. *Flicker* 29:43–63, 102–118.

Rusterholz, K. A. 1973. Island bird communities on Burntside Lake, Minnesota. M.S. thesis, University of Wisconsin, Madison.

Seabloom, R. W. 1960. La Salle trail bird census [Itasca State Park]. *Flicker* 32:38–40.

Sims, P. K., and G. B. Morey, eds. 1972. *Geology of Minnesota: A centennial volume.* Minnesota Geological Survey.

Smith, R. L. 1966. *Ecology and field biology.* New York: Harper and Row.

Swanson, G. 1940a. List from Kawishiwi and Isabella rivers, Lake County, July 1–6, 1940. Manuscript on file in the Bell Museum of Natural History, University of Minnesota, Minneapolis.

———. 1940b. Wildlife in the canoe country [Lake County]. *Flicker* 40:24–28.

———. 1943. Summer birds of Itasca Park. *Flicker* 15:25–28.

Swanson, G., and K. Carlander. 1940. Summer bird observations at Lake of the Woods. *Flicker* 12:1–5.

Swedenborg, E. D. 1939. Summer birds of the Lake Vermilion region. *Flicker* 11:14–16.

Voelker, Bro. T. 1969a. Survey of nesting birds in St. Yon Valley [Winona County]. *Loon* 41:87–89.

———. 1969b. Birds in Winona County. *Loon* 41:100–105.

Warner, D. W. 1950. Summer bird life of Carimona Woods, Fillmore County. *Flicker* 22:27–34.

Wood, M. 1967. *Birds of Pennsylvania*. Agricultural Experiment Station, Pennsylvania State University, University Park, Pennsylvania.

Index

Index